Towards Gender Equality in Law

Gizem Guney • David Davies
Po-Han Lee
Editors

Towards Gender Equality in Law

An Analysis of State Failures from a Global Perspective

palgrave macmillan
LYRASIS®

Editors
Gizem Guney
University of Portsmouth
Portsmouth, UK

David Davies
University of Sussex
Brighton, UK

Po-Han Lee
National Taiwan University
Taipei, Taiwan

With the support of more than 30 libraries, the LYRASIS United Nations Sustainable Development Goals Fund has enabled this publication to be available fully open access.

ISBN 978-3-030-98071-9   ISBN 978-3-030-98072-6 (eBook)
https://doi.org/10.1007/978-3-030-98072-6

This Palgrave Macmillan imprint is published by the registered company Springer Nature Switzerland AG.

The registered company address is: Gewerbestrasse 11, 6330 Cham, Switzerland

To Ada, Vida and Poppy

Foreword

It is a genuine pleasure to witness this important book come to fruition. Congratulations to Gizem, David and Po-Han, who worked tirelessly to organise the extremely successful conference from which this book blossomed, *Towards Gender Equality: Clashes in Law*, at the University of Sussex in summer 2018.

This timely book articulates a counter voice to the assumption that because we have gender equality laws, gender equality has been achieved. This book urges us to listen to the realities and materialities that know through the lived everyday that gender equality remains elusive. The book forces a reflection on, a coming back to, what we mean by gender equality in law. How do intersectional, colonial and trans considerations interact with the liberal, radical instruments that have been promulgated nationally, transnationally and internationally as a sign of normative gender equality? Invaluably, this book exposes and puts into question retrograde iterations of national(istic) legislation that intentionally restrict gender equality and rights, alongside the rise of gender criticality in the academy.

The book is replete with clashes and deliberately so, to highlight the contradictions, paradoxes and dichotomies inherent in the project of pursuing gender equality through law. In the words of Joanne Conaghan, "no-one said it would be easy". However, this book provides impeccable guidance through the many debates on gender equality in law, importantly from a global perspective. The book forms an indispensable contribution to the ongoing, determined project of gender equality through law. It was an honour to be invited as keynote to the conference. It is all the more pertinent to contribute a fragment to this book, edited by my first PhD student and close colleagues. Their perseverance, editorial skill and substantive knowledge have enabled them to fulfil this exceptional achievement at an early career stage and hold attention to this project in turbulent coronavirus times. The book puts the normative project of gender equality through law into question, not to undermine it but to provide a vital, robust and original analysis and companion to debates on possible futures looking towards gender equality in law.

University of Leicester, Leicester, UK Kimberley Brayson
28 June 2021

Acknowledgements

Many people have been involved along the way in the making of this book. Firstly, we would like to thank all the contributors for all their determination and patience in the process. Their passion and commitment to the book is testament that the project was of value and importance. We would also like to thank all those who participated in the 'Towards Gender Equality: Clashes in Law" conference held at the University of Sussex in June 2018, the event that provided a starting point for this book. The contributions and the discussions that followed after the conference and into the evening enriched the analysis of this book. Many thanks to the Doctoral School at the University of Sussex for funding the conference through the Researcher-Led Initiative Fund. Finally, we would like to also thank our colleagues in the School of Law, Politics, and Sociology at the University of Sussex, in particular Professor Nuno Ferreira, for taking the time to read and comment on our early thoughts and ideas.

Contents

Notes on Contributors

Kimberley Brayson is an associate professor at the Leicester law School, and prior to that was Senior Lecturer and Co-Director of the Sussex Centre for Gender Studies at the University of Sussex. She was a legal researcher at the College of Europe, Bruges (2007–2008), and a Research Fellow on an EU Framework 6 project entitled Juristras (2008–2009) based at the University of Sussex. Her research is interdisciplinary in nature and draws on diverse theoretical approaches to interrogate complex legal/material realities. She is currently working on a monograph entitled *Law and Islamic Dress: Rights and Fascism in Europe* (Hart Publishing).

David Davies is a lecturer in criminology and sociology at the University of Sussex, and his research is focused on a sociolegal exploration on how to combat the use of gender stereotypes in advertising. Before that, he taught EU law at the University of Essex.

Pia Eskelinen is a doctoral candidate at University of Turku's Faculty of Law. Eskelinen is writing a dissertation on rural women's land rights in China. Her main research interests are in gender and family relation, social change in contemporary China and Chinese feminism. Eskelinen has done fieldwork in various parts of China.

Olga Frańczak is a gender equality expert and feminist practitioner. Her research focuses on human rights and gender stereotyping with a specific interest in the Council of Europe. Her work employs interdisciplinary approach of law and political science. The research for this chapter was conducted during her doctoral studies at the University of Surrey.

Sarah Grosso holds a PhD in Anthropology from the London School of Economics in 2014. Her doctoral research explored women's rights in Ben Ali's Tunisia based on extensive ethnographic fieldwork in a neighbourhood and a family court in Tunis. She is a lecturer and researcher at Webster University Geneva, based in the Media Communications Department teaching various undergraduate and graduate courses in communication, media, anthropology and gender studies. Sarah also works as an independent consultant on gender and communications for clients including MSF, the WHO, UNICEF and UNESCO.

Gizem Guney holds an LLB degree from Eskişehir Anadolu University and LLM degree in Public Law from Queen Mary University of London. She holds a PhD from the University of Sussex (2019), which analysed the Istanbul Convention from a radical feminist perspective, particularly in the light of the dominance theory developed by Catherine A. MacKinnon. She is a teaching fellow in criminology and criminal justice at the University of Portsmouth. Before joining Portsmouth, she taught law, criminology and sociology modules at the University of Sussex for four years.

Po-Han Lee is an assistant professor at the Global Health Program and the Institute of Health Policy and Management, National Taiwan University, at which he also serves to coordinate the "Inclusion, Diversity, and Equality" Initiative of the College of Public Health. Previously, he taught sociology/criminology, human rights and gender studies at University of Sussex. He has been interested in queer, decolonial and other critical approaches to the politics of human rights and global health. He is also a senior editor for "Plain Law Movement" in Taiwan.

Gillian Love is a lecturer in sociology at the University of Sussex. Her work focuses on gender, abortion, reproductive rights and gender-based violence.

MaryFrances Lukera is a lecturer in law in the School of Law, Politics and Sociology at the University of Sussex. She is an advocate in the High Court of Kenya. She holds an LLB degree from University of Pune, an LLM degree in human rights specialising in reproductive and sexual health and rights from the University of the Free State, and a PhD from the University of Sussex. She has research interests in human rights, sexual violence, sexual and reproductive health and rights.

Jen Neller is a lecturer in law at Manchester Law School, Manchester Metropolitan University. She holds a PhD from Birkbeck University of London (2020). Her forthcoming book, *Stirring Up Hatred: Myth, Identity and Order in the Regulation of Hate Speech*, is due to be published in the Palgrave Macmillan "Hate Studies" series.

Amna Rashid is an assistant professor and Founding Director Center for Human Rights and Justice (CHRJ) at University of Management and Technology (UMT), Lahore, Pakistan.

Umar Rashid is a PhD candidate in law at the Adelaide Law School, University of Adelaide. He is on study leave from University of Management and Technology (UMT), where he was the associate director of the School of Law and Policy.

Julia Winstone is a sociolegal researcher. She is currently researching "Understanding Restorative Justice (RJ) with Children in Practice from Professional Perspectives: A Socio-Legal Approach" for her ESRC-funded PhD at the University of Sussex. This charts a child's journey to RJ from first contact with the Youth Justice System in England and Wales through to Out of Court and Court Ordered RJ. Julia also conducts sociolegal research in equality and diversity issues arising in legal and educational settings. Before entering academia, she spent several years as a legal aid clinical negligence and inquest solicitor (currently non-practising), and has also taught in schools.

CHAPTER 1

Introduction

Gizem Guney, David Davies, and Po-Han Lee

1.1 The Context

This book is the product of an international and interdisciplinary conference that was held at the University of Sussex, UK, in 2018. The primary aim of the conference was to have a closer look at the reasons and impacts of numerous problematic legislation and policies that have been adopted across the world over the last decade and which had a destabilising effect on gender equality and justice. There have been some notable examples in this regard: Poland has reintroduced restriction on women's right to abortion in 2020 (Calkin & Kaminska, 2020); the debate over the so-called foetal "heartbeat" bills in Taiwan (Liu, 2020) and the ephemeral unconstitutional anti-abortion state laws have been heated in the US and

G. Guney (✉)
University of Portsmouth, Portsmouth, UK
e-mail: Gizem.Guney@port.ac.uk

D. Davies
University of Sussex, Brighton, UK
e-mail: D.Davies@sussex.ac.uk

P.-H. Lee
National Taiwan University, Taipei, Taiwan
e-mail: pohanlee@ntu.edu.tw

G. Guney et al. (eds.), *Towards Gender Equality in Law*,
https://doi.org/10.1007/978-3-030-98072-6_1

internationally since 2019 (Bakst, 2019; Evans & Narasimhan, 2020); Russia has partially decriminalised domestic violence in 2016, despite the outcry from activists and victims (Semukhina, 2020). As a pandemic swept Europe (Kuhar & Paternotte, 2017), the mobilisation of "anti-gender", anti-feminist and misogynist discourse in the political and policy domains has its global resonance in, for instance, Brazil (Hunter & Power, 2019), India (Rothermel, 2020) and South Korea (Kim, 2021). In this light, it would not be an exaggeration to contend that the last decade marks a global crisis of gender equality.

All of these problematic *anti-gender* laws and policies came into existence during the same decade in which new international laws and initiatives were simultaneously adopted to promote women's rights and gender equality. The positive international developments include, just to name a few, the following: the Council of Europe adopted its first legally binding instrument that is specifically devoted to gender-based violence against women ("the Istanbul Convention"); the Committee on the Elimination of Discrimination against Women updated its blueprint General Recommendations No. 19 with No. 35 on gender-based violence against women in 2017; the Committee on Economic, Social and Cultural Rights adopted a comprehensive General Comment No. 22 for the right to sexual and reproductive health; the UN Human Rights Council appointed an Independent Expert on protection against violence and discrimination based on sexual orientation and gender identity in 2016, whose mandate has been renewed in 2019. In addition, the national delegates, at the UN venues, also adopted a Political Declaration on the occasion of the 20th Anniversary of the Fourth World Conference on Women in 2020, not to mention the significant attention given to "gender equality" as one of the 17 Sustainable Development Goals (Esquivel & Sweetman, 2016).

At the international level, the efforts to promote gender equality continued ambitiously in the face of states' problematic attitudes towards restricting gender equality at the domestic level. This is not the first time that our contributors have observed the contradiction between international and domestic systems. The tension between international and national norms has been persistent, and the question regarding which of these two normative systems should have superiority in protecting individual rights has been discussed previously. Traditionally, the internationalist camp has taken the stand for the integration of international norms into the domestic laws and their judicial interpretation, which is recently rebranded as "global constitutionalism" (Wiener et al., 2012; Peters,

2009). At the other end of the spectrum, the constitutionalist school advocated for a more restrictive approach towards integration based on democratic accountability, self-governance and state sovereignty (Powell, 2008). Benvenisti and Harel (2017) suggested an alternative approach based on the "discordant parity" hypothesis, which claims that neither international nor domestic laws are superior to the other, and, moreover, the tension between the two systems should be embraced as it contributes to the evolution and development of individual rights at the end.

The tension, friction and disharmony are not unique to the interaction between international and domestic laws; they can be found within international law as well. Marjan Ajevski (2014) has identified this as "fragmentation" where different international texts and bodies developed different principles towards the identification and realisation of human rights. Moreover, the same tension can also be observed within the domestic normative systems—between national, subnational and local levels—which has been explored with the approach of legal pluralism (Merry, 1988; Benda-Beckmann & Turner, 2018). Ashford and Maine (2020) has also noted the inconsistencies despite the states' repetitive recognition of their human rights obligations in relation to mainstreaming and promoting gender equality. Overall, it becomes clear that the concept of *law* that is to be used in achieving gender equality is a multidimensional, multilayered and, to an extent, a contradictory phenomenon, and this book starts off by acknowledging this.

In the face of this complex nature of law, this book casts its focus on state failures in gender equality. In other words, this book aims to find out how and why states fail in their gender equality laws and policies, and, in doing this, it holds a broad perspective. Namely, the book sheds a light on states' failures in their legal systems that include different levels and forms of law, namely domestic laws, local regulations and the implementation of international law, individually or in combination. While taking state failure seriously and thus holding the governments responsible seems self-evident, once gender equality is not achieved, as noted by Vasiljević et al. (2017), the nuances between how states "failed" is nevertheless an under-researched topic. Considering that various problematic legal reforms have been observed across the globe over the last decade as exemplified above, for this project we feel the need to better understand these backlashes against gender justice and women's rights in law and life.

1.2 Rethinking State Failures

Against the background where tensions and sometimes contradictions between laws at different levels occur, this book represents an eagerness to interrogate the political, social and cultural contexts from which these states' failures have emerged, in contrast to the renewed and even advanced commitments of international agencies to gender equality. Our main purpose is to investigate whether there are similarities, namely repeating patterns, in the way in which the states are unable and/or unwilling to keep their promises to realise gender and sexuality justice. Gender inequality is one of the most discussed topics of this decade, and there is a broad literature on how states individually fail in ensuring gender equality in their laws and policies. This provides a broad basis for a series of case studies (Örtenblad et al., 2017). However, there is a pressing need for an analysis approaching these failures from a perspective that looks beyond written words of different laws, as if these legal systems exist and run independently on their own, as held by the conventional approach to comparative law. Rather, acknowledging the connectedness and interrelatedness between the contexts in which these failures happened, we consider "law as written/stated" versus "law as applied/practised" within a given culture, to use Edward Eberle's (2011) words, and its global implication.

Moreover, the question concerning how gender equality law has *failed* should be answered not only by examining related legal developments; it also requires an analysis of the social norms and trends that have allowed for such legislative change. Informed by such an interdisciplinary approach to the contextualisation of law, in this book, the authors have drawn on data from ethnographic studies, sociolegal studies, the sociology of law, and media and cultural studies. This book, therefore, deploys a methodology where the law is located at the centre while exploring and uncovering the interactions between law and social norms in other forms (Banakar, 2011).

Therefore, while taking sociocultural dynamics into account, all the contributors to this book also consider that, rather than treating the failing of national systems for gender equality as individual cases, to situate the questions in the global context would be vital for developing better policy responses to the problem on both the international and domestic planes. This is to respond to Ratna Kapur's (2018) call for taking into account the non-juridical factors that influence progressive politics and legal agenda and also paying attention to the globalisation of the rights discourse. Thus, eventually, this book pursues its analysis based on a wide geographical spectrum by including societies that are less represented in academic literature, such as Kenya, Pakistan, Tunisia, China, Spain, Turkey and Israel, in order to properly represent the diversity in the circumstances where the states are or have become reluctant or even resistant to realising gender equality and sexuality justice.

As "gender equality" is the focal point of the book, this collection draws upon various feminist approaches. However, it is also important to highlight that, above all, the book has adopted an intersectional perspective, proposed by Kimberlé Crenshaw (1991) 30 years ago and developed greatly over the past decades, regarding the marginalisation and exclusion of women and sexual and gender minorities. Namely, the disadvantages that women and sexual and gender minorities face are understood to stem from their intersecting social identities (see Mouffe, 1995), such as race, religion, sexuality, class, nationality and so on. Hence, this book challenges the dominant discourse concerning "discrimination" and "inequality" as along a single, independent axis. It does this by paying attention to how discrimination on the grounds of class, race, sexual orientation and gender identity interplays and exacerbates discrimination on the grounds of sex and gender.

The chapters in the volume are organised according to the themes regarding the neutrality, coherence and practicality of law, respectively. That is, this book consists of three parts, and each part will present different states' failures in achieving gender equality under their legal frameworks. In conclusion, we identify the overarching and repeating patterns between states in how they fail in achieving women's rights and gender justice.

1.3 Law Is Neutral, or Is It?

Part I sheds light on the gendered foundations of law, upon which rights and responsibilities are assigned according to a binary spectrum that favours men's interests under a gender-neutral disguise (also see Gina, 2018). To open up the discussion with theoretical engagement, Olga Frańczak's chapter, drawing on feminist legal theory, critically attends to the role of law—including human rights discourse—in tackling gender stereotypes. Frańczak demonstrates that human rights are not gender-neutral, although they are presented as "value-free" in their "universalistic" preposition. Frańczak also detects the complicity of the Anglo-American liberal feminist approach in sustaining the hegemonic structure that is characterised as patriarchal and paternalistic and positions women as "victims". The ideas around justice represented in and by law are thus androcentric; in this light, Frańczak argues for "soft" law and policy measures as an alternative in addition to the conventional, prohibitive and punitive means of law.

Gillian Love's chapter considers that although the UK and Israel laws recognise the diversity of gender identity categories, by allowing individuals to change their legal gender, they are blind to transgender people's desire for the self-determination of their bodies and reproductive rights. More specifically, Love demonstrates that the relevant legal frameworks do not allow childbearing transgender men to be registered as fathers. Overall, this chapter demonstrates that despite the recognition of gender identity within the law to an extent, the law, as a whole, still holds a very much *gendered* position when it comes to parenthood; motherhood is still defined by the physical and biological experience of carrying a pregnancy. The law also follows an exclusively *binary* route, where parenthood is defined through the lines of motherhood and fatherhood. Identifying this as "repronormativity" of law, Love demonstrates how the laws still reproduce gendered legal subjects (i.e. mothers and fathers) as a result of the states' biopolitical projects.

Echoing the previous two chapters, Sarah Grosso's chapter explores the gendered divorce procedures and experiences as well as women's growing rights consciousness in Tunisia and uncovers that, though aiming to become gender-neutral in addressing family disputes, relevant legal practices have turned out to be blind to women's subjugated positions. The imbalanced relationship between wives and husbands in Tunis has been maintained due to the judges' gendered opinions regarding family, despite the progressive development of marriage and family law reform. Drawing upon anthropological accounts, Grosso has identified the tension in law in multiple forms, such as that between law and cultural norms, between different agents of law and between law (the purpose of law) and legal practices (the application of law). The interpretation and enforcement of law in this regard have become, as observed in the field, not just a legal but also a moral work, which involves judgements about what is good and bad about family and society.

1.4 Law Is Coherent, or Is It?

Part II of the book moves to the question of whether the law is a coherent entity that has consistent implications to gender equality within the jurisdiction where it is applicable. Amna Rashid and Umar Rashid explore the legal reforms that have taken place in Pakistan to ensure equality for transgender individuals initiated by the Constitutional Court in 2009, which recognised "third gender" as a distinct identity category. Their chapter puts these positive developments in context, where they at the same time contradict other legal regulations, such as inheritance laws and penal laws that criminalise homosexuality. This demonstrates the fragmentation and incoherence between positive and problematic laws and policies with regard to gender equality in Pakistan.

Similarly, Pia Eskelinen's chapter portrays how Chinese women's land rights recognised in national legislations are inconsistent with local councils' rulings in practice. The chapter, based on Eskelinen's fieldwork study, explores the barriers facing Chinese rural women for "not having" or "losing" their rights to own, use and dispose of lands, and locates the question in a larger politico-economic context—such as the capitalist economy and urban expansion—that has influenced women's role in China. The tension between law in books (legal rules for equality) and law in action (the inertia of law enforcers at the village level) is obvious. The general practice that deprives women of contractual rights in rural areas and negative legal implications of the change of marital status (e.g. divorcee and widow) have placed these women in a precarious position. Eskelinen thus argues that both legal and social recognition of women's rights relating to land use are the key to empowering rural women and promoting their status in households and communities.

This is followed by Gizem Guney's chapter, which attends to how Turkey has been taking progressive legal steps to eliminate gender-based domestic violence in order to comply with its obligations under the Istanbul Convention while adopting policies that undermine women's equality. As the first state to ratify the Istanbul Convention and the first signatory to withdraw from it after implementing it for six years, Turkey has manifested ambivalent attitudes towards international human rights legal rules regulating gender-based domestic violence. Observing from the various changes in law, Guney finds that Turkey always oscillated between two ends—progressive versus conservative—even before its withdrawal. This situation not only reflects the Turkish government's insincerity in its political commitment to addressing gender-based violence; it also implies that law can be instrumentalised for political considerations. That is, rather than a single and harmonious body of authority, law is a body that contains multiple principles and practices, which are sometimes contradictory.

Jen Neller's chapter problematises the conundrum regarding the "conflict" between values of gender equality and others such as free speech and multiculturalism. This is both a theoretical and an ethical contradiction. Situating the debates on hate speech legislation in England and Wales, Neller identifies that discourse has been dominated by the overemphasis on potential conflicts between the freedom of expression and the freedom from the harms of hate. Also, Neller argues that the tolerance of misogynistic narratives and the persistent absence of gender in the UK anti-hate law excludes the gender aspect of hate and deprives women of legal protection from hate. With a critical review of the UK parliamentary debate, Neller finds that the Parliament has pretended to be neutral in negotiating and balancing "competing" interests. However, the fact that such a need exists also represents potential *incoherence* inherent to the human rights-based approach to gender equality discourse.

1.5 Law Is Practical, or Is It?

Part III of the book is concerned with gender equality in practice by comparing what the law has pronounced in statutes and the experiences of women in reality. Julia Winstone's chapter draws upon the law's attempts to remove invisible barriers and hurdles women experience within the legal profession in the UK and shows how these attempts have failed due to structural and cultural factors against women's inclusion in this professional field. Despite the numerous legal initiatives to improve the career progression of women in the solicitor profession in England and Wales over the last five decades, in reality the gap persists between participation rates for women and men, with the number of women active in the profession reducing with age and experience. Drawing upon an approach that incorporates the theoretical accounts of intersectionality into sociolegal studies, Winstone explores the barriers faced by women solicitors and argues for practical measures to be developed to bring about a meaningful change.

Drawing on individual and group interviews with sex workers and other stakeholders in Kenya, MaryFrances Lukera's chapter identifies the tension between the upheld international human rights standards and everyday challenges that sex workers encounter. Lukera underlines the lack of understanding of laws not only by sex workers but also by social workers. Lukera demonstrates how this lack of understanding has resulted in sex workers' distrust in state service providers that makes them tend to look out for non-state, alternative solutions to their problems. Lukera, therefore, advocates a human rights-based approach to sexual health, which requires decriminalising sex work, promoting civil education and cultivating human rights awareness in Kenyan society. These strategies are also crucial in addressing stigmas and discrimination against sex workers by health workers, state officials and community members.

David Davies' chapter offers insights into Spain's legal regulations concerning sexist content in advertising. Spain is often viewed as a pioneer in combatting violence against women for its egalitarian laws of the Zapatero era. This is to an extent that Spain brought specific measures for gender stereotypes in advertising through Gender Violence Act (2004). In the European Union where most member states opt for self-regulation, Spain's attitude is an unorthodox approach. Analysing the advertisements of RyanAir and Cillit Bang as case studies, Davies demonstrates how the law fails in practice, and it complements, rather than counteracts, self-regulation. Davies' chapter also puts these trends in a sociohistorical context by portraying how Spanish society transformed from dictatorship to democracy and the politics of "the new way" has emerged since the 1970s.

1.6 The Vision of the Book

Overall, this book aims to find out the contradictions between different forms of laws concerning gender equality (namely international, national or regional), as well as the social and political factors that play a part in facilitating and promoting problematic gender policies. More importantly, this project also unravels whether there are any similarities/patterns regarding the way in which states define and utilise policies and laws that harm gender equality. In this way, this book proposes to contribute to the efforts to devise holistic policies to address gender inequalities across the world.

References

Ajevski, M. (2014). Fragmentation in International Human Rights Law: Beyond Conflict of Laws. *Nordic Journal of Human Rights, 32*, 87–98.

Ashford, C., & Maine, A. (Eds.). (2020). *Research Handbook on Gender, Sexuality and the Law*. Edward Elgar.

Bakst, L. (2019). Constitutionally Unconstitutional: When State Legislatures Pass Laws Contrary to Supreme Court Precedent. *UC Davis Law Review Online, 53*, 63–92.

Banakar, R. (2011). Having One's Cake and Eating It: The Paradox of Contextualisation in Socio-Legal Research. *International Journal of Law in Context, 7*, 487–503.

Benda-Beckmann, K. V., & Turner, B. (2018). Legal Pluralism, Social Theory, and the State. *The Journal of Legal Pluralism and Unofficial Law, 50*, 255–274.

Benvenisti, E., & Harel, A. (2017). Embracing the Tension Between National and International Human Rights Law: The Case for Discordant Parity. *International Journal of Constitutional Law, 15*, 36–59.

Calkin, S., & Kaminska, M. E. (2020). Persistence and Change in Morality Policy: The Role of the Catholic Church in the Politics of Abortion in Ireland and Poland. *Feminist Review, 124*, 86–102.

Crenshaw, K. (1991). Mapping the Margins: Intersectionality, Identity Politics, and Violence Against Women of Color. *Stanford Law Review, 43*, 1241–1299.

Eberle, Edward, J. 2011. The Methodology of Comparative Law. *Roger Williams University Law Review, 16*(1), 51–72.

Esquivel, V., & Sweetman, C. (2016). Gender and the Sustainable Development Goals. *Gender and Development, 24*, 1–8.

Evans, D. P., & Narasimhan, S. (2020). A Narrative Analysis of Anti-Abortion Testimony and Legislative Debate Related to Georgia's Fetal "Heartbeat" Abortion Ban. *Sexual and Reproductive Health Matters, 28*, 1686201.

Gina, H. (2018). Article—On Feminist Legal Methodologies: Spilt, Plural and Speaking Subjects. *feminists@law*, p. 8.

Hunter, W., & Power, T. J. (2019). Bolsonaro and Brazil's Illiberal Backlash. *Journal of Democracy, 30*, 68–82.

Kapur, R. (2018). *Gender, Alterity and Human Rights: Freedom in a Fishbowl*. Edward Elgar.

Kim, Y. (2021). Mirroring Misogyny in Hell Chosŏn. Megalia, Womad, and Korea's Feminism in the Age of Digital Populism. *European Journal of Korean Studies, 20*, 101–133.

Kuhar, R., & Paternotte, D. (Eds.). (2017). *Anti-Gender Campaigns in Europe: Mobilising Against Equality*. Rowman & Littlefield.

Liu, P.-Y. (2020). A Discussion Between Competing Claims of Constitutional Rights and Legal Interest. *Angle Health Law Review, 41*, 173–180.

Merry, S. E. (1988). Legal Pluralism. *Law and Society Review, 22*, 869–896.
Mouffe, C. (1995). Feminism, Citizenship, and Radical Democratic Politics. In L. Nicholson & S. Seidman (Eds.), *Social Postmodernism: Beyond Identity Politics*. Cambridge University Press.
Örtenblad, A., Marling, R., & Vasiljević, S. (Eds.). (2017). *Gender Equality in a Global Perspective*. Routledge.
Peters, A. (2009). The Merits of Global Constitutionalism. *Indiana Journal of Global Legal Studies, 16*, 397–411.
Powell, C. (2008). Tinkering with Torture in the Aftermath of Hamdan: Testing the Relationship Between Internationalism and Constitutionalism. *New York University Journal of International Law and Politics, 40*, 723–802.
Rothermel, A.-K. (2020). Global–Local Dynamics in Anti-Feminist Discourses: An Analysis of Indian, Russian and US Online Communities. *International Affairs, 96*, 1367–1385.
Semukhina, O. (2020). The Decriminalization of Domestic Violence in Russia. *Demokratizatsiya: The Journal of Post-Soviet Democratization, 28*, 15–45.
Vasiljević, S., Marling, R., & Örtenblad, A. (2017). Introduction: Different Dimensions of Gender Equality in a Comparative Perspective. In A. Örtenblad, R. Marling, & S. Vasiljević (Eds.), *Gender Equality in a Global Perspective*. Routledge.
Wiener, A., Lang, A. F., Tully, J., Maduro, M. P., & Kumm, M. (2012). Global Constitutionalism: Human Rights, Democracy and the Rule of Law. *Global Constitutionalism, 1*, 1–15.

PART I

Law Is Neutral?

CHAPTER 2

(Stereo)typical Law: Challenging the Transformative Potential of Human Rights

Olga Frańczak

2.1 Introduction

In 2010, the United Nations Commission on the Status of Women stated that stereotypes are a "significant challenge to the practical realisation of women's human rights" and addressing them "must be a key element in all efforts to achieve the realisation of women's human rights" (CSW, 2010, paras. 10–11; Cusack, 2013b, p. 125). This argument is also reflected by the feminist legal scholars, who also indicate that there is a clear link between stereotypes and gender inequality (Fredman, 1997; Cook & Cusack, 2010; Timmer, 2011; Peroni & Timmer, 2016). Leading human rights organisations recognise gender stereotypes as a human rights concern and have introduced legal and policy instruments aimed at their elimination.[1] Yet, stereotypes continue to affect and limit people's lives (Fredman, 1997, p. 3). This paradox raises the question of whether law is an appropriate tool to tackle gender stereotyping.

O. Frańczak (✉)
University of Surrey, Guildford, UK

G. Guney et al. (eds.), *Towards Gender Equality in Law*,
https://doi.org/10.1007/978-3-030-98072-6_2

However, gender stereotyping has not sparked a wide debate within legal scholarship. This visible gap makes it difficult to address the clash between numerous legal commitments and the continuous harmful impact of gender stereotyping. This chapter aims to fill this gap and challenge the status quo by taking a critical look at the transformative potential of international human rights instruments. It challenges the idea that human rights are a "panacea" and argues that they will not automatically transform societies and eliminate the deeply rooted attitudes which make discrimination not only possible but also encouraged. The considerations included in this chapter provide a fresh perspective on the anti-stereotyping laws and policies, and contribute to the scholarly debates on anti-discrimination laws, human rights, gender equality, gender stereotyping and feminist legal theory.

Drawing on feminist legal theory, this chapter addresses the following question: Can and should law be used to challenge gender stereotyping? To answer this question, the chapter identifies two "failures" of legal instruments. Firstly, that law "fails" to embody its expected ideals. While law is considered to be "objective", it is not free of bias and prejudice (Fredman, 1997). Legal instruments are drafted by the people in power, and, therefore, they are deeply influenced by the existing patriarchal hierarchies (Fredman, 1997). Feminist legal scholars highlight that the "objectivity" of legal norms in fact represents male interests (Hunter, 2013; Smart, 1989). Legal definitions and procedures simplify diverse human experiences and behaviours to fit the pre-established legal frames (Smart, 1989, p. 34). Therefore, it is important to consider if such a multifaceted and deeply rooted issue like gender stereotyping can be addressed by legal norms (Smart, 1989, pp. 164–165).

Secondly, this chapter analyses how law "fails" to be transformative and reproduces existing patriarchal power structures. Human rights are no exception. Their focus upon "protection" reinforces hegemonic structures and stereotypes, for instance women's position as victims (Otto, 2005; Peroni & Timmer, 2016). Therefore, legal norms can target gender stereotypes but can also reinforce them (Ben-Asher, 2016, p. 1190). It is impossible to foresee the implications of even the most carefully drafted law reform (Smart, 1989). Introducing a new law is not enough to eliminate deeply rooted gender stereotypes (Auchmuty, 2012; Hester & Lilley, 2014). However, this does not mean that law has no role to play in the elimination of harmful stereotypes. It has the power to publicly acknowledge gender stereotyping as a problem, which is necessary for its effective elimination (Cook & Cusack, 2010).

This chapter begins with the meaning of gender stereotyping and recognition that major human rights instruments refrain from defining it. The following section highlights that gender stereotyping is recognised by human rights institutions, as well as feminist legal scholarship, as an obstacle for the full realisation of human rights. Whilst feminist legal scholars notice that law has a role to play in elimination of gender stereotyping, they remain critical towards law. This leads to the analysis of how law "fails" to live up to its presumed characteristics of universality and objectivity and the exploration of how law "fails" to be transformative and might actually reproduce patriarchal power structures. The chapter concludes with a brief discussion outlining that while law is not enough to bring about substantive change, it is crucial to publicly identify gender stereotyping as a problem that needs addressing.

2.2 Defining Gender Stereotyping

When discussing gender stereotypes, it is crucial to agree on the meaning of both "gender" and "stereotypes". The international human rights system is reluctant to provide legally binding definitions of gender stereotyping. Even though the Istanbul Convention (adopted by the Council of Europe), the Maputo Protocol (the African Union) and the Convention of Belém do Pará (the Organisation of American States) oblige states parties to address gender stereotyping, they do not define it. Importantly, such definition is also absent from the Convention on the Elimination of All Forms of Discrimination against Women (CEDAW), which also includes such obligation. This does not mean that the organisations refrain from defining these terms at all. For instance, the Council of Europe Gender Equality Strategy 2018–2023 (p. 16) contains a definition of gender stereotyping. However, its absence within major legally binding instruments, like the ones listed above, is a missed opportunity to unify and standardise the understanding of gender stereotyping.

It should be noted here that defining a term in law has its drawbacks. With a concept as multifaceted as gender stereotyping, a strict definition could drastically narrow down the scope of anti-stereotyping legislation (or research), thus limiting the transformative potential of such instruments. However, failing to define the term poses similar challenges, since in such a case a term can be (mis)interpreted with no limitations.

Opponents of anti-stereotyping legislations could freely define stereotyping in a way that would distort the meaning of the term. Therefore, this chapter employs a broad definition of stereotyping to encapsulate its versatile character while still providing a point of reference and focus for the analysis.

This chapter follows the definition of gender included in the Istanbul Convention which reads that gender is "socially constructed roles, behaviours, activities and attributes that a given society considers appropriate for women and men" (Art 3 (c)). It recognises that gender is more than a set of biological characteristics which makes it particularly useful for a study on stereotypes. Moreover, it is a legally binding definition drafted by the leading human rights organisation in Europe, providing it with a high degree of recognition within the European context.

The definition of stereotyping employed in this chapter draws on the work of Rebecca Cook and Simone Cusack (2010). Their research on gender stereotyping in the legal context forms a significant part of the academic debate (e.g. Cusack, 2013a, 2013b, 2016; Cook & Weiss, 2016; Cook et al., 2010), and has influenced many scholars in the field (e.g. Timmer, 2011, 2015; Fredman, 2016; Hester & Lilley, 2014; Šimonović, 2014). Cook and Cusack (2010, p. 9) define stereotype as "a generalised view or preconception of attributes or characteristics possessed by, or the roles that are or should be performed by, members of a particular group". Therefore, a stereotype assumes that all members of a group have a particular characteristic without reflecting on individual personalities, wishes and abilities. Importantly, this definition does not exclude stereotypes assigning "positive" traits, nor stereotypes that might be "true" in a specific case. For instance, just because a specific man is physically strong, or a woman loves to cook, it does not make it any less of a stereotype (Cook & Cusack, 2010, pp. 9, 11).

Thanks to these two definitions, in short, gender stereotypes are understood in this chapter as generalised views based on socially constructed ideas of femininity and masculinity. This wording reflects that gender stereotypes affect people of all genders and avoids reinforcing gender binary (Agius, 2015). Employing such approach provides an inclusive scope for the discussion on the relationship between gender stereotyping and human rights, which is the aim of this chapter.

Importantly, this chapter challenges the idea that gender stereotyping is solely a "women's issue". Patriarchal stereotypes, as well as toxic conceptualisations of masculinity, harm men and limit their ability to lead full lives and develop their personal potential (Connell, 1993; Council of Europe Gender Equality Strategy 2018–2023). At the same time, they reinforce men's dominant position in the society. Moreover, as pointed out by Cook and Cusack (2010), gender stereotypes of one gender can impact another as well. For instance, if stereotypically women's place is at home, in the private sphere, then public and professional life is designated to men (Council of Europe Gender Equality Strategy 2018–2023). Similarly, if mothers are considered better parents, then that paints a picture of fathers as inadequate and incapable. Both these sides create social expectations and pressure to conform. Gendered divisions of labour, particularly relating to the social function of care, do not happen in a vacuum (Caracciolo di Torella & Masselot, 2020). They support a very specific (patriarchal) socio-economic model with unpaid labour performed mostly by women and paid labour—by men. Therefore, deeply rooted gender stereotypes are the normative underpinnings that support these particular structures (Caracciolo di Torella & Masselot, 2020; Smart, 1989).

2.3 Why Bother?

This section explores the position of gender stereotyping within a human rights framework and feminist legal scholarship. It discusses human rights commitments to tackle gender stereotyping and positions gender stereotyping as a challenge for the realisation of human rights. This also highlights the urgency of raising awareness on gender stereotyping and the importance of conducting this research. In doing so, this section sets the context for identifying the key legal "failures" with regards to the elimination of gender stereotyping.

Gender stereotypes create a social climate of "intimidation, fear, discrimination, exclusion and insecurity which limits opportunities and freedom" where inequality and violence thrive (Recommendation CM/Rec(2019)1, p. 1). As highlighted by the Council of Europe in the Recommendation of Preventing and Combatting Sexism, acts of "everyday" sexism can incite "overtly offensive and threatening acts, including sexual abuse or violence, rape or potentially lethal action" (Recommendation CM/Rec(2019)1, p. 4). The "Everyday Sexism Project", which catalogues instances of sexism experienced on a day-to-day basis, is a sobering illustration of that (Bates, 2012). Consequently, gender stereotypes are a part of the "continuum of violence" (Recommendation CM/Rec(2019)1, p. 1). As such, they are not "harmless" or "benign", but a human rights concern recognised in several instruments drafted by major international organisations.

The most prominent example of such documents is CEDAW adopted by the United Nations (UN) in 1979. CEDAW draws a clear connection between gender stereotyping and discrimination against women and obliges states parties to address it (Arts 2(f), 5(a) and 10(c)). Currently 189 states are parties to CEDAW suggesting that there is a global agreement that gender stereotypes are a challenge for human rights. This is further reinforced by the fact that CEDAW is not the only legal instrument introduced by the UN aimed at the elimination of gender stereotypes. The Convention on the Rights of Persons with Disabilities (CRPD) is another excellent example. It recognises that stereotypes relating to persons with disabilities can also be based on "sex and age" and obliges states to combat them (Art 8). Therefore, CRPD acknowledges that different grounds of stereotyping can intersect with each other. Moreover, the general recommendations adopted by the Committee on the Elimination of Discrimination against Women (CEDAW Committee) also encourage states to address gender stereotypes in an array of different areas, like public and political life (General recommendation No. 23), conflict and post-conflict situations (General recommendation No.30), the justice system (General recommendation No. 33) and many others.[2]

Importantly, also other international human rights organisations have introduced legal and policy mechanisms aimed at the elimination of gender stereotyping. The Organisation of American States, the African Union, the Council of Europe, as well as the European Union have introduced an array of such instruments as well.[3] Similar commitments are also visible in Asia.[4] There are two main conclusions from these observations. Firstly, a recognition that gender stereotypes are a problem and should be eradicated. Secondly, the international community considers legal and policy instruments to be a valid tool for the eradication of gender stereotyping.

Feminist legal scholarship reaffirms the link between gender stereotyping and human rights violations, considering stereotyping to be one of the biggest challenges to the realisation of human rights in contemporary society (e.g. Fredman, 1997; Cook & Cusack, 2010; Timmer, 2011). Rebecca J. Cook and Simone Cusack (2010, pp. 2–3) highlight that in order to eliminate violations of the human rights of women, greater attention must be dedicated to eliminating harmful gender stereotyping. Rikki Holtmaat and Jonneke Naber (2011) argue that examining gender stereotyping is essential to grasp links between human rights violations and culture. In the words of Alexandra Timmer (2011, p. 737), "stereotypes are both cause and manifestation of the structural inequality that non-dominant groups suffer from". They hinder human dignity because they limit individuals' ability to exercise their own agency (Cook & Cusack, 2010; also, Council of Europe Gender Equality Strategy 2018–2023). Moreover, feminist scholarship recognises that gender stereotyping contributes to justifying violence against women (Peroni & Timmer, 2016; Clay-Warner & Edgemon, 2020).

Law is "an important and necessary means of dismantling" gender stereotypes (de Silva de Alwis, 2011, p. 314; Timmer, 2011). Cook and Cusack (2010, pp. 39–41) argue that without legal measures, gender stereotypes are legitimised and given authority through the law. Therefore, lawmakers should not omit or ignore the impact of gender stereotyping when designing human rights instruments. At the same time, feminist scholars remain critical of the law as a tool of substantive change and recognise that law is not a "panacea" for gender stereotypes (Smart, 1989; Fredman, 1997; Cook & Cusack, 2010). The next section reflects on these arguments and challenges the presumed "objectivity" of legal norms.

2.4 Failure to Be Objective

This section explores if the law (including international human rights) fails to live up to its "expected" characteristics, such as universality and objectivity. Following feminist legal scholarship, it represents a critical approach towards using legal norms as a tool for gender equality and rejects the liberal rhetoric of law as neutral. In fact, this section draws attention to the many ways law fails to be objective and reflects the views and goals of the people who draft it. As Carol Smart (1989) argues, while the power of law must not be disregarded, feminists should be careful when relying on law to bring forward social transformation.

To open up these considerations, it should be pointed out that even though law is not value-free, it enjoys a special position within the society (Smart, 1989; Fredman, 1997). Smart (1989, p. 10) warns that law "sets itself above other knowledges like psychology, sociology, or common sense" and claims to reflect the "truth". At the same time, the author highlights that legal language, procedures and methods are "fundamentally anti-feminist or (…) bear no relationship to the concerns of women's lives" (Smart, 1989, p. 160). There is an analogy between law and "what might be called a 'masculine culture'" (Smart, 1989, p. 2). Therefore,

Smart (1989, p. 2) cautions that "in taking on law, feminism is taking on a great deal more as well".

In a similar vein, Roberta Guerrina and Marysia Zalewski (2007, p. 7) point out that "the concept of rights might be so irredeemably tainted by its association with the Western liberal tradition that it cannot be useful to women". Hence, human rights can actually be perceived as a Western creation, with Western understanding of gender, equality, justice, culture as well as stereotypes. Therefore, feminist scholars argue that law fails to be neutral and highlight the influence of the dominant interests on its contents.

This challenges the idea of law as being above particular interests and expressing "universally" (in the national/regional context) accepted values. Sandra Fredman (1997, p. 2) notices that since law is made by the people in power, it is not "a disembodied force". Feminist scholars highlight that law is a product of the already-existing social, political and economic structures. As such, law reflects and perpetuates the patriarchal social order. Because men have constituted (and still do) a majority of lawmakers, but more importantly, because they have "dominated over women", the interests represented in the legal systems are generally male (Fredman, 1997, pp. 1–3). In fact, feminists argue that the "objectivity" of law highlighted by legal liberalism reflects "the male perspective" (Hunter, 2013; Smart, 1989). Even human rights instruments marginalise women's voices by considering the male position to be "universal" (Otto, 2005, p. 105). If law mirrors the current patriarchal order, can it be effectively used to eradicate deeply rooted gender stereotypes?

As Eva Brems and Alexandra Timmer (2016) highlight, in essence legal norms are based on generalisations. The authors point out that the legal driving age is based on an assumption that children are reckless (also: Timmer, 2011, p. 718). In this example, law does not take into account that a particular 15-year-old might be mature enough to drive or that a specific adult might be too reckless to be a responsible driver. In the same way, legal norms can reflect harmful gender stereotypes. For instance, the Irish Constitution states that through "her life within the home", woman gives the state support necessary for achieving the "common good" (Art 41 (2)). Therefore, being grounded in the stereotype that woman's main role is being a homemaker (Cook & Cusack, 2010, pp. 22–23).

Law limits and simplifies people's experiences to fit into fixed legal frames (Smart, 1989, p. 34). Perhaps it is not sufficient to provide effective solutions for such a deeply rooted and multifaceted issue like gender stereotyping (Smart, 1989, pp. 164–165). Legal reasoning aims at fitting complex and diverse human behaviours into pre-established legal definitions, procedures and nomenclature. A valid example is when human rights instruments refer to "women" without reflecting on the heterogeneity of women's lives, experiences and knowledges. For instance, CEDAW does not refer to the fact that other grounds of discrimination, like disability, sexual orientation, religion or age, intersect in important ways with gender. The reflection on diversity of women's experiences is limited to three cases (Fredman, 2016, p. 35). The Convention refers, firstly, to women in "situation of poverty" (preamble), and secondly, to rural women (Art 14). Thirdly, the preamble highlights that elimination of all forms of racism is "essential to the full enjoyment of the rights of men and women". While CEDAW recognises that women are not a homogenous group, the approach is rather fragmentary. However, the UN has taken steps to address this gap for instance in CRPD or through adoption of general recommendations by the CEDAW Committee.

Feminist legal theory reveals that the "universal" women's experience visible in legal norms is in fact an expression of gender essentialism. It assumes that there exists a "standard" women's experience, irrespective of race, age, religion, disability or other characteristics (Choudhry, 2016, p. 411). The law considers women to be a homogenous group, disregarding individual needs and abilities (Hirschmann, 2013, p. 54). The experiences of the dominant group of women (abled, middle aged, straight, white, cisgender) become a "default". This shows that when legal norms refer to "women", they refer to a very specific group, leaving out non-dominant and intersectional experiences (Crenshaw, 1989; Fredman, 2016).

The generalising nature of legal norms can pose serious challenges for drafting anti-stereotyping laws or equality laws in general. If such instruments do not recognise the diversity of women's experiences, it can severely limit their applicability and effectiveness (Crenshaw, 1989). Without acknowledging that gender intersects with other grounds of discrimination, anti-stereotyping laws would in fact reproduce stereotypes by representing the dominant experiences as the only valid experiences.

At the same time, this raises the question of whether aiming to include many different grounds of inequality would not compartmentalise anti-stereotyping laws, making them ineffective, especially considering that all these categories can intersect in infinite number of personal contexts and could not possibly be listed within a legal document. An intersectional approach developed by Kimberlé Crenshaw (1989) offers answers to these doubts. An intersectional interpretation of gender identifies that gender intersects with other social characteristics and identities without the need to list all of them. Instead, the focus is placed on targeting the power structures rendering some people vulnerable, not on who those people are (Fredman, 2016, p. 31; Cho et al., 2013; Crenshaw, 1989). As Fredman (2016, p. 34) highlights, women experience gender stereotyping in different ways without changing the fact that they are based on gender.

The last point in this section continues the above discussion on the "generalising" character of legal norms and focuses it specifically on international human rights. It remains highly problematic as to whether they are the best means to lead the way towards the elimination of gender stereotyping. Clearly, international institutions, like the United Nations, the Council of Europe, the African Union or the Organisation of American States bring countries together allowing them to work towards shared goals. They provide a platform to identify common problems and make commitments beyond the borders of just one country. However, international human rights instruments are drafted by complex institutions detached from the everyday realities of people's lives (Zwingel, 2016, p. 223).

Since these norms must be applicable to a variety of vastly different contexts, they must ensure a sufficient level of flexibility. For instance, Art 14 of the Istanbul Convention obliges states parties to "include teaching material" on "non-stereotyped gender roles". While the article states that it must be a part of "formal curricula" and be included "at all levels of education", the wording is purposefully left without further details to allow maximum flexibility in the implementation of the article and to recognise "different possibilities between Parties in determining teaching materials" (CoE, 2011, p. 18). Therefore, since international norms must be applicable in different contexts, they remain quite general. However, the more specific the laws, the better protection they can offer (McGee Crotty, 1996, p. 322).

Moreover, international norms are usually the lowest "common denominator" that could have been agreed on by a variety of states with different traditions and agendas. CEDAW is an appropriate example. Due to its global reach, the implementation of the Convention faces significant challenges. CEDAW's effectiveness is hindered by numerous reservations, cultural differences and states interpreting its provisions to suit their own political, social and economic goals (Kimelblatt, 2016, p. 408).

The above considerations suggest that law does not truly embody its presumed characteristics of objectivity, universality and neutrality. Law is made by the people in power and reflects the existing patriarchal power structures (Hunter, 2013; Smart, 1989; Fredman, 1997). Fixed legal procedures and definitions make it difficult for law to fully encapsulate and address multifaceted and deeply rooted issues (Smart, 1989, p. 34). Through its "generalising" nature, anti-stereotyping norms can reinforce gender essentialism by acknowledging only the experiences of dominant groups of women (Hirschmann, 2013; Choudhry, 2016; Crenshaw, 1989). This allows scholars to question the transformative potential of anti-stereotyping laws. They can perpetuate the same discriminatory practices that they aim to eliminate. This paradox is explored in the following section of this chapter.

2.5 Failure to Be Transformative

Drawing on the previous section, which explored that law fails to be "objective", this section discusses how law might not only reflect but also reinforce the patriarchal gender order. It does so by exploring the disconnection between the perceived intent of lawmakers and the possible impact of anti-stereotyping laws. Therefore, this section argues that legal instruments aimed at improving women's situation can actually perpetuate discriminatory hierarchies.

Before commencing the discussion, it is crucial to remain vigilant that it is impossible to truly know the intent of lawmakers. It remains beyond the scope of academic research to compare the "true" intent with actual results of a legal norm. Therefore, references to "intent" are used figuratively. The aim of this section is to critically engage with the perceived intent or *ratio legis* of anti-stereotyping norms, namely the elimination of gender stereotyping, compared with the possibility that these provisions will simply perpetuate the existing patriarchal power structures. At the same time, it should be highlighted that this might not always be an "unintended" result. As discussed in the previous section, lawmaking is influenced by the existing social, political and economic power structures, and it is made by people in power (Fredman, 1997). Therefore, it is possible that the "actual" intent of the lawmakers is in fact to solidify gender stereotypes and patriarchal social order which secure their dominant position.

This argument is reflected in feminist critique of the "paternalistic" character of law (Otto, 2005). Even the human rights system tends to position women as victims or a "vulnerable group" who needs special help, not as active subjects who require rights. For instance, the laws aimed at elimination of violence against women can reinforce the patriarchal gender order, instead of dismantling it (Otto, 2005, p. 122). They can uphold the stereotypes sustaining "men's power over women" and women's position as victims (Clay-Warner & Edgemon, 2020, p. 42). This in turn reproduces hegemonic hierarchies and facilities male violence against women (Clay-Warner & Edgemon, 2020; Otto, 2005).

Recognising this benevolent paternalism of human rights is especially crucial when addressing the needs of non-dominant groups of women. As signalled in the previous section, the "allegedly universal" human rights system reproduces other forms of discrimination, including race, nationality and cultural background, which intersect with gender (Otto, 2005, p. 106). Lawmakers must avoid describing non-dominant groups of women as "abjectly oppressed by their cultures" (Peroni, 2016, p. 50), because this approach reinforces the stereotypical assumption of some cultures as unjust and "backward" (Gill & Walker, 2020).

This discussion of the patronising character of human rights shows that there are basically two kinds of legal norms with regards to gender stereotyping. Laws prohibiting stereotyping and those reinforcing it (Ben-Asher, 2016, p. 1190). That causes a clear clash within the law. Certain gender stereotypes are prohibited and considered discriminatory, while others are being given legitimacy through the law (Ben-Asher, 2016, p. 1190). For instance, it is "lawful to deny a female guard a position at an all-male prison but unlawful to refuse to hire a woman as a researcher for a physics clinic" (Ben-Asher, 2016, p. 1187).

This argument demonstrates that drafting truly transformative anti-stereotyping laws poses serious challenges. However, feminist legal scholars warn that even with the most carefully drafted legal reforms, it is impossible to predict their implications (Smart, 1989). Once a new law is in place its application, enforcement and interpretation "is in the hands of individuals and agencies far removed from the values and politics of the women's movement" (Smart, 1989, p. 164). This is especially true with regards to international law, including human rights. They are drafted on the international level; however, their implementation takes place on the national level. In the case of CEDAW, this means 189 countries which interpret and apply the Convention according to their social and political systems and structures. While the document that includes a reporting procedure by the CEDAW Committee is more a monitoring tool than an enforcing mechanism (Hodson, 2014, p. 563). Therefore, the real-life application and interpretation of CEDAW remains in the hands of individual countries which might not share the same values or ideas about gender equality as the drafters. For instance, when joining CEDAW some states expressed reservations that they shall implement it as long as it does not go against their constitutions (e.g. Pakistan, Qatar and Monaco) or Sharia law (e.g. Malaysia, Oman and Morocco), without providing much detail as to what it actually entails (UN Treaty Collection, 2021).

These doubts lead to an argument well established in feminist scholarship that introducing a new law, policy or institution is not enough to bring about sustainable social transformation (Cook & Cusack, 2010; Timmer, 2011; Auchmuty, 2012; Hester & Lilley, 2014). Law cannot be considered a sufficient solution to gender inequality and discrimination. What is needed is a structural shift within power relations together with the elimination of social attitudes which allow (or sometimes even encourage) continuous violations of the human rights of women (Chinkin et al., 2005, pp. 25–28). Rosemary Auchmuty (2012) brings forward an example of marital laws. The author argues that they are not the most appropriate tools for securing women's interests, and she proposes "empowerment through education and opportunities" as more promising solutions (Auchmuty, 2012, p. 84). Smart (1989, pp. 164–165) argues that the feminist involvement with law should go beyond simple reform which by itself does not offer effective and sustainable solutions to problems. At the same time, the author does not encourage ignoring law altogether (Smart, 1989, p. 2). The role that law can play in eliminating gender stereotyping is discussed below.

2.6 No Name: No Problem

The previous sections explained that law is far from being universal and objective and should not be automatically seen as a "panacea" for gender inequality. Keeping these observations in mind, this chapter now discusses if and how law can still be useful to tackle gender stereotyping. As noticed by Smart (1989), law holds a special position within societies, as it has the power to declare the "truth" and sets itself above different views. Therefore, while it is crucial to remain critical of the law and understand that a simple law reform is not enough to bring forth sustainable change, ignoring law is not advisable either (Smart, 1989, p. 2; Cook & Cusack, 2010).

Legal scholars working on stereotyping argue that a fundamental task law can fulfil is to "name" gender stereotyping (Cook & Cusack, 2010; Timmer, 2011; Brems & Timmer, 2016). Naming means publicly acknowledging gender stereotyping as a problem requiring action. Cook and Cusack (2010) notice that without naming it is impossible to address any issue. There is no problem without the name. As highlighted by Sara Ahmed (2015), naming sexism is a feminist obligation. Without publicly "naming" gender stereotyping, its harm remains unrecognised (Cook & Cusack, 2010, pp. 39–70). The special position that law holds in the society (as discussed in the previous sections) makes it particularly valuable in this context. Legal instruments can acknowledge gender stereotyping as a human rights concern and possible violation. Without legal measures, gender stereotyping is legitimised and given authority through the law (Cook & Cusack, 2010, pp. 39–41). Since naming allows for recognition of gender stereotyping as a problem, without naming it is impossible to design solutions.

Naming is just the beginning of the process of eradication of gender stereotyping (Cook & Cusack, 2010, p. 39). Acknowledging stereotypes as a problem does not equal a commitment to address it. It is an important first step; however, it must be accompanied by the will to actually eliminate gender stereotyping and the conviction that it can be done. Law is not a "panacea". Even feminist scholars who highlight the role of law in the elimination of gender stereotyping recognise the importance of other tools, like the media and education (Cook & Cusack, 2010, p. 39; de Silva de Alwis, 2011, p. 333). Leading human rights organisations also propose an array of solutions, for instance awareness raising, trainings for media professionals and teachers, gender mainstreaming or changes in textbooks (CEDAW; the Istanbul Convention; the Maputo Protocol; Convention of Belém do Pará; European Parliament Resolution (2012/2116(INI)); Recommendation CM/Rec(2019)1).

2.7 Concluding Remarks

Gender stereotypes are a serious obstacle to the full realisation of human rights (Cook & Cusack, 2010; Timmer, 2011; Fredman, 1997; Peroni & Timmer, 2016). There exists a rich variety of international human rights instruments obliging states parties to take action against gender stereotyping. Leading human rights organisations, like the United Nations, the African Union, the Organisation of American States or the Council of Europe, have introduced legal and policy instruments aimed at elimination of gender stereotyping. These commitments suggest that the international community considers law to be an appropriate tool to address gender stereotyping. Similarly, legal scholarship notices the connection between gender stereotyping and human rights violations (Cook & Cusack, 2010; Peroni & Timmer, 2016). Yet, despite the legal commitments, gender stereotypes continue to shape and limit the lives of people across the globe (Fredman, 1997, pp. 1–3). Due to this paradox, this chapter engaged critically with using legal instruments to eradicate harmful gender stereotyping.

This chapter studied two "failures" with regards to using law to eliminate gender stereotyping. Firstly, it challenged the idea of law as "objective" and "neutral" and explored that law is shaped by the existing patriarchal hierarchies. This led to the second "failure" which focused on the limited transformative impact of legal instruments. The discussion revealed that "benevolent" laws can in fact reproduce existing power structures, including gender stereotypes. For instance, the position of women as victims who require special "help" and "protection", instead of realisation of rights (Otto, 2005).

Nevertheless, law does hold a special position in the society. It is considered to express universally accepted values, and, therefore, it should not be ignored when addressing gender stereotyping. Law has the power to publicly name gender stereotyping as a problem that requires addressing. Without legal recognition, the harm of gender stereotyping remains hidden (Cook & Cusack, 2010). And in turn, stereotyping becomes validated through law.

Nevertheless, as explained in this chapter, drafting anti-stereotyping laws remains a challenging task. "Naming" gender stereotypes in legal norms needs to be accompanied by addressing the roots of these harmful attitudes and proposing solutions. The most carefully drafted legal norms are not enough to bring about sustainable change. The deeply rooted and multifaceted character of gender stereotypes suggests that their eradication requires a coordinated effort of different sectors and institutions. Everyday individual behaviours should not be overlooked. Each day people can contribute to building a social climate where gender stereotyping is not tolerated.

It is crucial to recognise that this chapter is just a beginning of engaging with the complex topic of law and gender stereotyping. Certainly, it is an important debate to explore. The amount of legal and policy instruments aimed at the elimination of gender stereotyping, together with the continuous negative impact of stereotypes, suggests that there is significant scope for improvement. Without further research into the anti-stereotyping laws and policies, as well as into the link between gender stereotyping and human rights violations, it will be very difficult to better grasp this complex phenomenon. More importantly, it will be much more challenging to design effective tools for eliminating gender stereotyping and in turn bring forward gender equality and put an end to violations of human rights.

Notes

1. See, for example: Protocol to the African Charter on Human and People's Rights on the Rights of Women in Africa; Inter-American Convention on the Prevention, Punishment, and Eradication of Violence against Women; the Council of Europe Convention on Preventing and Combating Violence against Women and Domestic Violence; A Union of Equality: Gender Equality Strategy 2020–2025 by the European Commission.
2. Also see, for example: General recommendations by the Committee on the Elimination of Discrimination against Women: No. 27, on older women and protection of their human rights; No. 28, on the core obligations of state parties under Article 2 of the Convention on the Elimination of All Forms of Discrimination against Women; No. 35, on gender-based violence against women, updating general recommendation No. 19; No. 36, on the right of girls and women to education; No. 37, on gender-related dimensions of disaster risk reduction in the context of climate change.
3. See Endnote 1.
4. For example, the Declaration on the Elimination of Violence against Women and Violence against Children in ASEAN; the SAARC Social Charter.

References

Agius, S. (2015). *Human Rights and Intersex People. Issue Paper Published by the Council of Europe Commissioner for Human Rights*. Council of Europe.

Ahmed, S. (2015). Introduction: Sexism, the Problem with a Name. *New Formations, 86*, 5–13.

Auchmuty, R. (2012). Law and the Power of Feminism: How Marriage Lost Its Power to Oppress Women. *Feminist Legal Studies, 20*, 71–87.

Bates, L. (2012). *The Everyday Sexism Project*. Retrieved June 9, 2021, from https://everydaysexism.com/

Ben-asher, N. (2016). The Two Laws of Sex Stereotyping. *Boston College Law Review, 57*(4), 1187–1235.

Brems, E., & Timmer, A. (2016). Stereotyping as a Human Rights Issue: Crosscutting Themes. In E. Brems & A. Timmer (Eds.), *Stereotypes and Human Rights Law* (pp. 2–4). Intersentia.

Caracciolo di Torella, E., & Masselot, A. (2020). *Caring Responsibilities in European Law and Policy: Who Cares?* Routledge.

Chinkin, C., Wright, S., & Charlesworth, H. (2005). Feminist Approaches to International Law: Reflections from Another Century. In D. Buss & A. Manji (Eds.), *International Law Modern Feminist Approaches* (pp. 17–46). Hart Publishing.

Cho, S., Crenshaw, K., & McCall, L. (2013). Toward a Field of Intersectionality Studies: Theory, Applications and Praxis. *Signs: Journal of Women in Culture and Society, 38*(4), 785–810.

Choudhry, S. (2016). Towards a Transformative Conceptualisation of Violence Against Women – A Critical Frame Analysis of Council of Europe Discourse on Violence Against Women. *The Modern Law Review, 79*(3), 406–441.

Clay-Warner, J., & Edgemon, T. G. (2020). Feminist Approaches to Victimology. In S. Walklate et al. (Eds.), *The Emerald Handbook of Feminism, Criminology and Social Change* (pp. 35–50). Emerald Publishing Limited.

CoE. (2011). *Explanatory Report to the Council of Europe Convention on Preventing and Combating Violence Against Women and Domestic Violence*.

Connell, R. (1993). *Masculinities*. Polity Press.

Cook, R. J., & Cusack, S. (2010). *Gender Stereotyping: Transnational Legal Perspectives*. University of Pennsylvania Press.

Cook, R., & Weiss, C. (2016). Gender Stereotyping in the Military. Insights from Court Cases. In E. Brems & A. Timmer (Eds.), *Stereotypes and Human Rights Law* (pp. 175–198). Intersentia.

Cook, R. J., Cusack, S., & Dickens, B. M. (2010). Unethical Female Stereotyping in Reproductive Health. *International Journal of Gynecology and Obstetrics, 109*, 255–258.

Crenshaw, K. (1989). Demarginalizing the Intersection of Race and Sex: A Black Feminist Critique of Antidiscrimination Doctrine. *Feminist Theory and Antiracist Politics, University of Chicago Legal Forum, 1989*(1), 139–167.

CSW. (2010). *Commemorating 30 Years of the Convention on the Elimination of All Forms of Discrimination Against Women: Moderator's Summary*. UN Doc. E/CN.6/2010/CRP.12.

Cusack, S. (2013a). *Gender Stereotyping as a Human Rights Violation*.

Cusack, S. (2013b). The CEDAW as a Legal Framework for Transnational Discourses on Gender Stereotyping. In A. Hellum & H. Sinding Aasen (Eds.),

Women's Human Rights: CEDAW in International, Regional and National Law (pp. 124–157). Cambridge University Press.

Cusack, S. (2016). Building Momentum Towards Change. How the UN's Response to Stereotyping Is Evolving. In E. Brems & A. Timmer (Eds.), *Stereotypes and Human Rights Law* (pp. 11–38). Intersentia.

de Silva de Alwis, R. (2011). Examining Gender Stereotypes in New Work/Family Reconciliation Policies: The Creation of a New Paradigm for Egalitarian Legislation. *Duke Journal of Gender Law and Policy, 18*, 205–334.

Fredman, S. (1997). *Women and the Law*. Clarendon Press.

Fredman, S. (2016). *Intersectional Discrimination in EU Gender Equality and Non-Discrimination Law*. European Commission.

Gill, A. K., & Walker, S. (2020). On Honour, Culture and Violence Against Women in Black and Minority Ethnic Communities. In S. Walklate et al. (Eds.), *The Emerald Handbook of Feminism, Criminology and Social Change* (pp. 157–176). Emerald Publishing Limited.

Guerrina, R., & Zalewski, M. (2007). Negotiating Difference/Negotiating Rights: The Challenges and Opportunities of Women's Human Rights. Forum Introduction. *Review of International Studies, 33*, 5–10.

Hester, M., & Lilley, S. J. (2014). *Preventing Violence Against Women: Article 12 of the Istanbul Convention. A Collection of Papers on the Council of Europe Convention on Preventing and Combating Violence Against Women and Domestic Violence*. Council of Europe.

Hirschmann, N. J. (2013). Freedom, Power and Agency in Feminist Legal Theory. In M. Davies & V. E. Munro (Eds.), *The Ashgate Research Companion to Feminist Legal Theory* (pp. 51–64). Ashgate Publishing Company.

Hodson, L. (2014). Women's Rights and the Periphery: CEDAW's Optional Protocol. *European Journal of International Law, 25*(2), 561–578.

Holtmaat, R., & Naber, J. (2011). *Women's Human Rights and Culture from Deadlock to Dialogue*. Intersentia.

Hunter, R. (2013). Contesting the Dominant Paradigm: Feminist Critiques of Liberal Legalism. In M. Davies & V. E. Munro (Eds.), *The Ashgate Research Companion to Feminist Legal Theory* (pp. 13–30). Ashgate.

Kimelblatt, M. (2016). Reducing Harmful Effects of Machismo Culture on Latin American Domestic Violence Laws: Amending the Convention of Belém do Pará to Resemble the Istanbul Convention. *The George Washington International Law Review, 49*(1), 405–439.

Mcgee Crotty, P. (1996). Legislating Equality. *International Journal of Law, Policy and the Family, 10*, 317–333.

Otto, D. (2005). Disconcerting 'Masculinities': Reinventing the Gendered Subject(s) of International Human Rights Law. In D. Buss & A. Manji (Eds.), *International Law Modern Feminist Approaches* (pp. 105–130). Hart Publishing.

Peroni, L. (2016). Violence Against Migrant Women: The Istanbul Convention Through a Postcolonial Feminist Lens. *Feminist Legal Studies, 24*, 49–67.

Peroni, L., & Timmer, A. (2016). Gender Stereotyping in Domestic Violence Cases. An Analysis of the European Court of Human Rights Jurisprudence. In E. Brems & A. Timmer (Eds.), *Stereotypes and Human Rights Law* (pp. 39–65). Intersentia.

Šimonović, D. (2014). Global and Regional Standards on Violence Against Women: The Evolution and Synergy of the CEDAW and Istanbul Conventions. *Human Rights Quarterly, 36*, 590–606.

Smart, C. (1989). *Feminism and the Power of Law*. Routledge.

Timmer, A. (2011). Toward an Anti-Stereotyping Approach for the European Court of Human Rights. *Human Rights Law Review*, 707–738.

Timmer, A. (2015). Judging Stereotypes: What the European Court of Human Rights Can Borrow from American and Canadian Equal Protection Law. *The American Journal of Comparative Law, 63*(1), 239–284.

UN Treaty Collection. (2021). *Status of the Convention on the Elimination of All Forms of Discrimination Against Women*. Retrieved April 30, 2021, from https://treaties.un.org/Pages/ViewDetails.aspx?src=TREATY&mtdsg_no=IV-8&chapter=4

Zwingel, S. (2016). *Translating International Women's Rights: The CEDAW Convention in Context*. Springer.

CHAPTER 3

Trans Pregnancy in a Repronormative World

Gillian Love

3.1 Introduction

In 2008, Thomas Beatie produced a media sensation in the US after publishing a first-person essay in *The Advocate*, a prominent LGBT publication, about his impending parenthood (Beatie, 2008). Beatie was a trans man, and he was pregnant with his and his wife Nancy's first child. In his *Advocate* article, he explained that as part of his transition[1] he had undergone top surgery[2] but had retained his ability to give birth. His wife, suffering from endometriosis, had undergone a hysterectomy years before, so was unable to carry a child. The couple therefore made the decision that Beatie should carry their child, conceived with an anonymous sperm donor. The photograph accompanying the *Advocate* essay of Beatie, shot naked from the waist up caressing his pregnant stomach, was widely reproduced. The media dubbed Beatie "the first pregnant man", and he was recognised by the Guinness Book of World Records as "the first married man to give birth" (Guinness World Records, n.d.). Beatie thus became, figuratively, *the* pregnant man (Pearce & White, 2019), "something exotic, different, a symptom of the modern age" (Lester, 2017, p. 146). Several other countries have since had their "first" pregnant men (the UK has had two "first"

G. Love (✉)
University of Sussex, Brighton, UK
e-mail: G.Love@sussex.ac.uk

G. Guney et al. (eds.), *Towards Gender Equality in Law*,
https://doi.org/10.1007/978-3-030-98072-6_3

pregnant men, in fact), and each time the media have responded with sensationalism, shock and a narrative of novelty (Pearce & White, 2019).

Beatie was certainly not the first trans man to go through the experience of pregnancy or childbirth. In 1999, Matt Rice, a trans man, gave birth to his son Blake (Califia-Rice, 2000), and trans men who give birth have been the focus of academic research before (More, 1998). More recent research has indicated that the number of trans pregnancies may be increasing. One 2014 study recruited 41 trans respondents who had conceived post-transition (Light et al., 2014); another study found that young trans people had similar rates of pregnancy as the general population (Veale et al., 2016). More recently, the international Trans Pregnancy Project has interviewed 50 trans participants from the UK, Australia, Canada and the US who have given birth, have been pregnant or may want to in future ("Trans Pregnancy", n.d.; Riggs et al., 2020, 2021).

Trans people who give birth or want to conceive face a number of social, medical and legal barriers. Some jurisdictions require trans people to be sterilised if they wish to gain legal recognition of their gender (Dunne, 2017; Repo, 2019), and options for preservation of fertility are not always well understood (Chen et al., 2017; Nixon, 2013). Furthermore, when trans people do become pregnant and give birth, they are subject to stigma and legal bureaucracy that struggles to recognise someone who gives birth as anything other than a woman or a mother (Pearce et al., 2019).

This chapter explores how current legal frameworks across the globe make it difficult or impossible for transmasculine and non-binary (TMNB)[3] people to give birth and be recognised as a "father" or a "parent". It begins with trans sterilisation requirements in Europe and beyond and frames these requirements as overt biopolitical regulation of trans bodies. It then uses case studies of two trans men—Yuval Topper-Erez (Israel) and Freddy McConnell (England)—who have given birth and have struggled to navigate legal and bureaucratic systems that erase the possibility of the pregnant man. Finally, the chapter addresses three common objections to legal reform for trans parents: that trans pregnancy is "unnatural"; that trans pregnancy is undesireable; and that trans rights clash with women's rights. In examining these arguments, the chapter concludes that the failure to protect trans people's reproductive rights and desires across the globe is a result of the perceived threat trans reproduction poses to the dominant *repronormative* order: the preservation of heteropatriarchal standards of sexuality in which only reproductive sex between cis men and -women is deemed legitimate (Franke, 2001; Weissman, 2017).

3.2 Understanding Sex, Gender and Being Trans

The term "trans" is an umbrella term, the widely accepted definition of which is a person whose gender identity is incongruent with the one they were assigned at birth (Stonewall, 2019). A cisgender or cis person is one whose assigned gender matches their gender identity. Gender is assigned at birth based on visible characteristics, usually the presence of either a penis and testicles or a vulva and vagina. If the former, a baby is assigned male and is assumed to be a man; if the latter, a baby is assigned female and is assumed to be a woman.

Some find it is useful to separate gender—a complex set of physical, psychological and social characteristics—from biological sex. Biological sex is usually captured by a cluster of characteristics, including chromosomes, gonads, reproductive organs, balance of hormones and secondary sex characteristics. We define biological sex along the binary of male and female. Some therefore argue that sex is an immutable, biological fact, whereas gender is a social and cultural identity (Oakley, 1972). In this sense, one can have a "female" body but identify as a man.

However, the distinction between sex and gender is often murkier than this. Feminist and queer theorists have pointed out that the terms "male" and "female" are *already gendered* concepts we use to describe clusters of biological traits, and furthermore that only one biological trait (visible sex organs) is used to assign someone's *gender*, not simply their *sex* (Butler, 1994; Fausto-Sterling, 2000). When expecting parents receive an ultrasound scan, they are told they are having a *girl* or a *boy*, not that their baby has a penis or is an "anatomic female".

Those babies grow into children, teenagers and adults whose identities do not match the gender they were assigned at birth. A person assigned female at birth may identify as a trans man, for example, and someone assigned male at birth may identify as a trans woman. However, one's gender identity does not have to fall neatly at one pole of the binary gender spectrum; there are a wealth of other identities that fall along this spectrum including non-binary, genderqueer, gender non-conforming and so on. In general, all of these identities can be thought of under the "trans" umbrella.

3.3 Understanding Trans Pregnancy

Being trans does not necessarily require a change to one's reproductive organs or any other anatomical features. Some trans people choose to medically transition, which can consist of hormone therapy and/or surgical interventions. Statistics suggest, however, that most trans people do not undergo surgeries to transform their reproductive organs (Nolan et al., 2019; Quinn et al., 2017). This chapter focuses on trans people who have the capacity to get pregnant and give birth. In general, they are people who were assigned female at birth, but identify either as trans men or another label like transmasculine or non-binary (someone who does not identify along the man/woman gender binary at all). I use the acronym TMNB (trans men/masculine and non-binary) throughout this chapter in order to capture this group of people. If a TMNB person wants to conceive, they are advised to stop taking testosterone (if they are undergoing hormone therapy). They then have the same options as any person who wants to conceive, namely through sex with their partner who can produce sperm, using a sperm donor or conceiving through assisted reproductive technologies.

3.4 The Legal and Medical Gatekeeping of Trans Reproduction

The road to trans pregnancy is not necessarily easy or even possible for all. Trans people's civil rights vary greatly across the globe, as does discrimination and stigma. Even in jurisdictions where trans people enjoy legal protection (e.g. through anti-discrimination laws) and relatively straightforward mechanisms to have their gender legally recognised, there persists a lack of understanding of trans pregnancy in the medical community and more generally (Hoffkling et al., 2017). Furthermore, there are many jurisdictions where the ability for trans people to reproduce at all is curtailed or even removed entirely.

For example, in 16 European jurisdictions, sterilisation is a requirement for any person who wishes to change their legal gender (Dunne, 2017). Legal recognition means one's gender marker on passports and other official documents match one's identity and presentation. In some jurisdictions, like Malta (TGEU, 2015), Luxembourg (Intersex and Transgender Luxembourg, 2018), Argentina and Ireland (Open Society Foundations, 2014), legal recognition is obtained through a self-declaration framework.

These jurisdictions do not require medical interventions of any kind to gain legal gender recognition. Other jurisdictions do have medical requirements, for example the UK, which requires diagnosis of gender dysphoria by a registered medical practitioner or psychologist; living in the "acquired gender" for at least two years prior to the application; and the intent to live in the acquired gender until death (Gender Recognition Act, 2004).

Finally, some jurisdictions require trans people to be sterilised if they want their legal gender to be changed. In Finland (Repo, 2019), trans people are required to prove they are sterile either through natural infertility or through medical interventions from hormone therapy or surgical sterilisation to gain legal gender recognition. The Czech Republic also requires a "termination of reproductive function" through removal of ovaries or castration, a requirement that the European Committee of Social Rights has noted "lacks an objective and reasonable justification" and is a situation that "has a serious impact on a person's health and ability to give free consent" to a significant medical procedure (European Committee of Social Rights, 2018). In 2017, the European Court of Human Rights found that requiring sterilisation for gender recognition violates Article 8 of the European Convention on Human Rights (A.P., Garçon and Nicot v. France, 2017).

Despite this, 16 EU states enforce a requirement the ECHR has deemed a violation of human rights. Furthermore, trans people face coercive sterilisation in many other parts of the globe including Japan (The Lancet, 2019), Hong Kong, Singapore, South Korea (Open Society Foundations, 2014) Uzbekistan, Kazakhstan and Tajikistan (TGEU, 2019). Sterilisation requirements are defended for a number of reasons including the avoidance of "legal confusion", fears that children of trans parents will face discrimination and abuse, and aversion to reproduction outside of traditional understandings of sex and gender (Dunne, 2017). The latter argument is perhaps the most explicit example of repronormativity—the preservation of heteropatriarchal standards of sexuality in which only reproductive sex between cis men and -women is deemed legitimate (Franke, 2001; Weissman, 2017). The possibility of the pregnant man poses a challenge to these repronormative values that form the basis of legal and social understandings of sex and gender.

3.5 The Legal and Bureaucratic "Solutions" to the Pregnant Man

Compulsory sterilisation is at the explicit end of the spectrum when it comes to the gatekeeping of trans reproduction; repronormativity also results in social, legal and bureaucratic barriers to those who reproduce outside of the bounds of traditional, heteronormative structures. Even in countries without a sterilisation requirement, the legal and bureaucratic elision of pregnant men causes distress and inconvenience. This section presents two case studies, the first (in Israel) exemplifying the experience of trans men in contexts where the act of giving birth and being a woman are fundamentally intertwined. The second example (in the UK) shows that even in contexts where pregnancy and childbirth do not invalidate a TMNB person's gender identity, the category of "mother" is strictly enforced as a matter of reproductive, biological fact.

Yuval Topper-Erez, a trans man, gave birth in 2011 to his first child in Israel with his partner Matan Topper-Erez. The new parents registered their newborn son with Israel's Interior Ministry as required, but the ministry refused to recognise both men as the biological fathers. Gender reassignment was possible in Israel, and both Yuval and Matan were legally recognised as male. Israel had also previously recognised same-sex couples as parents; in 2005, a same-sex couple was granted the right to adopt one another's children (Yaros Hakak v the Attorney General, 2005), and in 2008 the right for same-sex couples to adopt was confirmed in a decision by the attorney general Menachem Mazuz (Yoaz, 2008). However, although in the past the state had recognized same-sex couples as parents to children through adoption orders, there had never been a same-sex couple both registered as a child's *biological* parents (Efraim, 2013).

After a protracted legal battle, the Interior Ministry settled on a bureaucratic solution: they re-registered Yuval as female in order to register him as his son's biological mother, and Matan as his biological father. Yuval was subsequently re-re-registered as a man (Efraim, 2013). Yuval went on to have more children, each time having to go through the same process of registering as female and re-registering as male, leading him to joke in a conference talk that he must hold the record for number of legal gender reassignments in the world (Beatie et al., 2020).

The *Times of Israel* noted that while this was presented as a groundbreaking case in Israeli media, the Interior Ministry's solution could be described as "a bureaucratic sleight of hand" that the couple were forced to accept (Santo, 2013). Confirming this, Matan in an interview with media outlet YNet called the move "bureaucratic stupidity, made up of lack of respect and sensitivity to the fact that there are a variety of ways and identities through which to express yourself" (Efraim, 2013). When confronted with Yuval's existence as a man who had given birth, the Israeli state simply denied the possibility of his existence. Only after a great deal of legal pressure from Interior Minister Gideon Sa'ar and the chairman of the Knesset Interior Committee Miri Regev (JTA, 2013) were the Topper-Erezes offered a convoluted solution that arguably increases the "legal confusion" that trans parents are often positioned as creating (Dunne, 2017). Furthermore, there seemed to be little recognition from the state or the judiciary that this process had a personal and social cost for the Topper-Erezes. A legal and bureaucratic solution to the "problem" of Yuval's existence was the priority, not the dignity or recognition of trans parents.

The problems with this kind of solution were finally recognised by the Israeli High Court of Justice on 5 May 2021. The Court heard the case of another couple, Yonatan and Daniel Martin Marom, two men who had a son together (Parsons, 2021). After giving birth to their son, Yonatan found that his gender in the population registry had been changed without his permission from male to female and that he had been registered as the child's mother (Joffre, 2021). The court ruled that, instead, trans parents can opt to appear on their children's birth certificates with the non-gendered designation "parent" rather than "mother" or "father". The court argued that regardless of Yonatan's gender in the population registry, "that does not justify the harm caused by registering him on the child's birth certificate as a 'mother'" (Joffre, 2021).

TMNB people who give birth in Israel can therefore remain registered as male and avoid being registered as the "mother" of their children. However, they must also confirm to a Gender Adjustment Committee that their gender is unchanged after the birth, an element that has attracted some criticism. Dr Ido Katri, Assistant Professor of Law at Tel Aviv University and trans advocate, was quoted in *PinkNews* and *The Jerusalem Post* as arguing that "the ruling continues to reflect outdated perceptions and conditions the recognition of trans parenting on its appeal to a medical committee" (Joffre, 2021; Parsons, 2021). Despite this, he also noted this was a clear decision "in favor of the trans community's right to parenthood and equality", and the ruling has been welcomed as a step forward for trans parents in Israel. In the UK, journalist Freddy McConnell recently lost his own legal battle to be recognised as his child's father or parent rather than "mother". McConnell, a trans man who gave birth to his son, was told by the General Register Office (responsible for registration of births and deaths in England and Wales) that he would have to be registered as the child's mother, although the registration could be in his current (male) name. McConnell challenged this in high court in 2019 (The Queen (on the Application of TT) v Registrar General for England and Wales, 2019). His primary claim was that he should be entitled to be registered as a "father, "parent" or "gestational parent" on his child's birth certificate. His secondary and alternative claim, on the basis that domestic law requires his registration as "mother", was for a declaration of incompatibility under Section 4 of the Human Rights Act (1998) on the ground that UK law is incompatible with his and his child's Convention rights under Articles 8 and 14 of the European Convention on Human Rights. The high court judge Sir Andrew McFarlane ruled against McConnell, arguing that the only way McConnell can be registered on his child's birth certificate is as the mother, a decision that was upheld on appeal (R (Alfred McConnell) v The Registrar General for England and Wales and Others, 2020).

Unlike in Topper-Erez's case, the high court judgement did not conclude that giving birth made McConnell a woman. In fact, the judgement explicitly notes that McConnell is legally a man and that "[f]or all other purposes, be they social, psychological or emotional, [McConnell] will be a male parent to his child and therefore his 'father'" (para. 147). However, the judgement states that the term "mother" "is the status afforded to a person who undergoes the physical and biological process of carrying a pregnancy and giving birth" (para. 279). The terms "mother" and "father" are simply "a matter of the role taken in the biological process, rather the person's particular sex or gender" (para. 139). The judgement cites the Human Fertilisation and Embryology Act (HFEA) (2008), Section 33 of which specifies that "the woman who is carrying or has carried a child as a result of the placing in her of an embryo or of sperm and eggs, and no other woman, is to be treated as the mother of the child". In other words, the person who carries a child is legally considered to be the mother of that child.

Interestingly, despite the gendered language in the HFEA (i.e. "the woman who is carrying or has carried a child"), the judgement in McConnell's case divorces the category of "mother" from the sexed or gendered subject, instead arguing that "mother" is defined entirely by reproductive experience (para. 139) (Pearce et al., 2019). Furthermore, the Appeal judgement notes that the term "parent" is defined elsewhere in law (paras 65-66) and so cannot be used on a birth certificate in the place of "mother" as McConnell desired.

The idea that the term "mother" is divorced from a sexed or gendered subject, of course, stands in tension with the social and cultural understanding of the term. Beyond the specific reproductive experience of childbirth, motherhood is an inherently gendered concept which denotes a familial role defined by heteropatriarchal society (Fineman, 1992). McConnell's legal representatives argued that being identified as "mother" on his child's birth certificate undermines his legal status as a man, and effectively "outs" McConnell as trans to anyone who reads that document. Indeed, the high court judgement notes there is likely to be "a tension" (para. 147) between the legal definition of motherhood and the social and psychological understanding of the term, but neither the high court nor the Appeal judgement were able to identify a legal remedy for this tension.

Both McConnell and Topper-Erez's cases demonstrate the embedded legal understanding of "mother" as discursively inseparable from a person's biology and the specific reproductive experience of childbirth. In these jurisdictions, deviating from parental roles and markers was more difficult than reassigning one's legal gender. Thus, the regulation of trans reproduction begins at birth with one's assignment of sex which carries with it a future parental role (Katri, 2019). However, the reversal of position in Israel, where TMNB parents can now register as "parent" rather than "mother", demonstrates one of several legal and bureaucratic solutions to the "problem" of TMNB people giving birth, possibilities that have been modelled already in various parts of the globe. In the Canadian province of Quebec, up to four people of any gender can be assigned as a parent to a newborn child (Katri, 2019), and the Swedish system allows trans men who give birth to be listed as father on birth certificates, and trans women who contribute sperm as mothers (TGEU, n.d.). Rather than generating contradiction and paradox—like registering and re-registering a person as a different gender six times over or designating someone a "male mother"—these solutions model a helpful and coherent way forward for trans parents. Despite this, barriers to the recognition of trans parenthood persist.

3.6 The Repronormative Barriers to Legal Reform

This section turns attention to the common objections raised to legal reform, analysing their underlying theoretical constructions of sex, gender and reproduction. "Legal reform" here refers to changes in legislation that make trans reproduction possible (e.g. removing sterilisation requirements) and that allow for the recognition of trans parents (e.g. allowing a trans man to be registered as his child's father). The objections presented here are not only legal arguments but also social, cultural and political ones that draw upon a number of common discursive ideas. The first, the "nature" argument, is an explicitly essentialist argument that cis women instinctively desire motherhood due to their biology, and the ideal family consists of a cis mother and a cis father. This is analysed through the concept of repronormativity. The second argument is an implicitly eugenic one that positions trans (and other "deviant") bodies reproducing as undesirable. Finally, I turn attention to the argument put forward by trans-exclusionary radical feminists (TERFs) that positions an expansion of trans rights as an attack on (cis) women's rights. Despite these three positions appearing incompatible (most feminists would balk at the suggestion that women are biologically wired to desire motherhood, for example), they share a rhetoric appeal to "common sense" understandings of gender and reproduction that are in fact expressions of conservative repronormative values.

3.6.1 The "Nature" Argument

In general, there exists a "common sense" discursive framing of reproduction based on heteropatriarchal values that exist in most parts of the world. In this framework, women have the reproductive organs that enable pregnancy and childbirth, and it is expected that motherhood is the desired state for most women; indeed, womanhood and motherhood are so discursively linked that "women's health" is almost always used to refer to reproductive health (Waggoner, 2017). Men have the capacity to produce sperm but not to carry children; thus, fatherhood is a role decoupled from the act of carrying and giving birth to children. A cis woman and a cis man having children together is the natural, normative state against which other acts of reproduction are measured (Fineman, 1992; Weissman, 2017).

This framework that understands biological sex to be a determinant of gender and therefore of parental role is deeply embedded into many legal systems. For example, there persists a biologically determinist understanding in European law that every person has unambiguous biological traits that are male or female; only those with female reproductive organs can give birth; therefore, that person is a woman (Dunne, 2017) or at least, as in McConnell's case, a mother.

While the socially constructed nature of gender is now a relatively uncontroversial concept, the distinction of sex as immutable and natural (therefore untouched by social and cultural norms) persists. Furthermore, reproduction as an act discursively tied to the heterosexual family unit remains the norm even in liberal contexts (Fineman, 1992; Karaian, 2013). Weissman (2017) notes that countries with liberal attitudes towards same-sex marriage have generally lower levels of acceptance towards same-sex adoption and assisted reproduction, indicating a discomfort with non-reproductive sexuality. This is something Edelman terms "reproductive futurism": the privileging of sexual acts that propagate the species and are thus granted legitimacy that most queer people cannot achieve (Edelman, 2004).

It is therefore only when reproduction happens within the bounds of legitimacy and "nature" that it is socially accepted. Franke (2001) coined the term "repronormativity" to describe hegemonic social forces that incentivize motherhood and erase the possibility of non-reproductive desire and pleasure. Any reproduction that falls outside of heteronormative conceptualisations of the family is framed as illegitimate, and therefore a legitimate target of state sanction (Eggert & Engeli, 2015). This argument against legal recognition of trans reproduction can be found in a number of legal jurisdictions (Dunne, 2017).

3.6.2 *The Eugenic Argument*

The overt curtailing of reproduction in certain sections of the population (e.g. requiring the sterilisation of trans people) can usefully be thought of as a *biopolitical* project, and also as a eugenic one. "Biopolitics" is the term Foucault used to describe the mechanism through which nation states implicitly or explicitly manage populations (Foucault, 1998). A dimension of *biopower*—"a power to foster life or disallow it to the point of death" (Foucault, 1998, p. 138)—biopolitics encourages the proliferation of life through diffusive and pervasive means, but also works in tandem with disciplinary power that is exerted upon unruly bodies (Foucault, 2008). The result is regulation of populations and individual bodies that is sometimes overt but is often implicit, framed through concepts like reproductive choice and responsibility (Rabinow & Rose, 2006).

Eugenics—the practice of improving the population by control of inherited qualities (Shakespeare, 1998)—could be conceived of as a particularly overt form of state power. However, Shakespeare (1998) differentiates between "strong eugenics"—"population-level improvement by control of reproduction via state intervention" (p. 669)—and "weak eugenics". He frames weak eugenics as "promoting technologies of reproductive selection via non-coercive individual choices", for example using antenatal testing to present pregnant people with the decision to end an otherwise wanted pregnancy due to the detection of an abnormality (Shakespeare, 1998, p. 669). It is my contention that trans people face both strong and weak eugenics.

The sterilisation requirements for trans people seeking legal recognition in many parts of the world is a clear example of strong eugenics (Lowik, 2018). Beyond explicit practices like sterilisation, the barriers to legal recognition of trans parenthood demonstrate the working of weak eugenics and biopolitics. TMNB people who give birth are often blamed for making an "irresponsible" choice to have children in a way that causes legal and bureaucratic problems. For example, Freddy McConnell's legal battle to be recognised as his child's father has been framed by some sections of the media as a selfish and harmful situation for his son who would be "without a mother" (Ditum, 2019; White, 2020). Furthermore, the potential effects of prior testosterone use on a pregnancy is framed as a selfish risk (Jeffreys, 2014), even though the current medical advice for TMNB people who want to conceive is simply to stop taking testosterone in the absence of evidence prior use affects birth outcomes (Brandt et al., 2019; Obedin-Maliver & Makadon, 2016). This frames individual reproductive choice as a way to avoid stigma and distress rather than locating the problem within flawed legal structures, a neoliberal biopolitical move that places responsibility on the individual rather than the state.

The argument that the barriers to trans reproduction are both eugenic and biopolitical is contextualised by similar strong and weak eugenic practices levelled against minority groups throughout history. In the US, Women of Colour have historically been discouraged from reproduction through involuntary sterilisation and more diffuse barriers like systemic poverty and vilification as poor mothers (Forward Together, 2005; Silliman, 2004). Canadian provinces instituted laws in the 1930s that sanctioned involuntary sterilisation of women who were institutionalised for mental health issues (Amy & Rowlands, 2018), as did Sweden (Boréus, 2006). Indigenous women were also targeted by sterilisation programmes until the late 1970s in the US and Canada (Pegoraro, 2015), and French doctors performed involuntary sterilisation and abortions on thousands of Black women in French foreign territories in the 1960s and 1970s (Vergès, 2018). In the UK, screening technology and directive advice from medical professionals has arguably created a weak eugenic climate in which aborting pregnancies with "abnormalities" and therefore potential disabilities is considered desirable (McLaughlin, 2003; Shakespeare, 1998). Furthermore, in February 2020 controversy was ignited in the UK when a blog post from a Conservative government aid was unearthed supporting "enforced contraception" for those in the "permanent underclass" (Proctor, 2020). Academic and journalistic commentary on the incident expressed concern that Conservative Prime Minister Boris Johnson did not explicitly condemn the remarks (Bienkov & Payne, 2020; Bush, 2020; Wester, 2020; Woodcock, 2020).

In each of the examples above, minority groups are identified who present some threat to the repronormative order (Weissman, 2017). Repronormativity does not just produce children; it *re*produces *values*, the heteropatriarchal and nationalist values upon which nation-states are often built (Yuval-Davis, 1996). Heteronormative reproduction between cis women and -men is so embedded into many social and legal landscapes that to reproduce outside of this framework is to attack the foundations upon which society is built (Fineman, 1992; Weissman, 2017). Women of Colour and working-class women are characterised as promiscuous, irresponsible and a burden on the welfare state (Hawkes, 1995; Jones, 2013; Tyler, 2008), and those with physical and mental disabilities are "unfit" to reproduce (Boréus, 2006). Through overt sterilisation requirements and legal barriers to recognition as parents, trans people are subject to "eugenic logics" that position their reproductive capacity as confusing, undesirable or even dangerous (Lowik, 2018).

3.6.3 The "Women's Rights" Argument

The resistance to recognition of trans parenthood becomes more complex when supported by those with ostensibly feminist values. A vocal minority of feminists have argued against legislative and political efforts to expand trans people's civil rights, positioning these rights as clashing with those of cis women. Called "gender critical" feminism by its supporters and "trans-exclusionary radical feminism", or TERFism, by its detractors, this strand of feminism has gained increasing popularity in recent years, particularly in the UK (Hines, 2019). Some TERFs[4] argue, following earlier work by feminist theorists like Sheila Jeffreys (1997) and Janice Raymond (1994), that gender is functionally indistinguishable from biological sex, and therefore one cannot identify as a woman if one is not born a woman. In Jeffrey's words, "[t]he inferior sex caste status of women is assigned with reference to their biology, and it is through their biology that their subordination is enforced and maintained through rape, impregnation and forced childbearing" (Jeffreys, 2014, p. 6). Others accept that gender can be self-defined, but that *femaleness* is an immutable and unchangeable fact determined by chromosomes and reproductive organs (Stock et al., 2019). In this iteration of the argument, gender is a social identity, whereas sex is a biological fact. A trans woman can identify as a woman if she likes, but she does not possess the *female* attributes that make her a "real" woman.

While the focus of TERFs tend to be on trans women and their "infiltration" of women's spaces (Bindel, 2019; Joyce, 2018; Richards, 2018), the logic underpinning this ideology is also applied to trans masculine and non-binary people. While there is little to no academic work published on "gender critical" views of trans pregnancy, TERFs in mainstream media have argued against calls to be inclusive of TMNB parents by using gender-neutral terms in relation to pregnancy like "pregnant persons" and "chest-feeding" (rather than breastfeeding) (Glosswitch, 2015; Moore, 2020). It is argued that this gender-neutralisation is irrational because the terms "mother" and "breast-feeding" are simply labels for biological realities (O'Neill, 2017). Again, this argument is easily challenged by troubling the gender/sex distinction upon which it is based: "motherhood" and "breast-feeding" are discursive and linguistic constructs that make our biology intelligible to us rather than immutable, independent truths (Butler, 1994).

However, another element of this argument is that legal reform and "gender-neutralisation" of the law runs the risk of ignoring the gendered nature of reproductive experiences and the social inequalities that stem from them. Abandoning the term "mother" in relation to pregnancy and childbirth limits our ability to frame them as political issues that primarily affect women, it is argued, and thus trans rights are pitted against (cis) women's rights (Glosswitch, 2015). This argument has been made in academic work on family law, albeit outside the framework of "gender critical" feminism. Fineman, in 1992, argued that the push towards gender neutrality in family law was part of a "male backlash" which aimed to reassert patriarchal control over the family. As the figure of the Mother rhetorically disappeared from family law in favour of gender neutrality, she argues, legal discourse became "Mother-purged" and no longer reflected the real gendered inequalities that women experienced (Fineman, 1992). The TERF argument against recognising trans birth parents as anything other than mothers can be framed as another iteration of this position: pregnancy, childbirth and reproductive rights are framed as *women's* issues for salient political reasons, so "gender-neutralising" motherhood glosses over the gendered inequalities cis women experience.

Fineman's paper, however, ends with a call to build family law from the perspective and lived experience of women and mothers (Fineman, 1992). If this principle were extended to trans parents, it would quickly become clear that on the issue of reproductive rights, trans and feminist activists share a great deal of ground. The argument that trans rights "clash" with those of cis women are challenged by examples of trans and women's organisations mobilising together. In Argentina, trans and women's groups have used the country's liberal legal and political framework around gender recognition (TGEU, 2013) to act as a platform to support abortion rights, using the same arguments around bodily autonomy and civil rights that had reformed gender identity laws (Junco & Fernández, 2020). In 2018, an abortion rights bill was discussed in congress, and trans and feminist interventions changed the wording of the bill to "women and gestating persons", modelling inclusive language that does not "de-gender" the issue of reproductive rights (Sutton & Borland, 2018). Similarly, in Northern Ireland, more recently, the campaign to decriminalise abortion saw mobilisation of trans and feminist groups to create a gender-inclusive abortion law that recognised TMNB people's need for abortion as well as cis women's (Moore & McIlwaine, 2020; TransgenderNI, 2019).

Here, TERF objections to inclusive legal reform become both unconvincing and counterproductive. In so fiercely defending the essentialist understanding of motherhood as a biological category, TERF arguments reinforce the repronormative framework that not only denies the existence of trans birth fathers but also discursively entwines cis women's bodies with the role of motherhood. As Weissman argues, "by determining who is considered illegitimate to reproduce, there is a reification of who can (and must) produce" (Weissman, 2017, p. 291): repronormativity mandates that cis (and white, affluent, middle-class) women *should* be mothers (Franke, 2001). Allying with trans activists' efforts to resist the idea that pregnancy is necessarily sexed as female would, rather than depoliticise reproductive rights, "further dismantle the normative and socially constructed sexed and gendered roles that govern us" (Karaian, 2013, p. 224). The TERF argument may be framed as a feminist position; however, its *effects* are indistinguishable from those of heteropatriarchal, repronormative politics that equate recognition of TMNB birth parents with social disorder and disgust.

3.7 Conclusion

Legal and social barriers persist in many contexts that prevent or make it difficult for TMNB people to become parents. For those who can have children, the legal systems in many countries do not accommodate an understanding that a person can give birth and yet not be a woman or want to be referred to as a mother. This is not simply an individual inconvenience for TMNB people who give birth, nor can it be dismissed as an innocuous quirk of law that often was not designed with trans people in mind. Trans reproduction destabilises the often deeply embedded "truth" in law and wider society that pregnancy is necessarily sexed as female, and trans fathers and birth parents therefore challenge the heteropatriarchal assumptions that many legal systems are built on.

Trans birth parents are framed by various actors and institutions as disruptive to nature and the biological order, legal certainty (Dunne, 2017), reproductive legitimacy (Lowik, 2018; Weissman, 2017), and cis women's rights (Bindel, 2019; Jeffreys, 2014; Stock, 2018). This chapter suggests that a reframing is in order. Seeing the "problem" of trans parents through the lens of repronormativity shifts focus from the individual experiences of TMNB parents—whose stories are nevertheless worthy of attention—to a wider hegemony that frames "deviant" reproduction as undesirable. Rather than locating the problem with TMNB parents, attention should continue to be turned to legal solutions that protect the reproductive and civil rights of trans people and their children.

Notes

1. Transitioning is the process a trans person goes through to live in their gender identity. This process differs for everyone but can include medical interventions like hormone therapy and surgery, social elements like "coming

out" to friends and family, and legal processes like changing one's name and gender marker on official documents.

2. Reduction or removal of breast tissue: the term "top surgery" is commonly used to refer to this procedure when undertaken as part of gender transition.
3. Not all trans people who were assigned female at birth identify as men—some prefer the term "transmasculine" (identifying more with the "masculine" end of the spectrum) or non-binary (identifying outside of the gender binary altogether). The term "transmasculine and non-binary" (TMNB) acts as an umbrella term for this group of trans people who may be able to get pregnant and give birth.
4. Some argue that the term "TERF" is a slur. I do not agree, and I use it here in recognition that (a) it was coined as a technical, neutral and descriptive term (Williams, 2014 in Hines, 2019) for an ideology that is weaponised by cis women against a marginalised group and (b) it is widely used and recognised to refer to the ideology under discussion.

References

A.P., Garçon and Nicot v. France. (2017). European Court of Human Rights, 79885/12, 52471/13 and 52596/13. HUDOC [Online]. Retrieved May 2, 2021, from https://hudoc.echr.coe.int/spa#%22itemid%22:[%22001-172913%22]

Amy, J.-J., & Rowlands, S. (2018). Legalised Non-consensual Sterilisation – Eugenics Put into Practice Before 1945, and the Aftermath. Part 1: USA, Japan, Canada and Mexico. *The European Journal of Contraception & Reproductive Health Care, 23*(2), 121–129.

Beatie, T. (2008). Labor of Love: Is Society Ready for This Pregnant Husband? *The Advocate*, 14 March. Retrieved January 28, 2020, from http://www.advocate.com/news/2008/03/14/labor-love.

Beatie, T., Freddy, M., & Topper-Erez, Y. (2020). Pregnancy in the Limelight, presented at the Trans Pregnancy, Fertility, Reproduction, and Body Autonomy: An International Conference, The Carriageworks, Leeds, UK, 14 January.

Bienkov, A., & Payne, A. (2020). The Andrew Sabisky Eugenics Scandal Is the Latest in Boris Johnson's History of Racism, Sexism, and Homophobia, *Business Insider*, 17 February. Retrieved May 19, 2020, from https://www.businessinsider.com/andrew-sabisky-boris-johnson-alleged-racism-sexism-homophobia-2020-2.

Bindel, J. (2019). How Transgender Turf Wars Put Lives in Danger, *UnHerd*, 20 March. Retrieved May 19, 2020, from https://unherd.com/2019/03/how-transgender-turf-wars-put-lives-in-danger/.

Boréus, K. (2006). Discursive Discrimination of the 'mentally deficient' in Interwar Sweden. *Disability & Society, 2*(5), 441–454.

Brandt, J. S., Patel, A. J., Marshall, I., & Bachmann, G. A. (2019). Transgender Men, Pregnancy, and the 'New' Advanced Paternal Age: A Review of the Literature. *Maturitas, 128*, 17–21.

Bush, S. (2020). The Andrew Sabisky row raises questions for Dominic Cummings, *New Statesman*, 17 February. Retrieved May 18, 2020, from https://www.newstatesman.com/politics/uk/2020/02/andrew-sabisky-row-raises-questions-dominic-cummings.

Butler, J. (1994). Contingent Foundations: Feminism and the Questions of 'Postmodernism'. In *The Postmodern Turn: New Perspectives on Social Theory*. Cambridge University Press.

Califia-Rice, P. (2000). 'Family Values', *The Village Voice (Online)*, 20 June. Retrieved February 4, 2020, from https://www.villagevoice.com/2000/06/20/family-values/.

Chen, D., Simons, L., Johnson, E. K., Lockart, B. A., & Finlayson, C. (2017). Fertility Preservation for Transgender Adolescents. *Journal of Adolescent Health, 61*(1), 120–123.

Ditum, S. (2019). 'Transgender 'motherlessness' Is a Chilly Fiction to Impose on Children', *The Telegraph*, 17 July. Retrieved May 6, 2020, from https://www.telegraph.co.uk/politics/2019/07/17/transgender-motherlessness-chilly--fiction-impose-children/.

Dunne, P. (2017). Transgender Sterilisation Requirements in Europe. *Medical Law Review, 25*(4), 554–581.

Edelman, L. (2004). *No Future: Queer Theory and the Death Drive*. Duke University Press.

Efraim, O. (2013). State Recognizes 2 Biological Fathers for First Time, *YNET News (Online)*, 15 September. Retrieved May 14, 2020, from https://www.ynetnews.com/articles/0,7340,L-4430009,00.html.

Eggert, I., & Engeli, I. (2015). Rainbow Families and the State: How Policies Shape Reproductive Choices. In *The Ashgate Research Companion to Lesbian and Gay Activism* (1st ed.). Routledge.

European Committee of Social Rights. (2018). *Decision on the Merits: Transgender Europe and ILGA-Europe v. the Czech Republic: Complaint(117/2015)*. Retrieved February 11, 2020, from https://hudoc.esc.coe.int/eng.

Fausto-Sterling, A. (2000). *Sexing the Body: Gender Politics and the Construction of Sexuality*. Basic Books.

Fineman, M. (1992). The Neutered Mother. *University of Miami Law Review, 46*(3), 653–669.

Forward Together. (2005). *A New Vision for Advancing Our Movement for Reproductive Health, Reproductive Rights and Reproductive Justice*. http://forwardtogether.org/assets/docs/ACRJ-A-New-Vision.pdf.

Foucault, M. (1998). *The History of Sexuality I: The Will to Knowledge*, Trans. Hurley, R., new edition, Penguin, London.

Foucault, M. (2008). *The Birth of Biopolitics: Lectures at the Collège de France, 1978-1979*, ed. Senellart, M., and Trans. Burchell, G., Palgrave Macmillan, New York.

Franke, K. M. (2001). Theorizing Yes: An Essay on Feminism, Law, and Desire. *Columbia Law Review, 101*(1), 181–208.

Gender Recognition Act. (2004). *C. 7*, Retrieved February 11, 2020, from http://www.legislation.gov.uk/ukpga/2004/7/contents.

Glosswitch. (2015). The Problem with Talking About 'pregnant people', *The New Statesman*, 29 September. Retrieved May 7, 2020, from https://www.newstatesman.com/politics/feminism/2015/09/what-s-matter-talking-about-pregnant-people.

Guinness World Records. (n.d.). First Married Man to Give Birth, *Guinness World Records.* Retrieved May 13, 2020, from https://www.guinnessworldrecords.com/world-records/first-married-man-to-give-birth?fb_comment_id=970743489607836_1597668960248616.

Hawkes, G. (1995). Responsibility and Irresponsibility: Young Women and Family Planning. *Sociology, 29*(2), 257–273.

Hines, S. (2019). The Feminist Frontier: On Trans and Feminism. *Journal of Gender Studies, 28*(2), 145–157.

Hoffkling, A., Obedin-Maliver, J., & Sevelius, J. (2017). From Erasure to Opportunity: A Qualitative Study of the Experiences of Transgender Men Around Pregnancy and Recommendations for Providers. *BMC Pregnancy and Childbirth, 17*(2), 332.

Human Fertilisation and Embryology Act. (2008). *HFEA 2008*, 22.

Intersex and Transgender Luxembourg. (2018). Communiqué de presse : Loi relative à la modification de la mention du sexe et du ou des prénoms à l'état civil, *ITGL*, 27 July. Retrieved February 11, 2020, from https://itgl.lu/legal/loi-relative-a-la-modification-de-la-mention-du-sexe-et-du-ou-des-prenoms-a-letat-civil/.

Jeffreys, S. (1997). Transgender Activism. *Journal of Lesbian Studies, 1*(3–4), 55–74.

Jeffreys, S. (2014). *Gender Hurts: A Feminist Analysis of the Politics of Transgenderism*, Taylor & Francis Group, London, UK. Retrieved May 7, 2020, from http://ebookcentral.proquest.com/lib/suss/detail.action?docID=1682231.

Joffre, T. (2021). Transgender Parents Can Be Agender 'parent' on Child's Birth Certificate, *The Jerusalem Post | JPost.Com*, 5 May. Retrieved May 10, 2021, from https://www.jpost.com/israel-news/transgender-parents-can-be-agender-parent-on-childs-birth-certificate-667265.

Jones, C. (2013). 'Human Weeds, Not Fit to Breed?': African Caribbean Women and Reproductive Disparities in Britain. *Critical Public Health, 23*(1), 49–61.

Joyce, H. (2018). The New Patriarchy: How Trans Radicalism Hurts Women, Children—and Trans People Themselves, *Quillette*, 4 December. Retrieved May 18, 2020, from https://quillette.com/2018/12/04/

the-new-patriarchy-how-trans-radicalism-hurts-women-children-and-trans-people-themselves/.

JTA. (2013). Israeli Transgender Man Recognized as Child's 'Father' in Same-Sex First, *The Forward*, 16 September. Retrieved April 29, 2021, from https://forward.com/news/breaking-news/183968/israeli-transgender-man-recognized-as-childs-fathe/.

Junco, D., & Fernández, F. (2020). Breaking the Barrier: Transmasculine Inputs in the Argentinean Abortion Law, Presented at the Trans Pregnancy, Fertility, Reproduction, and Body Autonomy: An International Conference, The Carriageworks, Leeds, UK, 16 January.

Karaian, L. (2013). Pregnant Men: Repronormativity, Critical Trans Theory and the Re(conceive)ing of Sex and Pregnancy in Law. *Social & Legal Studies, 22*(2), 211–230.

Katri, I. (2019). Transparental Designations and the Limits of Legal Recognition, Presented at the Trans Pregnancy, Fertility, Reproduction, and Body Autonomy: An International Conference, Leeds, UK, 16 January.

Lester, C. N. (2017). *Trans Like Me: A Journey for All of Us.* Virago.

Light, A. D., Obedin-Maliver, J., Sevelius, J. M., & Kerns, J. L. (2014). Transgender Men Who Experienced Pregnancy After Female-to-Male Gender Transitioning. *Obstetrics & Gynecology, 124*(6), 1120–1127.

Lowik, A. J. (2018). Reproducing Eugenics, Reproducing while Trans: The State Sterilization of Trans People. *Journal of GLBT Family Studies, 14*(5), 425–445.

McLaughlin, J. (2003). Screening Networks: Shared Agendas in Feminist and Disability Movement Challenges to Antenatal Screening and Abortion. *Disability & Society, 18*(3), 297–310.

Moore, S. (2020). Women Must Have the Right to Organise. We Will Not Be Silenced, *The Guardian*, 2 March. Retrieved May 19, 2020, from https://www.theguardian.com/society/commentisfree/2020/mar/02/women-must-have-the-right-to-organise-we-will-not-be-silenced.

Moore, A., & McIlwaine, C. (2020). Abortion rights in Ireland, Presented at the Trans Pregnancy, Fertility, Reproduction, and Body Autonomy: An International Conference, The Carriageworks, Leeds, UK, 16 January.

More, S. D. (1998). The Pregnant Man—an Oxymoron? *Journal of Gender Studies, 7*(3), 319–328.

Nixon, L. (2013). The Right to (Trans) Parent: A Reproductive Justice Approach to Reproductive Rights, Fertility, and Family-Building Issues Facing Transgender People. *William & Mary Journal of Women and the Law, 20*(1), 73.

Nolan, I. T., Kuhner, C. J., & Dy, G. W. (2019). Demographic and Temporal Trends in Transgender Identities and Gender Confirming Surgery. *Translational Andrology and Urology, 8*(3), 184–190.

O'Neill, B. (2017). The Word 'woman' Is Being Erased from Public Life, *The Spectator*, 23 October. Retrieved May 7, 2020, from https://www.spectator.co.uk/article/the-word-woman-is-being-erased-from-public-life.

Oakley, A. (1972). *Sex, Gender & Society*. Temple Smith, London.

Obedin-Maliver, J., & Makadon, H. J. (2016). Transgender Men and Pregnancy. *Obstetric Medicine, 9*(1), 4–8.

Open Society Foundations. (2014). *License to Be Yourself: Forced Sterilization*, Open Society Foundations. Retrieved May 19, 2020, from https://www.opensocietyfoundations.org/publications/forced-sterilization.

Parsons, V. (2021). Trans dad wins right to be named 'parent' on birth certificate – but not 'father', *PinkNews*, 7 May. Retrieved June 14, 2021, from https://www.pinknews.co.uk/2021/05/07/trans-dad-parents-israel-high-court-birth-certificate-legal-gender/.

Pearce, R., & White, F. R. (2019). Beyond the Pregnant Man: Representing Trans Pregnancy in a Deal with the Universe. *Feminist Media Studies, 19*(5), 764–767.

Pearce, R., Hines, S., Pfeffer, C., Riggs, D. W., Ruspini, E., & White, F. R. (2019). Of Trans Fathers and Male Mothers – the Importance of Centering Experience, *Trans Pregnancy*, 26 September. Retrieved April 30, 2020, from https://transpregnancy.leeds.ac.uk/2019/09/26/of-trans-fathers-and-male-mothers-the-importance-of-centering-experience/.

Pegoraro, L. (2015). Second-rate Victims: The Forced Sterilization of Indigenous Peoples in the USA and Canada. *Settler Colonial Studies, 5*(2), 161–173.

Proctor, K. (2020). Calls for Tory aide to Be Sacked Over 'enforced contraception' Remarks, *The Guardian*, 16 February. Retrieved May 18, 2020, from https://www.theguardian.com/politics/2020/feb/16/tory-aide-wants-enforced-contraception-to-curb-pregnancies.

Quinn, V. P., Nash, R., Hunkeler, E., Contreras, R., Cromwell, L., Becerra-Culqui, T. A., Getahun, D., et al. (2017). Cohort profile: Study of Transition, Outcomes and Gender (STRONG) to Assess Health Status of Transgender People. *BMJ Open, 7*(12), e018121.

R (Alfred McConnell) v The Registrar General for England and Wales and others. (2020). Court of Appeal (Civil Division), C1/2019/2730 and C1/2019/2767. *Courts and Tribunals Judiciary* [Online]. Retrieved April 30, 2021, from https://www.judiciary.uk/judgments/r-alfred-mcconnell-v-the-registrar-general-for-england-and-wales-and-others/.

Rabinow, P., & Rose, N. (2006). Biopower Today. *BioSocieties, 1*(2), 195–217.

Raymond, J. (1994). *The Transsexual Empire: The Making of the She-Male*, new edition, Teachers' College Press, New York.

Repo, J. (2019). Governing Juridical Sex: Gender Recognition and the Biopolitics of Trans Sterilization in Finland. *Politics & Gender, 15*(1), 83–106.

Richards, A. (2018). Female Campaigners 'self-identify' as Men to Infiltrate Male Only Pool at Hampstead Heath, *Evening Standard*, 29 May. Retrieved May 18, 2020, from https://www.standard.co.uk/news/uk/female-campaigners-selfidentify-as-men-to-infiltrate-male-only-pool-at-hampstead-heath-a3850556.html.

Riggs, D. W., Pearce, R., Pfeffer, C. A., Hines, S., White, F. R., & Ruspini, E. (2020). Men, Trans/masculine, and Non-binary People's Experiences of Pregnancy Loss: An International Qualitative Study. *BMC Pregnancy and Childbirth, 20*(1), 482.

Riggs, D. W., Pfeffer, C. A., Pearce, R., Hines, S., & White, F. R. (2021). Men, Trans/masculine, and Non-binary People Negotiating Conception: Normative Resistance and Inventive Pragmatism. *International Journal of Transgender Health, 22*(1–2), 6–17.

Santo, O. (2013). Transgender? Judaism's Got a Blessing for You, *The Times of Israel (Online)*, 25 September. Retrieved May 14, 2020, from https://www.timesofisrael.com/transgender-judaisms-got-a-blessing-for-you/.

Shakespeare, T. (1998). Choices and Rights: Eugenics, Genetics and Disability Equality. *Disability & Society, 13*(5), 665–681.

Silliman, J. M. (2004). *Undivided Rights: Women of Color Organize for Reproductive Justice*. South End Press.

Stock, K. (2018). Changing the Concept of 'woman' Will Cause Unintended Harms, *The Economist*, 6 July. Retrieved May 19, 2020. from https://www.economist.com/open-future/2018/07/06/changing-the-concept-of-woman-will-cause-unintended-harms.

Stock, K., Allen, S., Jones, J. C., Lawford-Smith, H., Leng, M., & Reilly-Cooper, R. (2019). Doing Better in Arguments About Sex and Gender, *Medium*, 25 July. Retrieved May 7, 2020, from https://medium.com/@kathleenstock/doing-better-in-arguments-about-sex-and-gender-3bec3fc4bdb6.

Stonewall. (2019). What Does Trans Mean?, *Stonewall*, 27 March. Retrieved May 14, 2020, from https://www.stonewall.org.uk/what-does-trans-mean.

Sutton, B., & Borland, E. (2018). Queering Abortion Rights: Notes from Argentina. *Culture, Health & Sexuality, 20*(12), 1378–1393.

TGEU. (2013). Argentina Gender Identity Law: English Translation of Argentina's Gender Identity Law as Approved by the Senate of Argentina on May 8, 2012, 12 November. Retrieved May 19, 2020, from https://tgeu.org/argentina-gender-identity-law/.

TGEU. (2015). Malta Adopts Ground-breaking Trans and Intersex Law – TGEU Press Release, *Transgender Europe*, 1 April. Retrieved February 11, 2020, from https://tgeu.org/malta-adopts-ground-breaking-trans-intersex-law/.

TGEU. (2019). TGEU Trans Rights Europe & Central Asia Map 2019, *TGEU*. https://tgeu.org/wp-content/uploads/2019/05/MapB_TGEU2019.pdf.

TGEU. (n.d.). Sweden Recognises Trans Parenthood. Retrieved April 30, 2020, from https://tgeu.org/sweden-recognises-trans-parenthood/.

The Human Rights Act. (1998). 42. https://www.legislation.gov.uk/ukpga/1998/42/introduction.

The Lancet. (2019). Editorial: Coercive Sterilisation of Transgender People in Japan. *The Lancet, 393*(10178), 1262.

The Queen (on the application of TT) v Registrar General for England and Wales. (2019). High Court of Justice Family Division and the Administrative Court, FD18F00035.*Courts and Tribunals Judiciary* [Online]. Retrieved April 30, 2021, from https://www.judiciary.uk/judgments/r-on-the-application-of-tt-v-the-registrar-general-for-england-and-wales-and-others/.

Trans Pregnancy. (n.d.). Retrieved May 14, 2020, from https://transpregnancy.leeds.ac.uk/.

TransgenderNI. (2019). TransgenderNI's Response to the Public Consultation Abortion Services in Northern Ireland, *TransgenderNI*, 16 December. Retrieved May 18, 2020, from https://transgenderni.org.uk/abortionconsultation/.

Tyler, I. (2008). 'Chav Mum Chav Scum': Class Disgust in contemporary Britain. *Feminist Media Studies, 8*(1), 17–34.

Veale, J., Watson, R. J., Adjei, J., & Saewyc, E. (2016). Prevalence of Pregnancy Invement Among Canadian Transgender Youth and Its Relation to Mental Health, Sexual Health, and Gender Identity. *International Journal of Transgenderism, 17*(3–4), 107–113.

Vergès, F. (2018). On Women and Their Wombs: Capitalism, Racialization, Feminism. *Critical Times, 1*(1), 263–267.

Waggoner, M. (2017). *The Zero Trimester: Pre-Pregnancy Care and the Politics of Reproductive Risk*. University of California Press. https://www.ucpress.edu/book/9780520288072/the-zero-trimester (accessed 14 May 2020)

Weissman, A. L. (2017). Repronormativity and the Reproduction of the Nation-State: The State and Sexuality Collide. *Journal of GLBT Family Studies, 13*(3), 277–305.

Wester, G. (2020). The Eugenics Debate Isn't Over – But We Should Be Wary of People Who Claim It Can Fix Social Problems, *The Conversation*, 26 February. Retrieved May 18, 2020, from https://theconversation.com/the-eugenics-debate-isnt-over-but-we-should-be-wary-of-people-who-claim-it-can-fix-social-problems-132055.

White, F. R. (2020). Media Representations, Presented at the Trans Pregnancy, Fertility, Reproduction, and Body Autonomy: An International Conference, The Carriageworks, Leeds, UK, 14 January. https://transpregnancy.leeds.ac.uk/conference/.

Woodcock, A. (2020). Downing St refuses to Say If Boris Johnson Agrees with Adviser Who Suggested Black People Are Mentally Inferior and Backed Compulsory Contraception, *The Independent*, 17 February. Retrieved May 19, 2020, from https://content.jwplatform.com/previews/A8cRaPxK-9ygSIn9G.

Yaros Hakak v The Attorney General. (2005). Supreme Court of Israel, CA 10280/01. *Versa* [Online]. Retrieved April 30, 2021, from https://versa.cardozo.yu.edu/opinions/yaros-hakak-v-attorney-general.
Yoaz, Y. (2008). Israel Recognizes Sex Changes Without Operation - Haaretz Com - Haaretz.com, *Haaretz*, 11 February. Retrieved April 29, 2021, from https://www.haaretz.com/.premium-israel-recognizes-sex-changes-without-op-1.5362107.
Yuval-Davis, N. (1996). Women and the Biological Reproduction of 'the nation'. *Women's Studies International Forum, 19*(1), 17–24.

CHAPTER 4

Judging Divorce in Ben Ali's Tunisia

Sarah Grosso

During my fieldwork in Tunisia under Ben Ali's regime,[1] I spent time with Karima, a court clerk in the office dealing with personal status cases in a court in the suburbs of Tunis. One morning, a man in his 30s asked her for advice about changing the type of divorce he had filed for; his wife had left the marital home and refused to come back—a possible ground for divorce. She explained that the issue was finding proof. He had employed a notary to visit his in-laws' house to certify that she was living there, but at the time of the visit there was no one at home. The only convincing truth would be if his wife were to tell the judge that she would not return. "She knows the law", Karima said. "She will lie and say she does not want a divorce. It is a tactic. It is all about money." (If she does not agree, her husband will have to pay her compensation.)

"This", Karima concluded, "is the problem now with Tunisian women today. They have taken all their rights and the men suffer".

S. Grosso (✉)
Webster University Geneva, Geneva, Switzerland
e-mail: grosso@webster.ch

G. Guney et al. (eds.), *Towards Gender Equality in Law*,
https://doi.org/10.1007/978-3-030-98072-6_4

4.1 Introduction

Karima had been working on divorce cases for years. Their exchange embodies some of the tensions that surrounded Tunisia's Personal Status Code (PSC) and, more specifically, its divorce law.

Tunisia is well known for its PSC that promotes the equality of women and men by banning polygamy and extending equal rights in divorce to women. Promulgated by the new president Bourgiba in 1956, shortly after the country gained independence from France, the PSC was seen as a progressive move to advance women's rights (Murphy, 1996) and has been used to inspire reforms elsewhere such as in Algeria and Morocco (Chedly, 2007). Although presented by Bourguiba as a modern interpretation of Islamic law, it entailed a radical reform of family law, in particular women's status in marriage and divorce, moving family matters from the jurisdiction of Islamic courts to that of the state.

Whether or not the laws on marriage and divorce were in harmony with Muslim values remained hotly contested during my fieldwork (2004–2008) and a matter of great concern as the Tunisian state sought to reinforce its legitimacy with the predominantly Muslim population. Bourguiba's successor, Ben Ali,[2] was accused of instrumentalising the country's image as a supporter of women's rights to bolster Tunisia's reputation abroad as "the most modernized and westernized country in the Maghrib" (Layachi, 2000, p. 32). Simultaneously, Tunisia was accused by human rights organisations of using this as a cover for human rights abuses (Labidi, 2010). Furthermore, the association of this law with "western" values accentuated the doubts within the country and the Middle East and North Africa (MENA) region about the PSC's religious and moral legitimacy.

Karima's reaction hints at the moral uncertainty that continued to shroud divorce and the changing status of women in marriage and at a tension inherent in the intention and purpose of the law. Although the PSC had granted women the right to file for divorce unilaterally on the same basis as men, the common sentiment remained that they should not. She immediately assumed that the wife would lie in court, questioning her moral character. If the wife is prone to conceal the truth, it is also because of a further tension inherent in the law. As we shall see, the difficulties of providing proof in the intimate domain of marriage meant that, in this personal status law, it was often the people and their perceived moral character that were being judged in ways that were highly gendered.

Based on an ethnographic study of a court house and lower middle-class neighbourhood in the urban suburbs of Tunisia's capital under Ben Ali's authoritarian regime, this chapter follows anthropological approaches that study the law in practice. It seeks to trace some of the tensions that were revealed as Tunisia's divorce law translated into practice, highlighting the importance of the legal processes. It focuses on the experiences of the actors (judges, lawyers, litigants, court clerks) who were instrumental in breathing life into the law. To do this, it draws on participation observation in the court, where I spent 19 months in the office which dealt with personal status cases, including divorce (2007–2008). I observed the confidential reconciliation sessions that litigants must attend, interviewed litigants, lawyers, judges, clerks and other court staff, and read divorce files. During this time, I also spent six months in total living with a lower middle-class family in the jurisdiction of the court and interviewed people in the neighbourhood about marriage and divorce.

After placing this research in the context of how anthropologists have approached studying the law and, more specifically, family law in the Middle East and North Africa, this chapter will begin by outlining some of the tensions that exist within the Tunisian legal framework and procedures that set the stage for the interactions between litigants and the judge. We shall then use the reconciliation sessions as a magnifying glass to reveal some of the tensions that must be resolved in these moments of judgement, as the litigants, evolving social norms and the law itself are placed under scrutiny in the court house.

4.2 Tensions in the Law: (Re)defining Gendered Persons and Things

Anthropologists studying the law have explored how the law interacts with society, culture or "normative orders" as it is translated into practice (Goodale, 2006; Riles, 2002). Through the specificities of its procedures, the law becomes a productive space where normative categories and forms of personhood and identity are constructed (Riles, 2006; Strathern, 2018; Pottage, 2004). Increased attention has been paid to the technicalities of the law that provide the framework in which knowledge and truth are produced (Riles, 2006), as well as the role of legal actors who interpret and implement the law within those frameworks, such as the judge (Bowen, 1998; Rosen, 2000). These technicalities set the stage, delimiting the space in which individuals (litigants, lawyers and the judge) perform the continual work of interpreting these legal categories which contribute to the "fabrication of persons and things" (Pottage, 2004, p. 25). It is also through these processes that norms are able to enter the work of the law through shared criteria or assumptions (Bowen, 1998).

This chapter draws inspiration from anthropologists who have studied how international legal regimes have been translated in local contexts (Goodale, 2006; Riles, 2006), in particular Goodale's approach to studying human rights through "ethical theory": "the development of normative ideas through the dynamic interaction between … many different sources" (Goodale, 2006, p. 29). Considering how international human rights are brought to life in Bolivia through the work of multiple actors, Goodale argues that human rights are never separate from "the swirl of other sources of normative inspiration" (2006, p. 29), which include community rules, national law and religious standards.

This articulation between the law and ethics has been emphasised in work on family law in Muslim contexts (Asad, 2001; Bowen, 2001; Joseph, 2000), in particular where this law is codified and brought under the auspices of the state, raising ethical questions about the respective roles of the state and religion in organising family life and maintaining public morality. This scholarship has stressed the need to examine the impact of family law reforms in the context of broader political, social and economic processes (Moors, 1998). The law is viewed as a productive site: "rather than taking the meaning of gender for granted, the focus is on the ways in which gender is constructed in particular local contexts" (Moors, 1998, p. 26). Increased focus has been placed on women's agency, narratives and strategies as they navigate these laws in practice. Legal practice is understood within the context of broader political processes, in which gender and family law may be potent political symbols (Moors, 1998, p.26). The tensions between the ideals and the reality of contemporary marital life, such as the difficulty of maintaining the model of a sole male breadwinner when there is an economic necessity for both spouses to work, bleed into the operation of the law.

Consequently, legal practice is a site where actors are required to engage with existing tensions between sometimes competing normative frameworks as legal categories are "translated" (Merry, 2006) to make them meaningful in local settings and relevant to individual circumstances and cases. The construction of categories in this way is a political process, as actors make choices between alternatives (Merry & Coutin, 2014): "Legal and technical knowledge systems thus make particular versions of social reality visible, even as they obscure others, rendering them unknowable" (Merry & Coutin, 2014, p. 3). In this way, the court becomes a forum where matters of public morality are debated (Murphy, 1997; Kelly, 2011; Goodale, 2006).

Anthropologists have also stressed the role played by various intermediaries as the law is "translated" (Merry, 2006; Messick, 1993). Elsewhere, I have described how divorce lawyers interpret the law as they craft petitions translating the facts into legal arguments to appeal to the judge; as they do this, they simultaneously lend legitimacy to particular gender norms that are expected to appeal to the judge and carry weight in court (Grosso, 2019). This interpretative labour is made necessary as the court is itself a decontextualised space (Murphy, 1997), despite an understanding of context being vital for the judgement process, not the least in personal status cases. Judges (and lawyers), therefore, play a key role in bringing some of the relevant context back into view. They engage in a process I call recontextualisation, as they are required to use their moral and social, as well as their legal, judgement to interpret and rule on divorce cases; this "ethical work" is vital to the process of judging divorce cases.

Anthropologists have highlighted the potential for uncertainty and anxiety, in particular in areas where the law offers the least certainty, based on open norms or legal categories that are poorly defined or in instances when it is particularly difficult to establish the truth. For instance, Kelly (2012, p.753), in his study of how claims of torture are handled in the British Asylum Process, discussed the "widespread suspicions about the genuineness of their claims". He argued that these suspicions were based on the recognition of mutual humanity and with it "the mutual capacity to dissimulate", rather than a "denial of suffering" and othering, as might be assumed (2012, p. 743). As such, Kelly foregrounds the significance of the roles of the legal actors who interpret the law, as well as their perceptions and emotions, as the law is implemented and legal categories are defined. Crucially, these reactions contribute to "institutional receptivity", an element of the "rights consciousness" of litigants that shapes their willingness to access the rights granted in the legal code and turn to the law in the event of marital discord (Merry, 2003, p. 344).

4.3 Tensions in the Law: Legitimacy and Origins of the PSC

Tunisia's PSC enables us to observe the tensions that arise as a contested, morally dubious, national law is translated into practice. It is this national law that remains somewhat controversial and that creates a space where competing notions of gender and gender equality are debated.

It could be said that the PSC originated from an ideological and political clash. Promulgated rapidly after Independence in the wake of a violent period of civil war, Bourguiba—who had been trained as a lawyer in France—was able to pass this law that was considered a radical move in favour of women's rights after defeating his ideological opposition. The association of Bourguiba with the French did not help the acceptance of the new law locally, despite his attempt to position the PSC as a modern reading of Islamic law. Ben Youssef, Bourguiba's opponent during the civil war, questioned the PSC's compatibility with Islam from his exile in Egypt, claiming that it had "prohibited what God had authorized and authorized what God had forbidden" (Perkins, 2004, p. 137). This is a phrase that I heard often during fieldwork; supposedly, by preventing a man from taking a second wife (seen by many as permitted in Islam), the PSC made it more likely for men to commit adultery (forbidden in the religion). Through this reform, Bourguiba also enabled the state to intervene in intimate, family matters which had previously been the preserve of Islamic courts. Passing this radical legal reform top-down thanks to the power vacuum that emerged as he gained victory in the civil war, Bourguiba turned women and women's rights into a potent political symbol in the identity of the nascent, independent nation state.

The PSC also represented a departure from the way in which family law was organised prior to Independence. Polygamy had been allowed under the religious law, and men could take up to four wives, although the limited data available suggests that it was rarely practised (Micaud, 1964, p. 145). Men could repudiate their wives, whereas women had to appeal to a religious judge (*qadi*) for a divorce and could only do so in specific circumstances such as abuse or neglect (Anderson, 1976, p. 103). The PSC required both men and women to divorce through a court. Women, like men, could file for divorce unilaterally; the judge could not refuse the divorce, but could require the petitioner to pay their spouse compensation. In this respect, the PSC introduced greater gender equality, enabling either party to end the marriage.

4.3.1 Clashes in Purpose

What does it mean that a woman could now file for a divorce? The ethnographic study of the law in practice can help grasp its impact on those it purports to empower. Anthropologists who study the law are often interested in the lived experiences of the people who are affected by those laws (Osanloo, 2009; Mir-Hosseini, 1993; Merry, 2003), the extent to which such laws fulfil their (alleged) purpose (Goodale, 2006) and the extent to which laws, such as personal status laws, empower women or reinforce gender inequalities (Würth, 2003; Osanloo, 2009; Mir Mir-Hosseini, 1993).

Paying attention to procedures and the formation of legal subjectivities may reveal potentially unexpected consequences of legal regimes. In her comparative study of divorce in Iran and Morocco, Mir Hosseini argued that women may find empowerment in seemingly unlikely places (Mir-Hosseini, 1993, p. 121). In Iran, where only women and not men had to petition a court to be granted a divorce, the legal procedures that required women to engage with the court opened up spaces of resistance where women could exercise their agency. This led Mir Hosseini to the counter-intuitive conclusion that this engagement with the law led Iranian women to feel empowered, despite the gender inequalities that remained in the legal system (Mir-Hosseini, 1998, p. XIV). In contrast, the Tunisian divorce law required both women and men to engage with the court system in order to divorce.

4.4 Legal Context

4.4.1 To Reconcile, or Not to Reconcile?

In Tunisia, all litigants must encounter a judge at least once for a compulsory reconciliation session before they are permitted to divorce. Judges could be male or female; my fieldwork took place under one female and one male family judge. As one of these family judges told me, "it is *personal* status law. You need to see the person." If there are children, the couple must attend three reconciliation sessions, each spaced one month apart, to allow more time for reflection and for the couple to potentially reconcile, an indication of the sanctity of the family and public fears about moral breakdown if children grow up in a "broken" family. The ostensible purpose of these sessions is to attempt to prevent the divorce, "the most hated by God of all permitted things". The state, therefore, plays a role both in facilitating and in preventing divorce.

If this was a unique moment when the litigants and judge met in person, it was because divorce cases are judged based on the documents in the case file (petitions and documentary evidence). These petitions were usually written by lawyers, less frequently by notaries; in contrast, the legal regime before independence had been based on oral testimony. Three types of divorce were available to both men and women (Art 31, PSC). Couples could divorce by mutual consent with no compensation payments. One party could file for a divorce without grounds; the judge could not prevent the divorce, but would rule on compensation payments to be paid to the spouse who did not want to divorce. These compensation payments were gendered. Wives only had to pay "moral compensation" for harm done, whereas husbands also had to pay "material compensation" to compensate for the wife losing her breadwinner. Finally, one party could file for a divorce for harm. If able to produce legally valid evidence of the harm done, the injured party would be entitled to receive compensation payments. A great deal—including the financial settlement and possibly custody of any children—hinged on the ability to produce convincing, valid evidence to justify a claim of "harm". In reality, in cases of divorce without grounds, litigants also strove to demonstrate to the court that they had suffered "harm" in order to mitigate the compensation they would owe to their spouse.

The reconciliation sessions played a vital role, not only due to the physical encounter between litigants and the judge, but also because they generated a written document that enters the divorce file and can be used as evidence. The judge or a clerk rapidly wrote out an account of what each litigant said during the session. This summary was signed by both parties. Given the difficulty of providing evidence for "harm" in such an intimate domain of life, these accounts could provide missing evidence to support a case of divorce for harm. This is why, although the judge may approach these sessions hoping to explore the "real reasons" that led to marital breakdown and reconcile the couple, litigants often approach them with the hope of producing evidence of their spouse's failures that could help them secure a favourable divorce settlement. Consequently, the intended purpose of the sessions that relies on transparency and honesty clashes with their role in the legal procedure that incentivises each litigant to conceal any wrongdoing and present themselves favourably to the judge. These legal technicalities frame the space in which legal actors interact and collectively interpret the meaning of the central categories that are relevant to divorce law (Riles, 2005) and in which their subjectivities are formed in interaction with the law and its officials (Merry, 2003).

4.4.2 Judging "Harm": Clarity v Ambiguity

What constituted "harm" in divorce cases? The most definitive types of "harm" were those that could be backed up with legally valid evidence; only these would lead to a ruling on divorce for harm. Typically, these involved cases in which another legal judgement could be produced,[3] such as for adultery or domestic violence, which were legislated against in the Penal Code.[4] In cases of divorce without grounds, the judge had more discretion and could determine the divorce settlement based on their appreciation of who had suffered most due to the breakdown of the marriage.

In divorce cases, litigants typically attempted to establish that they had been fulfilling their marital duties, whilst their spouse had not. Couples were expected to treat each other with kindness and to "fulfil their marital duties according to custom and habit" (Art 23, PSC). A further form of "harm", therefore, was a failure to fulfil these duties, which were highly gendered. Dispositions elsewhere in the legal code provided some clarity to help define "marital duties". For instance, the PSC defines the husband as the head of the household and expects him to provide for his family (Art 23 and Arts 37-53bis, PSC). In return, since her duty of obedience was removed from the PSC in 1993, a wife is expected to "cohabit" with her husband in the marital home, the site of her marital duties as defined by social norms (Art 23); legal procedures provide for a husband to file a complaint for "*nushuz*", a wife abandoning a marital home.

These categories remained nonetheless ambiguous, leaving considerable scope for interpretation and the judge's discretion. For some legal professionals I interviewed, this was a deliberate move by the legislator to leave flexibility for the judge to adapt to changes in the institution of marriage and in the gender norms that define what makes a "good" husband or wife. It is in these ambiguous categories that the judge is required to carry out ethical work interpreting which social norms are relevant to the case; in this way, this ethical work is brought into the practice of the law.

4.5 Reconciliation Sessions

4.5.1 Concealing v Revealing

The judge who conducted the reconciliation sessions I observed, a young man in his 30s who was married and the father to a young baby, told me that his job was "not to judge them, but to make them get on".[5] The four judges I spoke to at the court all cared deeply about trying to reunite couples, especially those who had children.[6] The cantonal judge found it difficult to rule on, in his words, "the breakdown of a family". His strategies during the sessions aimed to encourage the litigants to reveal the "real" reasons for their divorce: "I must make them feel I am not judging them", he told me. He did this by minimising his presence, even taking calls on his mobile phone, in the hope the couple would "forget" about him and open up. He was, however, all too conscious that they were more likely to tell me the truth than they were him. Speaking to the judge had potential repercussions for the divorce settlement; if a litigant were to admit they were at fault, this could be held in evidence against them. Ultimately, there was little he could do to make them forget his role as a judge and the power he had over them through the divorce settlement.

The couples who came to the court had a different perspective. Of the 61 reconciliation sessions[7] I observed, only 1 husband had come to tell the judge that he and his wife had reconciled. Litigants approached these sessions strategically with the aim of persuading the judge that the divorce should be blamed on their spouse in order to win the judge's sympathy and, hopefully, a favourable divorce settlement. Consequently, the reconciliation sessions created an emotionally charged stage where litigants could perform as "good" husbands or wives; through these performances, they also revealed their understanding of the kinds of arguments they believed would be legally authoritative and emotionally and morally persuasive to the judge. What did litigants reveal or conceal? And to what extent were these performances gendered?

4.5.2 (Not) Wanting a Divorce

Gearing these strategies to achieving a favourable settlement leads to the first contradiction inherent in these so-called reconciliation sessions. If one spouse files for divorce unilaterally, they will have to pay the other party compensation payments; the divorce could only proceed without such compensation if the couple agree to divorce by mutual consent. Consequently, if one spouse is filing for divorce unilaterally, it is very unlikely that the husband or the wife will come to the court and tell the judge that they agree to divorce; doing so would entail losing this financial compensation and would place them in a much weaker position to negotiate the divorce settlement.

> Fatima was a lawyer in her early 30s and used to working on divorce cases. She used this knowledge to her advantage when her own marriage started to break down. They both realised that they had become incompatible, despite the birth of their son, and their arguments had turned to violence. She knew that obtaining a final judgement for domestic violence could take time and did not want to wait for this to file for a divorce herself on the basis of harm. She was pleased when her husband finally decided to file for a divorce without grounds and remained firm in her refusal to divorce by mutual consent. After her suffering, she hoped the compensation payments he would be required to pay would give her some form of justice. To have a chance at this, however, she must attend the reconciliation sessions, hide her true feelings and say that she wanted the marriage to continue. She had to play the role of a patient wife and mother, willing to sacrifice herself and show forgiveness for the sake of the family; it is this position—in line with social norms and expectations—that would ultimately empower her to achieve the outcome she desired in the divorce case. Given that Fatima had started proceedings against her husband for violence, and that the judge may well have been aware of this, we can only speculate whether the judge would have truly been convinced by her performance.

The judge knew that that the legal proceedings were not conducive to revealing the truth. He may well have turned a blind eye, knowing that Fatima was pursuing a sensible course of action to end a violent marriage more rapidly. Consequently, the judge was performing both ethical and legal work as he presided over these sessions, judging the legal facts and also the moral character of the litigants who came before him. He too held "widespread suspicions about the genuineness of their claims" (Kelly, 2012, p. 753). These suspicions were also based on compassion: an ability to identify with her and her suffering and the recognition that, if pressed, perhaps he too would have done the same thing.

4.5.3 *Husband v Wife*

The performances of the litigants were articulated with the clearest legal definitions of "harm". The arguments put forward by wives most frequently revolved around their husband's failure to pay maintenance or domestic violence. As well as bearing legal weight, and being supported by social, moral and religious ideals of a husband's role, if so many litigants chose to reveal economic issues, it could also be because they preferred to conceal other, perhaps more intimate, issues affecting their marriage. In this way, they remained in control of the extent to which the state, via these procedures, could intervene in their marital affairs.

Although, in the 1993 reform, the PSC had been modified to mention that a wife should also contribute to the household's expenses "if she has the means", it remained very unclear what this meant in practice, and the husband clearly remained the head of the household with a duty to maintain the family. This tension between the continued duty of the husband to be a sole provider for the family and the suggestion that the wife could or should also contribute financially was played out in the reconciliation sessions. Several wives underlined the failings of their husbands as providers by highlighting the role they played in contributing to the family with their own salaries. In some cases, wives brought bills with them that they had paid and their husband had not. On the other hand, husbands disputed the wife's use of her salary or complained that their wives were too demanding materially. Such comments were (deliberately) wounding to husbands and their masculinity.

> One warring couple demonstrated how maintenance becomes an authoritative language through which to express marital dissatisfaction. In their mid-30s, they came to the court dressed smartly. Both of them had moved back in with their respective parents. Although both had finished high school, only the husband was working, earning a modest wage as a civil servant, and told the judge that his parents also "helped them," lamenting the high cost of the clinic where his daughter, still a baby, had been born prematurely. Their strained and angry exchange in the presence of the judge was peppered with the forms of "harm" that were mostly likely to hold weight legally. He accused her of hitting his mother and leaving the marital home. She accused him of lying: why was she not in prison, if she hit his mother? She also accused him of failing to pay any maintenance, not even money for milk for their daughter. Both claimed that they were the injured party. "I don't want your mother to pay. I want you to take your

> responsibility," she lamented. "I am in front of you a man," the husband simply replied. "Then why," she shouted," did I do a case for failure to pay maintenance?"

The judge did not react to this, visibly troubled by the tension in the room. The husband would be unable to argue with documentary evidence produced if the wife had indeed filed a case against him for failing to maintain her and the child. He would also find it difficult to argue with the material reality that would make it hard for him to afford to pay 200 dinars per month out of his (claimed) 330 dinar salary.

> Only rarely did the judge seem to see a possibility to help a couple reconcile. Saida and Mehdi, both in their 30s and with a daughter, had also been arguing about money. The wife worked as an accountant and earned slightly more than her husband who sold cars. Saida mentioned this fact frequently: "Each month I pay the rent alone and provide for our family alone!" However, the key tensions in their marriage appeared to start when they had moved into an apartment above his parents' house. Saida did not tolerate what she perceived as constant interference from her mother-in-law. The judge took the opportunity to empower Mehdi. He encouraged him to take charge and manage the relationship between his parents and his wife to make things go smoothly again. In this way, as the judge put it, "each man has power."

The judge's reaction to these cases implied that he was conscious of the economic strain on families and the need for two salaries to make ends meet; he seemed to acknowledge that it was not realistic for a husband to provide alone and sometimes even ignored these comments to focus on other ways of resolving marital stress that were more likely to be within the husband's grasp. He was required to "re-contextualise" these performances using his social and moral knowledge. In the process, he contributed to the legal recognition of the slow shifts in marital roles that could be observed in families in the neighbourhoods around the court.

The judge also relied on his moral and social knowledge and lent his legal authority to shifting gender norms when responding to husbands' complaints about their wives. Husbands most frequently complained about their wives' absences from the marital home and subsequent neglect of other, traditional wifely duties. Mehdi had tried to use this idea against Saida in the case mentioned above, accusing her of leaving the house all day and leaving the baby with his mother. Presumably, this was to go to work as an accountant for which, as we saw, she earned more money than him and her income was vital to the household. Furthermore, jurisprudence is clear that the law only sanctions wives who abandon the marital home without justification.

Therefore, these clashes between strongly gendered norms—in some cases backed up by the clearest definitions of marital duties in the legal code—also became clashes between the real and the ideal which, in turn, reveal how understandings of masculinity and femininity and gendered marital roles are changing in light of economic and social changes.

4.5.4 *Family v Freedom*

The reconciliation sessions also revealed changes in the meaning of kinship and the family in this urban setting in the suburbs of the capital city that was a melting pot of Tunisians, who originated from all over the country and had migrated in recent decades.

Another key source of tension in marriage was the relationship between the couple and their natal families. As I had observed in my interviews with people in the neighbourhood, recent decades of rapid urbanisation had led to more couples living neolocally, in contrast to the tradition of patrilocality after marriage. Female education and economic empowerment also encouraged a greater focus on the nuclear family; wives seemed less tolerant of interference from in-laws in light of their greater financial independence. The judge was conscious of class differences that led to some wives having greater expectations of living independently as a nuclear family, as well as the economic pressures that meant that this might not be possible, even when it was expected, as we saw with Saida and Mehdi above.

Also present in Saida and Mehdi's case and sometimes in the reconciliation sessions, tensions with the extended family seemed to be a greater driver of the divorce than issues between the couple themselves. As a working wife, Saida was caught up between the expectations her mother-in-law had of a "good wife" (who asked her if her husband's clothes had been washed) and her own expectations of being a well-educated, economically active woman expecting this to bring her more autonomy from her husband's family; he had reneged on his promise to live independently, and they moved into the flat above his parents when she was heavily pregnant.

As these issues were raised and debated in the privacy of the judge's office, the sessions become a litmus test of the potential for the law to support different gender roles that may be deemed more or less empowering to women (and men).

4.6 Conclusion

These highly personal and often emotional experiences of the law suggest how legal practice is connected with ethics and ethics with gender, as different expectations are placed on husbands and wives by the legal code and by the judge who strives to reconcile them. Karima, who we met at the start of this chapter, was correct: divorce cases were marred by the difficulties of telling right from wrong and the deceptive strategies litigants used to achieve a favourable outcome. These strategies were shaped by the legal procedures and contributed to making ethical work central to divorce cases as the judge also sought to read the gendered, moral character of the litigants as they came to the court.

The reconciliation sessions are, therefore, productive of a high degree of uncertainty and anxiety. Like the judge, the litigants were also unsure who they would encounter in the court; would they be able to win the judge's sympathy? In this Personal Status Law, much also hinges on the *person* of the judge who, within the constraints of the areas where the law more clearly defines marital roles, adjudicates on which husbands and wives are best fulfilling their duties. Clashes that exist outside the court are brought into the court and into the legal realm, notably those relating to changing gender roles and expectations of marriage. This is the context in which judges are required to make ethical and legal judgements that are necessarily gendered and that may stimulate their compassion for certain litigants over others. Consequently, judges may decide to support a wife who is a victim of domestic violence when she insists she wants to remain in the marriage (whether they believe her or not) or they may offer alternative ways for a husband to demonstrate his masculinity if they know it is impossible for him to support his family alone. By exercising their agency and sympathy in this way, judges effectively give legal backing to these changing marital roles. An inherent uncertainty remains, however; another judge may use his or her scope for discretion differently.

The emotional support provided by the judge also contributes to the "rights consciousness" of litigants and whether they feel they receive satisfaction through the law; it is part of their experience of the legal system that contributes to litigants seeing themselves as "rights-bearing subjects" (Merry, 2003, p. 343). These intimate proceedings, however, also have broader political implications; it is not only the litigants who are being judged. The morality and legitimacy of the divorce law are at stake as litigants come into contact with the law via its agents and through its procedures, whether the kindly judge, or the sometimes irate clerk, who had her own strong opinions on the morality of divorce and women's role in society. Behind the closed doors of the judge's office, the judge and litigants navigate the tensions between the impetuses to reveal and to conceal, between the ideal and reality of contemporary marriage and between the state's prerogative to enable whilst also prevent divorce. As they do so, the morality of the state, as well as of the litigants, is being judged.

Notes

1. Fieldwork took place between 2004 and 2008 in a suburb of Ben Arous close to the capital city of Tunis, in a family home in a lower-middle-class neighbourhood and in the chamber of the Court of First Instance of Ben Arous that dealt with personal status cases (2007–2008).
2. Ben Ali ruled Tunisia through an authoritarian regime from 1987 until he was ousted in the revolution of January 2011.
3. This must be a final judgement that is no longer subject to Appeal.
4. Article 218 of the Penal Code introduced a stronger sentence if the violence had been perpetrated by the victim's spouse.
5. Judges in Tunisia rotated around different roles rather than specialising in one field of law.
6. These included both family judges, the cantonal judge and the judge who presided over the reconciliation sessions I observed. This judge usually ruled on commercial law, but all judges in the court could be called upon to help with the large number of reconciliation sessions that had to be processed each week.
7. Both spouses were present in 44 of these cases; in the rest, only one party attended.

References

Anderson, N. (1976). *Law Reform in the Muslim World*. The Athlone Press.

Asad, T. (2001). *Thinking About Secularism and Law in Egypt*. ISIM Paper.

Bowen, J. (1998). You May Not Give It Away: How Social Norms Shape Islamic Law in Contemporary Indonesian Jurisprudence. *Islamic Law and Society*, *5*(3), 382–408.

Bowen, J. (2001). *Shari'a, State and Social Norms in France and Indonesia.* ISIM Paper.

Chedly, L. (2007). Les relations pécuniaires entre époux: cinquante ans après l'entrée en vigueur du Code du statut personnel tunisien. *Revue internationale de droit comparé, 59*(3), 551–593.

Goodale, M. (2006). Ethical Theory as Social Practice. *American Anthropologist, 108*, 25–37.

Grosso, S. (2019). Women's Rights on Trial: Gender Equality in a Family Court in Ben Ali's Tunisia. *The Asian Yearbook of Human Rights and Humanitarian Law, 3*, 219–242.

Joseph, S. (2000). Introduction. In S. Joseph (Ed.), *Gender and Citizenship in the Middle East* (pp. 3–30). Syracuse University Press.

Kelly, T. (2011). The Cause of Human Rights: Doubts About Torture, Law and Ethics at the United Nations. *Journal of the Royal Anthropological Institute, 17*, 728–744.

Kelly, T. (2012). Sympathy and Suspicion: Torture, Asylum, and Humanity. *Journal of the Royal Anthropological Institute, 18*, 753–768.

Labidi, K. (2010). Tunisia is Backtracking On Women's Rights. *The Guardian*, 25 August. Retrieved April 29, 2020, from https://www.theguardian.com/commentisfree/libertycentral/2010/aug/25/tunisia-backtracking-womens-rights

Layachi, A. (2000). Reform and the Politics of Inclusion in the Maghrib. *Journal of North African Studies, 5*(3), 15–42.

Merry, S. (2003). Rights Talk and the Experience of Law: Implementing Women's Human Rights to Protection from Violence. *Human Rights Quarterly, 25*(5), 343–381.

Merry, S. (2006). Transnational Human Rights and Local Activism: Mapping the Middle. *American Anthropologist, 108*(1), 38–51.

Merry, S., & Coutin, S. (2014). Technologies of Truth in the Anthropology of Conflict. *American Ethnologist, 41*(1), 1–16.

Messick, B. (1993). *The Calligraphic State: Textual Domination and History in a Muslim Society.* University of California Press.

Micaud, C. (1964). *Tunisia: The Politics of Modernization.* Pall Mall Press.

Mir-Hosseini, Z. (1993). *Marriage on Trial: A Study of Islamic Family Law.* I.B. Tauris.

Mir-Hosseini, Z. (1998). *Islam and Gender: The Religious Debate in Contemporary Iran.* Princeton University Press.

Moors, A. (1998). Islamic Family Law: Disciplinary Shift; Different Perspectives. *ISIM Newsletter*, p. 26.

Murphy, E. (1996). Women in Tunisia: A Survey of Achievements and Challenges. *The Journal of North African Studies, 1*(2), 138–156.

Murphy, W. (1997). *The Oldest Social Science? Configurations of Law and Modernity.* Clarendon Press.

Osanloo, A. (2009). *The Politics of Women's Rights in Iran*. Princeton University Press.
Perkins, K. (2004). *A History of Modern Tunisia*. Cambridge University Press.
Pottage, A. (2004). Introduction: The Fabrication of Persons and Things. In A. Pottage & M. Mundy (Eds.), *Law, Anthropology and the Constitution of the Social: Making Persons and Things* (pp. 1–39). Cambridge University Press.
Riles, A. (2002). Representing In-Between: Law, Anthropology, and the Rhetoric of Interdisciplinary. In M. Mundy (Ed.), *Law and Anthropology* (pp. 597–650). Ashgate.
Riles, A. (2005). *A New Agenda for the Cultural Study of Law: Taking on the Technicalities*. Cornell Law Faculty Publications, Paper 78.
Riles, A. (2006). Introduction: In Response. In A. Riles (Ed.), *Documents: Artifacts of Modern Knowledge* (pp. 71–89). University of Michigan Press.
Rosen, L. (2000). *The Justice of Islam: Comparative Perspectives on Islamic Law and Society*. Oxford University Press.
Strathern, M. (2018). Between the Devil and the Deep Blue Sea a Response to Nigel Rapport's 'Cosmopolitan Politesse'. *Journal of Legal Anthropology, 2*(1), 112–116.
Würth, A. (2003). Stalled Reform: Family Law in Post-unification Yemen. *Islamic Law and Society, 10*(1), 12–33.

PART II

Law Is Coherent?

CHAPTER 5

Constitutional and Legal Guarantees for Transgender in Pakistan: Reforms and Failures in Law

Amna Rashid and Umar Rashid

5.1 Introduction

The terms *Khawaja Sira*, *Hijra*, *khusras*, *zenanas* and eunuch have been traditionally used to refer to individuals who do not conform to the cis-gender identity in Pakistan. In recent years, the terms "third gender", "transgender" and "transsexual" have also begun to be used. Since the colonial era, they have been victims of social exclusion, public ridicule, discrimination, harassment and violence. For years, transgender people in Pakistan struggled for social acceptance and legal recognition of their gender identity and gender expression. This changed in 2009 following the first Order of the Supreme Court of Pakistan in the *Constitutional Petition No. 43 of 2009* on the rights of transgender people. For the first time in its

A. Rashid (✉)
University of Management and Technology, Lahore, Pakistan
e-mail: amna.rashid@columbia.edu

U. Rashid
University of Adelaide, Adelaide, SA, Australia
e-mail: umar.rashid@adelaide.edu.au

G. Guney et al. (eds.), *Towards Gender Equality in Law*,
https://doi.org/10.1007/978-3-030-98072-6_5

history, the legal system of Pakistan recognised the atypical gender identity of transgender people. Over the next three years, the Supreme Court directed the government to recognise the gender identity of transgender people and take action for the protection of their fundamental rights through a series of Orders under the *Constitutional Petition No. 43 of 2009*, reported as *Dr. Muhammad Aslam Khaki and Others vs. S.S.P. (Operations) Rawalpindi and Others* (2013) PLD 188 (SC). These Orders initiated a series of legal reforms over the following decade for the rights of transgender people in Pakistan, culminating in the enactment of the *Transgender Persons (Protection of Rights) Act 2018*.

This chapter analyses these legal reforms and their impact on the social and legal status of transgender people in light of the history of marginalisation and state failure in the protection of their rights. Following the introduction, Sect. 5.2 defines various terms used throughout the chapter, including the terms *Khawaja Sira* and *Hijra*, which represent indigenous development of gender identity for people who do not conform to cisgender identities. The next section provides a historical analysis of the systematic discrimination faced by such individuals, starting with their persecution under colonial rule. The chapter argues that their marginalisation under colonial rule continues to adversely impact transgender people post-independence, representing state failure. Section 5.4 analyses the series of Supreme Court Orders under the *Constitutional Petition No. 43 of 2009* and subsequent developments in case law for the protection of transgender rights. However, importantly, the chapter argues that the Orders misunderstood transgender identity, adopting an approach that failed to uphold the ideals of human dignity enshrined in the Constitution. The next section analyses the *Transgender Persons (Protection of Rights) Act 2018*. The final section, before the conclusion, analyses the primary data collected for this chapter to assess the impact of the legal reforms over the past decade and the immediate impact of the act on the social status and lives of transgender people in Pakistan.

This chapter demonstrates that despite improvements in the rights of transgender people in Pakistan because of the reform efforts, they have not been able to achieve full recognition of their rights and continue to face social stigma, discrimination and violence. The chapter shows that to overcome the historical marginalisation and negative portrayal of transgender people in Pakistan, the government would need to devise comprehensive strategies for the improvement of public perception about transgender people and ensure the proper implementation of the 2018 act.

5.2 Conceptual and Legal Definitions of *Hijra*, *Khawaja Sira* and Transgender

There is no single internationally recognised legal definition of a transgender person (ICJ, 2020, p.7). However, as an umbrella term "transgender" incorporates people who may have a gender identity different from the gender they were assigned at birth and describes a wide range of identities that are perceived as gender-atypical, such as non-binary, genderqueer, genderfluid and transexuals (Commissioner for Human Rights, 2011, pp. 22–23; UN Free & Equal, 2014). Some transgender people may desire medical treatment, including surgery, to align their bodies with their gender identity. However, transgender identity is not dependent on medical procedures or physical appearance.

Transgender identity is different from being intersex. Intersex people are those born with a wide range of natural variations in their sex characteristics that do not fit the typical binary notions of male and female bodies, such as genitals, gonads and chromosome patterns (Commissioner for Human Rights, 2011, p. 22). Being transgender is about a person's internal knowledge about their gender identity while being intersex relates to biological sex characteristics. As is the case with everyone else, an intersex person may identify as transgender. Because of ambiguous sexual characteristics and the fact that some intersex adults may be infertile, intersex people have often been seen through the framework of a "medical condition", "disorder" and "disability". Some intersex advocates have argued that this framework promotes the link between intersex and "abnormality", leading to stigmatisation and stereotyping that intersex people wish to avoid (Bauer et al., 2020; Cornwall, 2013, 2015; Briffa, 2014; Khetarpal & Singh, 2012; Orentlicher, 2010; Feder & Karkazis, 2008). Intersex people have often been subjected to non-consensual medical intervention to surgically alter their bodies in line with the binary conception of a male or female body.

Like transgender, *Khawaja Sira* and *Hijra* are also umbrella terms that encompass people with atypical gender identity and includes intersex people. However, *Khawaja Sira* and *Hijra* are broader concepts, encompassing a wider range of identities than "transgender", and have an older pedigree, dating back to the medieval period of South Asia (F. A. Khan, 2016a, pp. 158–159). The terms represent the unique cultural outlook of the South Asian Society towards individuals who do not fit into the traditional male/female binary of gender identities and biological bodies and individuals whose sexual orientation falls outside the ideals of heterosexuality (Nanda, 1999; Reddy, 2005; S. Khan, 2016b, pp. 219–220).

During the Mughal rule of India, the term *Khawaja Sira* referred to the eunuch officials of the royal and noble courts (Khan, 2014a, pp. 172–176; Reddy, 2005). They occupied an important social position and served as imperial officers, army generals and harem guards, and held powerful administrative positions. Outside of court titles, the term *Hijra* represented gender ambiguous people within the society. These included people who had ambiguous sexual characteristics, men who liked to dress as females or adopted female mannerisms, men who had sexual desires for other men and castrated men. Many such castrated men would engage in ritual castration as a more authentic means of expressing their identity as a *Hijra* (Nanda, 1990, pp. 24–37; Reddy, 2005, pp. 91–96).

Before the colonial period, *Khawaja Siras* and *Hijras* were an accepted part of the Indian society, living either as individuals or in social organisations based on *guru-chela* (master-disciple) relationships, and derived their legitimacy from both Quranic verses and Hinduism (Nanda, 1990, pp. 20–23; S. Khan, 2016b, pp. 219–220).[1] In many places in India, *Hijras* played an important role in celebrations, especially as dance performers. They also engaged in public performances and theatre to earn a livelihood. They were thought to be gifted by God with mystic powers, the ability to transition between both sexes, and the ability to bless familial celebrations, including marriages and births (Toppa, 2018; Zahra-Malik, 2017; Azhar, 2017; Nanda, 1986, p. 35; Khan, 2014b, p. 56).

This importance and acceptance began to change following the British colonisation of India, which is discussed in greater detail in the next section. The imposition of Victorian morality as regards gender identity and sexual orientation gradually marginalised *Khawaja Siras* and *Hijras*, with the term *Hijra* becoming pejorative. In recent years in Pakistan, activists and many members from amongst the transgender community have promoted the use of the term *Khawaja Sira* rather than *Hijra* because of its pejorative connotations (F.A. Khan, 2019a, para 17).

In contemporary Pakistan, the terms *Khawaja Sira* and *Hijra*, like the umbrella term "transgender", cover individuals whose gender identity does not conform to social norms based on the sex they were assigned at birth. In addition, they also cover all those individuals whose bodies do not fit the typical notions of male and female bodies. Since homosexuality is a crime in Pakistan and is considered a grave sin in Islam, *Khawaja Sira* communities also provide refuge to homosexual men to express their sexuality and form relationships (Khan, 2014b, pp. 71–74; Nanda, 1990, pp. 9–12). Thus, they encompass such individuals as transsexuals, transvestites, hermaphrodites, eunuchs, homosexuals, *khusra* (*khunsa*) and *zennana* (F.A. Khan, 2019a, para 19; Khan, 2014a, pp. 174–176; Nanda, 1990, p. 19). *Khusra* is an Urdu word that refers to intersex people. *Zennanaa* is also an Urdu word that refers to males who are believed to have a feminine spirit, are considered effeminate, display feminine mannerism and may dress up as females.

In recent years, some *Khawaja Siras* have also begun to identify themselves as transgender because of international exposure and overlap between the two concepts. Although the original Orders by the Supreme Court did not use the word "transgender", its use has become common practice in government documents since 2010. As "transgender" is the closest English term/identification for *Khawaja Siras*, it is also used in the 2018 act (Redding, 2019, p. 104). However, it is defined expansively under the 2018 act to include not only individuals with atypical gender identities but also those individuals who are covered by the indigenous terms *Khawaja Sira* and *Hijra*. In the following sections of this chapter, the word "transgender" is used to denote this expansive definition. Section 2(n) of the 2018 act gives a multipart definition of a "transgender person":

'Transgender person' is a person who is —

(i) intersex (khusra) with mixture of male and female genital features or congenital ambiguities; or
(ii) eunuch assigned male at birth, but undergoes genital excision or castration; or
(iii) a transgender man, transgender woman, *Khawaja Sira* or any person whose gender identity or gender expression differs from the social norms and cultural expectations based on the sex they were assigned at the time of their birth [original emphasis].

The next section discusses the historical discrimination and criminalisation suffered by *Khawaja Siras* and *Hijras* under British colonial rule. The section highlights their resulting social and economic exclusion and the failure of the Pakistani state over the next six decades to initiate any legal reforms to protect the rights of transgender.

5.3 Criminalisation Under Colonial Rule and Its Effects

The acceptance and prestige that *Khawaja Siras* and *Hijras* enjoyed in society began to change under British colonial rule (Abbas et al., 2014). The British with their ideas of sexuality and gender norms were incredibly uncomfortable with *Hijra* bodies and their way of life and imposed their ideals of sexuality to the detriment of *Hijras* (Loos, 2009, pp. 1315–1316; S. Khan, 2016b, pp. 222–223). British authorities displayed marked hostility towards *Hijras*, clearly demonstrated in the virulent language used to describe them. In their communications, British officials described *Hijras* as "immoral", "most shameless and abominable" and "wretches", and as individuals who resorted to "disgusting and cruel practices for the purpose of extorting money" (Nanda, 1990, pp. 48–51).

Hijras with their fluid sexuality and gender identity posed a challenge to Victorian-era British morality based on binary distinctions, between male and female, between "normal" heterosexual and "deviant" homosexual relationships (S. Khan, 2016b, pp. 222–223). *Hijras* eschewed these binaries, but for British officials engaged in the civilising mission, *Hijras* were seen as men who revelled in sexual "perversity" and engaged in vile practices (Hinchy, 2019). Disregarding the unique gender identity of *Hijras*, the British viewed Hijras as men who engaged in depraved practices, especially ritual castration, to fulfil their "perverse" desire to have sex with men. Official rhetoric during the 1850s and 1860s portrayed *Hijras* as inherently ungovernable and disorderly, as individuals who engaged in extensive criminality, sexual immorality and unnatural prostitution (Hinchy, 2019, pp. 27–43). Their traditional practices such as street performances, participation in celebrations, and ritual castration were labelled as a threat to public order and morality, and laws were enacted to combat this menace.

This was achieved through both medical regulation and criminal statutes. By the 1840s, discussion about *Hijras* had become popular in imperial medical journals. British doctors represented *Hijras* primarily as male-born castrates, who were symbolic of Indian sexual "perversity" (Hinchey, 2019, p. 30; S. Khan, 2016b, pp. 222–223). Over the ensuing decades, the process of medicalisation by the colonial state, though beneficial in many respects, portrayed *Hijras* communities through the language of disease, contagion, contamination and filth and as individuals suffering from various forms of disorder (Hinchy, 2019, p. 8; S. Khan, 2016b).[2]

This process of medicalisation categorised *Hijra* bodies as suffering from gender and sexual disorder, creating an image of *Hijras* as something less than normal. Post-independence, this language of disorder continues to plague *Khawaja Sira* and *Hijras* to their disadvantage and is discussed in greater detail in Sect. 5.4.

Under the *Cantonment Act 1864* and *Contagious Diseases Act 1868*, *Hijras* suspected of engaging in prostitution were subjected to compulsory registration, medical examinations and confinement (Hinchy, 2019, pp. 15–19, 50–61). The experience of registered *Hijras* with state officials was underpinned with violence and intimidation. This dynamic continued post-independence, and represents a major state failure. In fact, the immediate reason for the petition leading to the Supreme Court Orders was violence against transgender performers at the hands of police officers (discussed in greater detail in Sect. 5.4).

The criminalisation of *Khawaja Sira* and *Hijras* began in 1860, with the passing of the *Indian Penal Code 1860* (IPC). Section 290 criminalised public nuisance, and Section 294 criminalised obscene acts and songs in public. Colonial officials began to use these newly created crimes to target *Hijras* for being dressed in female clothes and for dancing and singing in public places (Hinchy, 2019, pp. 64–65). Victorian sexual morality also resulted in the promulgation of "unnatural offences" under Section 377 of the *Penal Code* which was also used to target *Hijras* (Hinchy, 2019, pp. 52–53). Section 377 criminalised acts that were labelled "unnatural", which included homosexuality, anal intercourse and sex with animals. *Hijras* were especially susceptible to investigations under Section 377 because British officials considered them men who desired other men. The hostility against *Hijras* culminated in the passing of *The Criminal Tribes Act 1871* and the *Dramatic Performance Act 1876*.

Using the term "eunuch" to refer to *Hijras*, the *Criminal Tribes Act* labelled *Hijras* as a criminal tribe, branding the entire community as innately criminal, subject to registration, surveillance and restrictions on movements. British hostility towards *Hijras* can be gauged from the fact that the colonial government devoted an entire part, Part II, of the act to deal with the "eunuch problem". This went beyond previous efforts under the IPC, which only applied to individual actions, as opposed to group designation, and was dependent on meeting the criminal burden of proof of "beyond reasonable doubt" for conviction. Section 24 empowered the local government to keep records of eunuchs and their property, who are "reasonably suspected" of engaging in castration, kidnapping of children and offenses contrary to Section 377. These records could be used by the colonial authorities to confine *hijras* to designated areas and regulate their movement and activities. Eschewing the criminal standard of proof made it far easier for the colonial state to regulate, marginalise and criminalise the *Hijra* communities in India.

Section 24 also defined "eunuch" to include "all persons of the male sex who admit themselves, or on medical inspection clearly appear, to be impotent", thus labelling individuals suffering from genetic disorders as criminals and making them vulnerable to invasive "medical" exams. Section 26 gave the power to arrest any eunuch without a warrant for dressing like a woman or wearing woman ornaments in public or for being seen wearing these articles from a public place. It also gave the power to arrest any eunuch who took part in any public exhibition, and who danced and played music either in public or for hire at a private venue. This criminalised the traditional means of livelihood of *Hijras*. Section 29, combined with Section 27, disenfranchised them from several legal rights—including the ability to adopt a male child, the ability to act as a guardian for a minor, the ability to make gifts and the ability to make a will. Section 30 gave sweeping powers to government officers to demand information from *Hijras* about their movable, immovable and trust properties.

The *Dramatic Performance Act 1876* had an indirect effect on *Hijras'* ability to earn a living. Section 3 gave the local government the power to prohibit any dramatic performance, play or pantomime in a public place that was of a "scandalous or defamatory nature" or likely to "deprave and corrupt" people. Even though the act did not directly address *Hijras*, the fact that colonial authorities considered *hijras* and their activities as depraved and perverse left their livelihood at the mercy of unsympathetic colonial officials.

The general disdain of colonial authorities and these laws profoundly affected the social status of people with atypical gender identities. Gradually, the Indian society began to categorise such individuals as "deviant", "dirty", "shameless", "aggressive", "criminal" and "sexual objects". They began to be stereotyped as people who suffer from gender and sexual disorders and who engage in perverted and immoral activities. Transgender people in India and post-independence Pakistan became victims of the worst form of social marginalisation and exclusion. Although the *Criminal Tribes Act* and the *Dramatic Performance Act* were eventually repealed, the legal treatment of *Khawaja Siras* and *Hijras* under the

British colonial rule left a legacy that has continued to impair their legal rights post-independence.

5.3.1 Post-Independence Situation

Representing a major state failure, this treatment of *Khawaja Siras* and *Hijras* continued after the creation of Pakistan. Their lifestyle was stigmatised for being contrary to the teachings of Islam, despite historical acceptance during the Muslim rule in India. They continued to face a steady decline in their social status, excluding them from mainstream economic and political activity. Their unique gender identity and gender expression became a subject of ridicule. Leaving them victims of frequent intimidation, harassment and violence, at the hands of both private citizens and government officials, especially the police (Khan, 2014b, pp. 117–127; Reddy, 2005, pp. 12–16; F.A. Khan, 2019a). They experienced significant hurdles in obtaining National Identity Card (NIC), which is essential for access to voting, passports, driving license, proper housing, education, health, banking and phone services. As a result, for most of them, especially transgender individuals from low-income backgrounds, the only viable way of earning livelihood became begging, dancing at parties and prostitution (Khan, 2014b, pp. 185–194). Such economic and social exclusion created a vicious circle that fed into the society's negative perception of transgender individuals further eroding their social status. Additionally, transgender individuals remain vulnerable to prosecution under Section 377 of *Pakistan Penal Code 1860*, which criminalises homosexuality.[3]

Due to the stigma and exclusion faced by people with ambiguous gender and bodies, many intersex children are abandoned by their parents often to be raised by *Khawaja Sira* and *Hijra* communities (Habib et al., 2017). Many others run away to these communities to seek refuge because of stigma, violence and sexual abuse (Wijngaarden et al., 2013). Social exclusion from mainstream society has meant that most *Khawaja Sira* or *Hijra* continue to live as part of a community that consists of others who do not fit into traditional binary gender identity. These communities have their own culture and traditions, and the members establish relationships in the form of a *guru* (master/teacher) and *chaela* (apprentice/follower) (F.A. Khan, 2019a, para 15–16; Khan, 2014b, pp. 90–103; Reddy, 2005, pp. 156–164).

This plight of the transgender community in Pakistan went unnoticed by the executive, the judiciary and wider civil society for more than six decades. It was only after 2009, following the First Order of the Supreme Court in *Khaki*, that transgender rights became part of the public discourse and led to several legal reforms over the next decade. In the following sections, the chapter analyses these reform efforts starting with the Supreme Court Orders.

5.4 Recent Developments in Law: The Supreme Court Orders and Subsequent Case Law

Almas Bobi the president of *Shemale Rights of Pakistan* (an association working for the advancement of the rights of transgender), alongside lawyer Aslam Kahki, filed a petition under Article 184 (3) of the *Constitution of Pakistan* in the Supreme Court in 2009 against the molestation and widespread humiliation of transgender individuals. The impetus for petition was the brutal attack against transgender individuals performing at a private function in the city of Taxila. They were robbed and sexually assaulted by the police. The petition argued that the state has failed to protect the rights of transgender individuals in Pakistan, leaving them vulnerable to violence at the hands of both private citizens and state officials. The petition asked for the recognition and protection of the rights of transgender people in Pakistan, especially the constitutionally guaranteed right to security (Art 9 of the Constitution), right to human dignity (Art 14), right to property (Art 24 (1)) and right to equality (Art 25). The petition resulted in a series of Orders by the Supreme Court between November 2009 and September 2012, with the final Order issued on 25 September 2012.

In the first Order, delivered on 4 November 2009, the Supreme Court ordered the attorney general of Pakistan to prepare a framework for federal and provincial governments to recognise transgender individuals as respectable citizens of Pakistan and to take steps to ensure that transgender individuals are able to enjoy the right to security, right to dignity and property rights like any other citizen of Pakistan. In the second Order delivered on 20 November 2009, the Supreme Court ruled that families cannot deprive transgender individuals of their legal inheritance by disowning them because of who they are. The Court directed the National Database and Registration Authority (NADRA) to devise a strategy to record the "exact status" of transgender individuals on passports and National Identity Cards, after conducting "medical tests based on hormones". The Court further ruled that transgender individuals have the right to register their names in the electoral list and have the right to cast a vote when they desire. The Court ordered all state ministries to collaborate and work together to provide respectable social status to transgender individuals.

The first Supreme Court Order recognised the unique gender identity of transgender individuals in Pakistan, but it recognised their unique gender identity as a result of a "gender disorder" and/or "disability". The Supreme Court stated that transgender individuals have been a target of systemic and pervasive abuse on account of the "gender disorder" of their bodies and required the attorney general to provide maintenance to transgender individuals on account of their "disability". The Court further opined that a system to facilitate "disabled persons" in finding employment opportunities already exists; therefore, the government can make similar arrangements to provide employment opportunities for transgender individuals and help them find work which "they can perform quite conveniently" (second Order para 3).

In the third Order, dated 23 December 2009, the Court read Article 22(4) of the Constitution of Pakistan, which allows any public authority to make "provision for the advancement of any socially or educationally *backward class of citizens*" (emphasis added), and Article 25 (the right to equality) and ordered the government to devise a special policy for the benefit of transgender people. To ensure that transgender people have access to educational and vocational opportunities (third Order para 4). As an example, the Court cited the steps taken by the District of Bihar in neighbouring India, where transgender individuals were employed by the government to collect payments from tax defaulters. These individuals were offered employment opportunities as part of a government "rehabilitation scheme" to provide literacy and vocational training to prepare them for respectable regular employment (third Order para 9).

In the final two Orders, the Court analysed policy initiatives taken by the federal and provincial governments in promoting the rights of transgender individuals in Pakistan, since its first Order. In its penultimate Order of 22 March 2011, the Court expressed satisfaction at the new NADRA policy, under which transgender individuals could register their non-binary gender identity as a separate gender category on their NIC. The Court also praised the policy efforts by the Provincial governments of Punjab, Sindh and Khyber Pakhtunkhwa to improve the situation of transgender in their provinces, and urged the government of Balochistan to do the same (*Muhammad Aslam Khaki v. SSP (Operation), Rawalpindi* (2013) SCMR 187, [3]). The Provincial efforts, lauded by the Supreme Court, included initiatives undertaken to increase enrolment of transgender students in educational institutions, hiring of transgender in certain government projects and devising a policy to increase employment opportunities for them in government departments. The Court expressed some concern regarding the police departments and the social welfare departments. The Court ordered the police departments to undertake greater efforts to improve the treatment of transgender individuals and ordered the Social Welfare departments to ensure better protection for their inheritance rights ((2013) SCMR 187, [5]-[7]). It also ordered the provincial and federal governments to appoint a focal person to bridge the communication gap between transgender individuals and government departments ((2013) SCMR 187, [5]-[7]). In its last Order dated 25 September 2012 (Dr. *Muhammad Aslam Khaki and others v. SSP (Operation), Rawalpindi and others* (2013) PLD 188 (SC)), the Court expressed satisfaction with the level of progress made at both the provincial and the federal level. Despite being immensely important, the Orders suffered from several shortcomings, which are analysed in the next section. Chief amongst them was the misunderstanding of transgender identity and reliance on the colonial language of "disorder" and "disability".

5.4.1 *Disability Approach of the Supreme Court Orders*

The Orders hold an important place in the history of the transgender struggle in Pakistan. They were essential in highlighting the vulnerable position that transgender people occupy in society and brought the debate surrounding the rights of transgender people to the forefront of the public discourse, laying down the foundations for subsequent legal reforms. They forced the federal and provincial governments to devise policies for the protection of transgender rights, including the first formal recognition of the unique gender identity of transgender people under the legal system in Pakistan. In spite of their significance, the Orders suffered from several problems.

Reminiscent of colonial language, the Court misunderstood transgender identity by perceiving all transgender people through the lens of disorder and disability. The conceptualisation of transgender identity as a "disorder" and a "disability" is neither new nor unique to the Supreme Court of Pakistan. Historically, transgender people have been seen as suffering from some kind of "disorder" or "disability" that can be cured and have been subjected to involuntary medical interventions (Spade, 2003). Transgender advocates have argued that the use of the word "disability" often invokes the image of an illness to be cured and can result in the pathologising of a transgender individual's expression of gender identity as "not normal" or "deviant" (Chung, 2011; Levi & Klein, 2006, p.75; Spade, 2003). By using the language of disability and ordering the use of medical exams, the Supreme Court was propagating this same approach. This focuses on imposing convenient legal labels on transgender individuals and usurping their autonomy over their bodies and minds, often through involuntary and invasive "medical" exams, regardless of the wishes of transgender individuals. The Court failed to take this opportunity to develop an approach towards transgender individuals that focused on self-identification and freedom to determine one's own gender identity, an approach that would have been in line with ideals of human dignity enshrined in the Constitution.

The Supreme Court's approach understood being transgender as a medical condition or a sickness, rather than an expression of gender identity. By offering jobs that transgender people could perform "conveniently", the Supreme Court categorised them as inherently impaired. Although the experiences of transgender people in the form of stigma, discrimination, prejudice and the creation of a disabling environment may have many similarities with the experience of people with disabilities, being transgender is different from having a physical or mental impairment (Carpenter, 2020; Safer et al., 2016). The Court seemed to be stating that transgender people have reduced mental or physical capacity than cisgender people, which might reduce their ability to perform certain functions, thus the focus on getting them "convenient" jobs. Rather than adopting this approach, the Court should have focused on the fact that the precarious condition of transgender is not the result of something inherent in them, but rather a result of the disabling environment that society creates. They do not need jobs that they can "conveniently" perform; they need access to equal opportunities and a society that does not revile and marginalise them, and treats them with respect and dignity.

Instead, the Court gave the example of the deeply problematic rehabilitation programme from Bihar as a paradigmatic example of jobs transgender can perform "conveniently". Such a programme perpetuates society's negative perception of transgender people. The transgender persons in Bihar were offered the work of debt collection precisely because they are "feared and reviled" and debtors would pay them to save themselves from the embarrassment of dealing with transgender individuals (Reuters, 2007). Such tactics by the government, instead of upholding the dignity of transgender individuals, exploits and perpetuates harmful stereotypes about transgender people.

The Court's direction to NADRA to create a policy on the use of medical exams for assigning gender to transgender individuals was also problematic. The reason for the direction lies in the Sharia Law of inheritance, which applies to Muslims in Pakistan. In Islam, the share of inheritance is different for male and female heirs. Female heirs receive half the share compared to male heirs in the same category. For example, if a person dies leaving a son and a daughter as their only heirs, the estate will be divided into three shares, with two shares going to the son and one share going to the daughter. In Pakistan, before the 2018 act, the traditional understanding of Sharia Law required that all heirs be categorised as either males or females, including those born with ambiguous sexual characteristics. Those born without ambiguous bodies were characterised as either male or female based on their biological sex, regardless of their gender identity. While those born with biological ambiguities were assigned a gender based on physical observation of their bodies after the onset of puberty. Gender was assigned based on the similarity with the "ideal" male or female form (Kugle, 2010, p. 257). This approach perpetuated negation of self-identity and invasion of privacy.

Rather than take this opportunity to mitigate the harmful effects of the traditional practice of assigning gender, the Supreme Court ordered NADRA to continue it, though garbed in the more palatable language of medical exams. Historically, the medicalisation of transgender and transexual individuals has been highly problematic, often used to justify non-consensual medical interventions (Rowlands & Amy, 2018). By ordering the creation of a system under which medical professionals would assign a gender to transgender people, the Court violated the privacy, autonomy and self-determination of transgender people.

Reliance on hormonal medical exams and use of colonial term "eunuch" (misspelled "unix" in some of the published Orders) also demonstrated the Court's misunderstanding about transgender identity in Pakistan. There is a common misconception in Pakistan that all *Khawaja Siras* and *Hijras* are people with ambiguous sexual characteristics, when in reality they only represent a small minority in the community (F.A. Khan, 2019a, para 22). The Court failed to realise that gender identity is different from biological sex characteristics. That people's gender identity is based on their own internal feelings, not on their bodies, and does not need to be assigned by an external entity. That people can have a gender identity different from their biological sex or a non-binary identity, and this has nothing to do with having ambiguous or unambiguous male or female sex characteristics.

The Court could have utilised this opportunity to state that a person's gender identity is a matter of self-determination and does not require assignment by the medical profession. As for the matter of inheritance, the Court could have adopted the same approach and held that the share would depend on whatever gender a transgender person identifies with. For those with non-binary identity, the Court could have decided that their inheritance share would be the average of the male and female share. For this, the Court could have drawn support from various pre-modern Muslim scholars who had argued that the Quran allows for the allocation of an average share for Muslims who do not fit in the binary male and female category, that is, half of the male share and half of the female share (Kugle, 2010, pp. 235–268; Gesink, 2018).

As a result of these problems, the Orders failed to meet the ideals of human dignity (Art 14) and equal treatment under the law (Art 25). Despite being aimed at improving the status of transgender people in society, protecting their rights and promoting equality, the Courts approach, based as it was on misunderstanding transgender identity and colonial language of "disorder" and "disability", was highly problematic. It disregarded their autonomy and perpetuated the common misconceptions about transgender people as "abnormal" individuals who suffer from an illness that needs a cure. The language and the example of "convenient" jobs treated transgender people as inferior to cisgender people with a reduced capacity to work while strengthening negative social perceptions about them. Despite these problems, the Orders led to immediate policy changes for the benefit of transgender people and created a precedent for future judicial enforcement of transgender rights. The subsequent development in the case law is discussed in the next section.

5.4.2 *The Legal Developments After the Supreme Court Orders*

Despite the problems with the Supreme Court Orders, the legal recognition of transgender identity finally started a process of legal reform for the recognition and enforcement of the rights of transgender individuals through case law and eventually legislation. One immediate benefit of the original 2009 Order was the policy change by NADRA, which gave transgender people the ability to register their gender as Gender X on various legal forms if they did not wish to identify as either male (Gender M) or female (Gender F). The Supreme Court Orders also opened the doors for transgender individuals to petition courts against discriminatory executive policies.

In 2016, a transgender individual petitioned the Lahore High Court in *Mian Asia v Federation of Pakistan through the Secretary Finance and two others*, Writ Petition No. 31581 of 2016 (reported as (2018) PLD 54 (LHC)) against a discriminatory executive policy. The petitioner alleged that the authorities had failed to provide him with a new NIC on the expiration of the previous one. The petitioner was denied renewal of his NIC because he was unable to provide the name of his father (he was abandoned at birth), and NADRA refused to accept the name of his *guru* as a substitute. It was argued before the high court that most transgender people are abandoned at birth and therefore are unable to provide proof of their parentage. This social reality should not be used to deprive them of their right to identity documents. The high court ruled that NADRA cannot deny NIC to a transgender person solely on the ground that they are unable to provide proof of their parentage. During the trial, NADRA changed its policy to accommodate such people.

However, this new NADRA policy remains problematic. It uses the same kind of shortcut that has been developed for orphans, namely picking of random strangers from the NADRA database to be put in the father column of the NIC (NADRA Policy, 2018; The Nation, 2017). Though the high court was concerned with upholding the dignity of transgender people, acceptance of NADRA's policy detracts from such aim. Requiring a name to be entered in the "Father Column" of a transgender person abandoned at birth fails to recognise such people as full citizens in their own right while perpetuating their trauma of abandonment.

The judgement itself is quite interesting, though it does demonstrate the disconnect between constitutional ideals of human dignity propounded by the courts and the ultimate policy decisions by the executive that often fails to live up to these ideals. It also demonstrates the improvements in judicial understanding about transgender people in the years that followed the landmark, but problematic, Supreme Court Orders. Rejecting the language of "disorder" and "disability", the high court recognised that gender identity is one of the most fundamental aspects of a person's life, referring as it does to an individual's "intrinsic sense of being male, female or transgender" ((2018) PLD 54 (LHC), para 11). The high court further reiterated that a person has a fundamental right to protection from discrimination on the basis of gender identity. The court stated that it was high time for the society to change its mindset towards transgender people and for the law to provide complete protection to them and formally recognise their gender identity. The judgement further stated that transgender people are respectable citizens of this country and as such entitled to the full recognition of their rights, including the right to education, the right to property and the right to live their lives in a dignified and secure manner.

The high court's approach was an improvement over the original Supreme Court's order, upholding the principle of human dignity, by emphasising gender identity as something intrinsic rather than a "disability". However, the court could do nothing about an executive policy that failed to uphold this principle. Judicial review powers of the courts are limited. The court had no jurisdiction to review the normative framework that informed NADRA's policy, as long as the alleged harm was remedied, namely provision of a new NIC to the applicant. This highlights the limits of judicial reform efforts. Without a corresponding legislative framework that is grounded in the principle of human dignity, courts cannot ensure that the policy option selected by the government will reflect this principle.

A similar failure in judicial reform efforts and the disconnect between the law and social realities can be observed in the 2014 judgement by the Supreme Court of Azad Jammu and Kashmir (AJ&K) (*Zafar alias Mumtaz & another v Mst. Sajjad Begum & Others* (2015) PLJ 14 (SC AJ&K)). This case concerned a property dispute between the legal heirs of a transgender *guru* (who had died issueless) and his *chelas* (disciples) The *chelas* argued that the deceased's property should go to them since that is the prevailing customary tradition amongst transgender individuals in Pakistan—the property of the *guru* devolves to the *chelas*, not to their legal heirs. This was opposed by the legal heirs on the ground that since the deceased was a Muslim, his property should be distributed based on Sharia Law and not on customs and traditions. The AJ&K Court agreed with the legal heirs and ruled that in AJ&K Sharia Law prevails over all customs and traditions, and hence the property of the deceased will devolve to the legal heirs and not to his disciples. For the court, it was irrelevant that the property in question was earned by the *guru* during his lifetime and was not ancestral property. It was also irrelevant that the *guru* had been abandoned by his family, who were now demanding a share in his estate. The plaintiff's application to apply established customs of the transgender community was denied by the court. Although AJ&K judgements are not binding on Pakistani courts, being only of persuasive authority, the same approach is likely to be adopted by the Pakistani courts. This is because of Article 227 of the Constitution of Pakistan under which all laws in Pakistan must be compatible with Islamic principles.

The decision by the AJ&K Court failed to take into account the social reality of transgender people, which makes it very difficult for most of them to inherit under Sharia Law. Inheritance under Sharia Law is based on biological relationships and marriage. For transgender people, this represents a problematic hurdle. They are shunned by their families and society. They are often abandoned at a young age and have no knowledge about their biological families. This means that in practice most transgender people will never inherit property from their biological families. The customary tradition under which *chelas* inherit from their *gurus* developed precisely because of this reason. By ignoring social reality and striking down the customary rule, the court created a situation where many transgender people will be unable to benefit from the right of inheritance, while family members who abandoned transgender individuals in life could claim their property after their death.

Because of the problematic approach adopted by the Supreme Court of Pakistan and the inherent limitations of judicial reform efforts, there remained a need for comprehensive legislative reform in the area. This was accomplished by the promulgation of the *Transgender Persons (Protection of Rights) Act 2018*, which is analysed in the next section.

5.5 The Transgender Persons (Protection of Rights) Act 2018

The Supreme Court Orders were successful in highlighting the bleak state of transgender rights and generating momentum for reforms. This ultimately led to the enactment of the *Transgender Persons (Protection of*

Rights) Act in 2018 by the National Assembly of Pakistan. Based on contemporary understanding of transgender people and gender identity, the act addresses many shortcomings in the jurisprudence developed by the courts. If implemented properly, it also provides a framework for the creation of a comprehensive rights regime for transgender people in Pakistan. Section 2(f) defines "gender identity" as the "innermost and individual sense of self as male, female or a blend of both or neither that can correspond or not to the sex assigned at birth", thus basing it entirely on one's choice. Section 2(e) defines "gender expression" as a "person's presentation of his gender identity and its perception by others". Similarly, Section 2(n), reproduced above, gives an expansive definition of "transgender person" to include all types of gender identities, in line with the unique cultural outlook of South Asian Societies. Section 3 of the act makes provisions for the recognition of the "self-perceived" gender identity of individuals in all relevant government documents. Additionally, Section 3(4) gives transgender people the power to apply for the modification of their existing identity documents to make them consistent with their chosen gender identity.

Section 4 prohibits discrimination against transgender individuals and contains a compressive list of nine subsections detailing the type of conduct prohibited, including discrimination in educational institutions, employment opportunities, healthcare services, access to public goods and services, public transport, use and ownership of movable or immovable property, holding of a public or private office, and accessing government or private establishments. Section 5 prohibits harassment against transgender individuals at home and in public, due to their sex or gender identity. Harassment has been expansively defined in Section 2(h) to include "sexual, physical, mental and psychological harassment", including conduct that may sexually demean, or conduct that may interfere with living, mobility, or work of a transgender individual, or may create a "hostile or offensive work or living environment".

Section 6 imposes obligations on the government to ensure full participation of transgender individuals in society and requires the government to establish "protection centres" and "safe houses", which would provide protection, rehabilitation, medical, counselling and educational services to transgender individuals, and to establish separate prison cells for them. It requires the government to launch training campaigns for government officials, law enforcement agencies and medical personal to improve the treatment of transgender people by government employees. It also opens up the possibility of launching public awareness campaigns to change the attitude of society towards transgender people. Furthermore, it imposes an obligation to launch financial and loan schemes to support entrepreneurship opportunities for transgender individuals, and any other measure that may be necessary to achieve the objectives of the act.

Section 7 reforms the law of inheritance and, to some extent, overcomes the shortcomings present in the judgement of the AJ&K Court. It allows inheritance share to be based on the self-declared gender on the NIC. In case a person does not declare themselves either as a male or a female, then Section 7, adopting the approach advocated by premodern Muslim scholars, gives them an inheritance share that is the average of the male and the female share. For heirs that are legal minors, and cannot declare their gender till they reach adulthood, their inheritance share would be based on the gender determined by a medical officer based on their predominant physical features. Section 3 makes it clear that this determination by the medical officer will not affect the individual's later declaration regarding their gender identity on reaching adulthood.

Despite these improvements in inheritance law, the act continues to perpetuate state failure by remaining silent on the legal validity of the customary tradition under which *chelas* inherit from their *gurus*. The act does not address the social reality—discussed above—which makes it impossible for many transgender people to inherit from their biological families. Thus, any attempt by *gurus* to leave their property to their *chelas* remains open to challenge by biological heirs of the *guru*, which under Sharia Law can include any male agnates of the *guru*, no matter how removed.

Sections 8 to 15 provide greater detail on the obligations imposed in Section 6. It imposes an obligation on the government to take steps to protect the right to education, employment, vote, holding a public office, assembly and access to public places, including places of religion, and property of transgender individuals. Section 10 (right to vote) further clarifies that access to polling stations for transgender would be based on gender identified on their NIC. These sections reiterate the duty of the government to provide proper funding and training to ensure that these rights are realised in practice. Section 16 reiterates that the fundamental constitutional rights guaranteed in Part II of Chapter I of the Constitution "shall be available unequivocally for every transgender person".

Section 17 provides imprisonment of up to six months and a fine of 50,000 rupees for any person who "employs, compels or uses" any transgender individual for begging. Section 18 provides enforcement mechanisms to protect transgender rights. It states that in addition to the remedies available under the Constitution, the *Pakistan Penal Code* 1860, the *Code of Criminal Procedure* 1898 and the *Code of Civil Procedure* 1908, transgender individuals can also complain directly to the Federal Ombudsman, National Commission for Status of Women and National Commission of Human Rights if their rights under the act are being denied.

One immediate positive impact of the act was that 13 transgender candidates ran for office in the 2018 general elections (Barker, 2018; Shah, 2018b). Nevertheless, the act suffers from several shortcomings. Firstly, the language used in the act is problematic. It misses the opportunity to sensitise the public about proper pronouns for transgender individuals. The act uses pronouns "him or her" to refer to transgender individuals, rather than using the gender-neutral "they".

Additionally, the act missed an opportunity to regulate gender confirmation surgery. At present, there is no Pakistani law on the matter. The act briefly touches on "necessary medical and psychological gender corrective treatment" in Section 12(c) but lays down no comprehensive and explicit right to gender confirmation surgery. Although in Pakistan there exists some ambiguity concerning the compatibility of gender confirmation surgery with Islamic principles, most Muslim scholars believe that Sharia Law allows such surgeries, which is legally practised in several Muslim countries, such as Iran, Syria and Egypt (Kugle, 2010, pp. 260–265; Sahqani et al., 2019). By explicitly recognising the right to seek medical help in law, the government can protect transgender individuals from the discretion of doctors and hospitals. Taking into account the general sentiments of the society towards transgender individuals and the ambiguity in Islamic rules on the matter, the absence of proper regulations on the availability of such surgery may leave many transgender individuals without access to proper medical facilities for gender confirmation surgeries (Shah, 2018a; Sahqani et al., 2019). For many, this would mean the continuation of the unsafe tradition, under which *chelas* undergo risky castrations performed by their *gurus* (Sahqani et al., 2019). Though the law is aimed at improving the status of transgender individuals in Pakistan, the lack of explicit recognition of the right to gender confirmation surgery leaves many transgender people at risk of discriminatory medical practices and risky traditions.

Similarly, though, the act imposes an obligation on the government to create a comprehensive framework for the betterment and protection of transgender people, especially in sections 4, 6 and 8 to15, it provides no detailed roadmap for such improvements, neither does it lay any mechanisms to evaluate the implementation of such improvements. It leaves it open to the government to devise policies for achieving these objectives. Unfortunately, in Pakistan, this is where most reform efforts flounder. The National and Provincial Assemblies in Pakistan regularly enact comprehensive statutes aimed at addressing various problems that the society is facing without much success, because of unsatisfactory implementation of the laws by the government. In addition to imposing an obligation on the government generally to improve the situation of transgender people in Pakistan, the act should have given the responsibility of the implementation to a new government department or office. Without a dedicated department/office, implementation is likely to be slow and uneven keeping in mind the already-heavy workload on existing government offices. Similarly, the act should have provided for a comprehensive policy for positive discrimination and affirmative action. This could have included employment quotas and financial uplifting schemes for transgender people as is the case with other vulnerable groups in Pakistan.

Notwithstanding these shortcomings, following the enactment of the act, several banks and microfinance institutions created low or no interest rate loan schemes for transgender individuals as a means for their economic betterment (State Bank of Pakistan, 2019; The News, 2019). Additionally, the Punjab Social Protection Authority created a comprehensive policy, the Transgender Persons Welfare Policy (2018), to address the needs of transgender individuals in Punjab. The actual implementation of the policy remains problematic, with little or no data available to assess its impact. Additionally, the Punjab Welfare Policy is only applicable in Punjab, with no comparable policy developed by other provinces.

The 2018 act puts Pakistan at the forefront in the protection of the rights of transgender people in the world, at least on paper. The framework envisaged in the act, despite the shortcomings identified above, has the potential to provide comprehensive protection to the rights of transgender people in Pakistan and uplift the community to a position where they can enjoy a life of dignity, social inclusion and equality as promised by the Constitution. It remains to be seen whether the government will be able to achieve the ideals. Based on the treatment of transgender people post-2018, and interviews of transgender people conducted by the authors in 2019, it is likely that the state would fail to achieve most of these ideals. The next section analyses the success of the decade-long reform efforts based on the data collected through the interviews.

5.6 Listening to the Transgender Individuals in Pakistan

A decade after the first Supreme Court Order and almost a year after the enactment of the 2018 act, in-depth interviews with some transgender individuals were conducted in Lahore. These interviews were conducted to assess the impact and effectiveness of the policies designed to improve the status of transgender individuals in Pakistan. A total of 79 transgender individuals were interviewed, with extreme care being taken to protect the privacy of the interviewees. Interviewers were under strict instructions to abstain from asking and recording the names of interviewees and from asking interviewees to sign anything. Interviewees were informed that their identity will not be disclosed, and no lasting records of the names were maintained to ensure privacy. Consent was orally taken in the preferred language of the interviewee. The interviewee's preference as to the form of address was recorded first. The primary research conducted follows the Ethics Policy at the University of Management and Technology (UMT).

The collected data has geographical limitations; it was only collected in Lahore. Lahore is the provincial capital of Punjab, the largest and richest province in Pakistan. It is the second-largest city in the country and acts as Pakistan's cultural centre, with a strong presence of an active civil society and NGOs working in the field of transgender rights. Legal reforms have the greatest chance of positive impact in Lahore. Interviewees were selected at random. Some interviewees were affiliated with Khawaja Sira Foundation, Akhuwat Foundation and Saima Foundation. These foundations are some of the leading organisations working towards the advancement of the rights of transgender people in Pakistan. Interviewees affiliated with, working with or under the care of the said foundations were approached at the offices of the foundations. Transgender individuals working on major streets/intersections in Lahore, not associated with any of these foundations, were also interviewed. The interviews were conducted based on a structured questionnaire but emphasised listening to the interviewees.

The first few questions were aimed at understanding the living situation of transgender people and their relationship with their biological families. Only 14% of the respondents lived with their biological families. The majority of the respondents lived with their *gurus* and other transgender individuals, and 16% lived on their own. About half of the respondents stated they were treated fairly by their families; however, the remaining half of the respondents reported bad and unfair treatment from their families, stating that they had no contact with their respective families.

The second part focused on their interactions with public officials and the ease of accessing government services. The findings were alarming. Twenty-three respondents stated that applying for and getting the NIC was easy; however, 20 reported that they found the process difficult. The difficulties they faced were primarily due to the hostile attitude of the NADRA officials. Interestingly, nine reported that they had no NIC and had no need for one. Considering the importance of the NIC for social and economic life in Pakistan, the responses demonstrate the extent of social exclusion experienced by certain transgender people and their fatalistic attitude about their place in society.

Similarly, 50% of the respondents stated that they are unable to get assistance from government officials and are treated harshly by them. More than half reported bad treatment from the police officials, with approximately two-thirds stating that they were harassed by police officials, and do not feel safe in asking them for help. Three respondents reported being sexually assaulted by police.

The next part focused on society's attitude towards transgender people, access to public spaces and the right to security. Social attitude towards transgender people remains problematic. Ninety per cent of the respondents stated that they had experienced hooting and harassment in public spaces. Two-thirds reported feeling unsafe moving in the society and stated that they had faced repeated harassment in public places. Half of the respondents categorically reported that society neither respects them nor treats them with dignity. Half of the respondents reported that they had been physically assaulted in public places, and half reported they had been sexually assaulted.

The next part focused on assessing their access to different services. This included healthcare, housing, banking, employment opportunities and religion. The situation was slightly better in access to healthcare and banking services. Most reported being treated with respect by healthcare professionals; however, 14% still reported being treated with disrespect in hospitals. Very few respondents faced antagonism from bank staff; however, an overwhelming majority faced difficulty in opening an account due to their inability to provide proper documentation and their low-income status. As a result, only 14% of the respondents had a bank account.

Two-thirds of the respondents found the process of renting and owning property extremely difficult. Half of the respondents believed that they would face discrimination in renting and buying property. The situation relating to economic opportunities remains grim. Sixteen per cent of the respondents stated that they had a bad experience when they applied for a job, and more than half believed they would be unfairly treated if they were to apply for a job. The majority of the respondents earned their livelihood through begging and dancing.

Concerning freedom of religion and access to religious places and services, 76% of the respondents reported that they were able to easily access religious places and were treated fairly by religious leaders. However, one-third stated that they faced difficulty in getting religious leaders to perform ceremonies for them.

As regards inheritance rights, despite no legal recognition of the customary tradition of *chelas* inheriting from their *gurus*, the majority of the respondents, about 67% believed that they would be entitled to their *gurus*' property. About 40% were sure they would not inherit anything from their parents, while 27% were not sure whether they would inherit anything from their parents. The rest of the respondents believed that they would receive an inheritance from their parents. Inheritance rights continue to be a significant area of state failure.

The last part of the interview questions focused on their awareness about the law and reforms introduced for the rights of transgender people. More than half of the respondents were not aware of the 2018 act. Half of the respondents did not know how to enforce their legal rights and believed that the government and the courts would not be able to protect their rights. Two-thirds of the respondents believed that there has been an improvement in the status of transgender individuals over the past ten years. Worryingly, 30% believed that there has been no improvement.

The data collected paints a depressing picture of transgender rights in Pakistan. Despite legal recognition of various rights in the last decade, including the right to gender identity, inheritance, non-discrimination and guaranteed access to government services, their experience continues to be shaped by pernicious social perceptions surrounding transgender people, which can be traced back to the colonial era. They continue to be treated with disrespect and hostility by both the general public and government officials, and social and economic exclusion remains the norm. Access to public places and public services remains limited. Their right to life and security remains severely curtailed, and they continue to face a serious risk of harassment and violence.

If the experience of transgender people in a major city like Lahore is so grim, the situation in other areas of the country will be far worse. This is borne out in various reports on violence against transgender in other cities. For example, since 2015 there have been 479 attacks reported against transgender people in Khyber Pakhtunkhwa province. At least 65 have been killed there since 2015 (Human Rights Watch, 2021; M.I. Khan, 2019b). The threat faced by transgender people from the police remains the most serious state failure. Our data and other reports amply demonstrate the complicity of police officials in violence against transgender persons. Many police officials are involved in violence or harassment, while many others fail to properly investigate reports of violence or provide adequate security to transgender people in need.

The data demonstrates the tragic irony of reform efforts of the past decade. Government officials, who carry the responsibility of implementing legal reforms, remain the most problematic group. The majority of transgender people are distrustful and afraid of government officials and continue to face hostility and harassment from them. The law relating to the protection of transgender people exemplifies one of the major problems within the Pakistani legal system. Repeated enactment of various rights protection legislation fails as a result of abysmal implementation by the government. Those who have the resources can go to court to have their rights protected, but for the vast majority, protection remains limited.

The major failure in the reform efforts has been the inability to change the attitude of society towards transgender people. More than a decade ago the Supreme Court ruled that to improve the status of transgender people in Pakistan, the government would need to create public awareness about the plight of transgender people and improve their treatment. This has been reiterated in Section 6 of the 2018 act, which imposes an obligation on the government to launch sensitisation and awareness campaigns for government officials and the general public. The federal and provincial governments have failed in this regard. Even piecemeal training provided to government officials has largely failed, as demonstrated by the experiences of interviewees. Though NGOs like Akhuwat, Khawaja Sira Society and Be Ghar Foundation, have continued their efforts in advancing transgender rights, without adequate government support, changing social perception about transgender people continues to be extremely slow and difficult (Akhuwat, 2020). The authors could not find evidence of a single government-sponsored campaign, on either the national print or the electronic media, to create awareness about transgender rights since 2018.

5.7 Conclusion

The Supreme Court Orders represented the first success of the long and arduous activism for the right of transgender people in Pakistan. The Orders provided legal recognition to transgender identity, led to some positive changes in government policy and opened the door for future transgender applicants to approach the courts. They also had a profound effect on the public discourse surrounding the rights of transgender people. They brought transgender issues to the public limelight, paving the way for future legal reforms and opening the door for possible positive change in society's perception about *Khawaja Siras* and *Hijras*. However, the Supreme Court Orders displayed several basic misunderstandings about transgender identity and relied on problematic colonial language. The Orders fell short of the ideals of human dignity and human rights, especially in the use of language that focused on "disorder", "disability" and the ability of transgender people to do "certain jobs conveniently".

The momentum generated by the Orders also made the enactment of the 2018 act possible, which remedied many problems with the Supreme Court Orders. These reform efforts had a positive impact, which can be gleaned from the participation of transgender candidates in the 2018 general elections and the belief amongst the majority of the interviewees that there have been improvements over the past decade. However, these improvements have been quite small, and many problems and failures continue to persist. There is a need to reform the law of inheritance and to design an effective regulation on sex-change procedures, a need for active efforts in changing social perception about transgender people, and improvements in their treatment by government officials, especially the police. There is a dire need for consistent efforts on part of the federal and provincial governments for ensuring proper implementation of these reforms, which have the potential to gradually improve the social and economic status of transgender people in Pakistan. Otherwise, transgender people in Pakistan will continue to face stigma, discrimination, harassment and violence, and the state will continue to fail one of its most vulnerable and marginalised groups.

Notes

1. The Quran explicitly recognizes the existences intersex people and people with fluid gender identities. In Sura 42, Verses 49–50, Quran states: "(42:49) The dominion of the heavens and the earth belongs to Allah. He creates whatever He pleases. He grants females to whomever He pleases and males to whomever He pleases, (42:50) or grants them a mix of males and females, and causes whomever He pleases to be barren. He is All- Knowing, All-Powerful." In Hinduism, several male gods take on dual-gender manifestation. For example, Lord Shiva has the female form *Ardhanarishvara* (the Half-Female Lord). Lord Vishnu transforms into a beautiful woman, Mohini. Additionally, *Hijras* claim to derive their power from ritual castration as a form of devotion to the incarnation Bahuchara of the Mother Goddess. For details, see Nanda (1990, pp. 19–23, 33–37) and Lal (1999, pp. 122–126).
2. For details on the process of medicalization, imposition of the British medical paradigm and enactment of Contagious Disease Act (1868) as a form of orientalism and colonization of the Indian body, see Arnold (1993) and Whitehead (1995). This paradigm led to repression of indigenous Indian mores on gender and sexuality and eventually led to a situation where people with ambiguous gender and bodies came to be seen as suffering from disorders and as socially and morally inappropriate, leading to their stigmatization and marginalization (S. Khan, 2016b).
3. Actual prosecution under Section 377 is rare, but it continues to pose a serious risk. Reform efforts over the last decade have been targeted to improve the rights of transgender people; there is no public demand or governmental attempt to decriminalise or legalise homosexuality in Pakistan (Baudh, 2013).

References

Abbas, T., Nawaz, Y., Ali, M., Hussain, N., & Nawaz, R. (2014). Social Adjustment of Transgender: A Study of District Chiniot, Punjab (Pakistan). *Academic Journal of Interdisciplinary Studies, 3*(1), 61–71.

Akhuwat, Khwajasira Support Program. Retrieved February 10, 2020., from https://akhuwat.org.pk/khwajasira-support-program/

Arnold, D. (1993). *Colonizing the body: State Medicine and Epidemic Disease in Nineteenth-Century India.* University of California Press

Azhar, M. (2017). Pakistan's Traditional Third Gender Isn't Happy with the Trans Movement. *The World*, 6 August. Retrieved February 20, 2020, from https://www.pri.org/stories/2017-07-29/pakistans-traditional-third-gender-isnt-happy-trans-movement

Barker, M. (2018). Once Ostracised, Now Pakistani Transgender People are Running for Parliament. *The Guardian*, 23 July. Retrieved February 16,

2020, from https://www.theguardian.com/world/2018/jul/23/pakistani-transgender-people-office-election

Baudh, S. (2013). Decriminalisation of Consensual Same-Sex Sexual Acts in the South Asian Commonwealth: Struggles in Contexts. In C. Lennoz & M. Waites (Eds.), *Human Rights, Sexual Orientation and Gender Identity in The Commonwealth* (pp. 287–312). University of London Press.

Bauer, M., Truffer, D., & Crocetti, D. (2020). Intersex Human Rights. *The International Journal of Human Rights, 24*(6), 724–749.

Briffa, T. (2014). Tony Briffa Writes on "Disorders of Sex Development". *Intersex Human Rights Australia*, 8 May. Retrieved April 4, 2021, from https://ihra.org.au/26808/tony-briffa-on-dsd/

Carpenter, M. (2020). Intersex: Intersectionalities with Disabled People. *Intersex Human Rights Australia*, 16 September. Retrieved April 4, 2021, from https://ihra.org.au/21214/intersex-and-disability/. [Note the content was first posted 29 October 2012, and the content last reviewed 16 September 2020].

Chung, J. J. (2011). Identity or Condition: The Theory and Practice of Applying State Disability Laws to Transgender Individuals. *Columbia Journal of Gender and Law, 21*(1), 1–45.

Commissioner for Human Rights. (2011). *Discrimination on Grounds of Sexual Orientation and Gender Identity in Europe: Background Document.* Council of Europe. Retrieved January 20, 2020, from https://rm.coe.int/discrimination-on-grounds-of-sexual-orientation-and-gender-identity-in/16809079e2

Cornwall, S. (2013). Asking About What Is Better: Intersex, Disability, and Inaugurated Eschatology. *Journal of Religion, Disability & Health, 17*(4), 369–392.

Cornwall, S. (2015). Intersex and the Rhetorics of Disability and Disorder: Multiple and Provisional Significance in Sexed, Gender, and Disabled Bodies. *Journal of Disability & Religion, 19*(2), 106–118.

Feder, E. K., & Karkazis, K. (2008). What's in a Name? The Controversy Over "Disorders of Sex Development". *The Hastings Center Report, 38*(5), 33–36.

Gesink, I. F. (2018). Intersex Bodies in Premodern Islamic Discourse: Complicating the Binary. *Journal of Middle East Women's Studies, 14*(2), 152–173.

Habib, F., Zaki, F., & Ajmal, S. (2017). Unprecedented Predicament: The Reality of Intersex Population in Karachi. *Shorthand Social*, 30 November. Retrieved February 15, 2020, from https://social.shorthand.com/fyzaahabib/nykl3BQPV3/unprecedented-predicament

Hinchy, J. (2019). *Governing gender and sexuality in colonial India: the Hijra, c. 1850–1900.* Cambridge University Press.

Human Rights Watch. (2021). *Pakistan: Events of 2020.* Retrieved July 10, 2021, from https://www.hrw.org/world-report/2021/country-chapters/pakistan#e81181

ICJ (International Commission of Jurists). (2020). *Pakistan: Transgender Persons (Protection of Rights) Act, 2018—A Briefing Paper*. Geneva: International Commission of Jurists. Retrieved January 15, 2021, from https://www.icj.org/wp-content/uploads/2020/03/Pakistan-Transgender-Advocacy-Analysis-brief-2020-ENG.pdf

Khan, F. A. (2014a). Khwaja Sira: Transgender Activism and Transnationality in Pakistan. In S. S. Wadley (Ed.), *South Asia in the World: An Introduction* (pp. 170–184). Routledge.

Khan, F. A. (2014b). *Khwaja Sira: Culture, Identity Politics, and "Transgender" Activism in Pakistan*. ProQuest Dissertations Publishing.

Khan, F. A. (2016a). Khwaja Sira Activism: The Politics of Gender Ambiguity in Pakistan. *Transgender Studies Quarterly, 3*(1–2), 158–164.

Khan, S. (2016b). What is in a Name? Khwaja Sara, Hijra and Eunuchs in Pakistan. *Indian Journal of Gender Studies, 23*(2), 218–242.

Khan, F. A. (2019a). Translucent Citizenship: Khwaja Sira Activism and Alternatives to Dissent in Pakistan. *South Asian Multidisciplinary Academic Journal (Sedition, Sexuality, Gender, and Gender Identity in South Asia)*, 20, (Online). Retrieved December 10, 2019, from https://journals.openedition.org/samaj/5034

Khan, M. I. (2019b). Transgender in Pakistan: Maya, The Woman Who Almost Broke Free. *BBC*, December 28. Retrieved February 22, 2020, from https://www.bbc.com/news/world-asia-50486439

Khetarpal, A., & Singh, S. (2012). Infertility: Why Can't We Classify this Inability as Disability? *The Australasian Medical Journal, 5*(6), 334–339.

Kugle, S. S. A. H. (2010). *Homosexuality in Islam: Critical Reflection on Gay, Lesbian, and Transgender Muslims*. Oneworld Publications.

Lal, V. (1999). Not This, Not That: The Hijras of India and the Cultural Politics of Sexuality. *Social Text, 61*, 119–140.

Levi, J., & Klein, B. (2006). Pursuing Protection for Transgender People Through Disability Laws. In P. Currah, R. M. Juang, & S. P. Minter (Eds.), *Transgender Rights* (pp. 74–92). University of Minnesota Press.

Loos, T. (2009). Transnational Histories of Sexualities in Asia. *The American Historical Review, 114*(5), 1309–1324.

NADRA. (2018, 21 August). *Policy on Issuance of CNIC to Eunuchs*. Author, NADRA.

Nanda, S. (1986). The Hijras of India: Cultural and Individual Dimensions of an Institutionalized Third Gender Role. *Journal of Homosexuality, 11*(3–4), 35–54.

Nanda, S. (1990). *Neither Man nor Woman: The Hijras of India*. Wadsworth.

Nanda, S. (1999). *Neither Man nor Woman: The Hijras of India* (2nd ed.). Wadsworth.

Orentlicher, D. (2010). Discrimination Out of Dismissiveness: The Example of Infertility. *Indiana Law Journal, 85*(1), 143–186.

Punjab Social Protection Authority. (2018, August). Transgender Persons Welfare Policy, Author Punjab Social Protection Authority (Government of Punjab, Pakistan). Retrieved August 8, 2019, from http://ljcp.gov.pk/tg/report.pdf

Redding, J. A. (2019). The Pakistan Transgender Persons (Protection of Rights) Act of 2018 and Its Impact on the Law of Gender in Pakistan. *Australian Journal of Asian Law, 20*(1), Article 8, 103–113. https://ssrn.com/abstract=3490418.

Reddy, G. (2005). *With Respect to Sex: Negotiating Hijra Identity in South India.* The University of Chicago Press.

Reuters. (2007). Dancing Eunuchs Taxing Red-Faced Shopkeepers. 20 January. Retrieved February 27, 2020, from https://www.reuters.com/article/us-eunuchs/dancing-eunuchs-taxing-red-faced-shopkeepers-idUSDEL302542006110

Rowlands, S., & Amy, J. J. (2018). Preserving the Reproductive Potential of Transgender and Intersex People. *The European Journal of Contraception & Reproductive Health Care, 23*(1), 58–63.

Safer, J. D., Coleman, E., Feldman, J., Garofalo, R., Hembree, W., Radix, A., & Sevelius, J. (2016). Barriers to Health Care for Transgender Individuals. *Current Opinion in Endocrinology, Diabetes, and Obesity, 23*(2), 168–171.

Sahqani, A., Dara, S., & Shaikh, A. F. (2019). Lust, Love and Longing for Change in the Transgender Community. *Herald*, February. Retrieved February 15, 2020, from https://herald.dawn.com/news/1398823

Shah, S. A. (2018a). Diamer's 18-Year-Old Ghazala Becomes 'Abdullah' After Sex-Change Surgery. *The Express Tribune*, 24 December. Retrieved February 15, 2020, from https://tribune.com.pk/story/1873892/1-diamers-18-year-old-ghazala-becomes-abdullah-sex-change-surgery/

Shah, S. K. H. (2018b). Transgender Persons in Pakistan and 2018 Elections. *The Financial Daily*, 4 July. Retrieved February 20, 2020, from ProQuest Central.

Spade, D. (2003). Resisting Medicine, Re/modeling Gender. *Berkeley Women's Law Journal, 15*(1), 15–39.

State Bank of Pakistan. (2019, 11 March). *Financing Facility for Low Cost Housing for Special Segments.* IH&SMEFD Circular No. 05 of 2019. Retrieved February 10, 2020, from http://www.sbp.org.pk/smefd/circulars/2019/C5.htm

The Nation. (2017). Nadra Introduces Policy to Register Transgender Persons. 29 August. Retrieved February 27, 2020, from https://nation.com.pk/29-Aug-2017/nadra-introduces-policy-to-register-transgender-persons

The News. (2019). Transgenders Incorporated into Loan Scheme. 28 October. Retrieved February 10, 2020, from https://www.thenews.com.pk/print/547202-transgenders-incorporated-into-loan-scheme

Toppa, S. (2018). Pakistan's Transgender Community Takes Another Step Forward. *Al Jazeera*, 6 March. Retrieved February 20, 2020, from https://www.aljazeera.com/news/2018/03/pakistan-transgender-community-takes-step-180305081113645.html

UN Free & Equal. (2014). *Definitions*. Retrieved January 14, 2020, from https://www.unfe.org/definitions/

Whitehead, J. (1995). Bodies Clean and Unclean: Prostitution, Sanitary Legislation, and Respectable Femininity in Colonial North India. *Gender & History, 7*(1), 41–63.

Wijngaarden, J. W., Schunter, B. T., & Iqbal, Q. (2013). Sexual Abuse, Social Stigma and HIV Vulnerability Among Young Feminised Men in Lahore and Karachi, Pakistan. *Culture, Health & Sexuality, 15*(1), 73–84.

Zahra-Malik, M. (2017). Transgender Pakistanis Win Legal Victories, But Violence Goes On. The New York Times, 19 August. Retrieved February 20, 2020, from https://www.nytimes.com/2017/08/19/world/asia/pakistan-transgender-bill.html

CHAPTER 6

Rural Women's Land Use Rights in China: Acceptance and Enforceability

Pia Eskelinen

6.1 Introduction

Legal control of land as well as social recognition of women's use of and rights to land can have catalytic effects of empowerment, increasing women's influence and status in their homes and communities (Araujo, 2017; Beijing Declaration and Platform for Action, 1995). In other words, land is a powerful asset, because of its strong social function. Its economic and social aspects are central in advancing gender equality. As land is Chinese rural peoples—and especially women's—only lifeline that forms the basis of their social security and economic independence, land tenure rights play a significant role. However, in China, with which this chapter is concerned, it is not always the case that people can fully enjoy the right to land.

Social norms strongly steer the land-rights situation in rural areas of China, even though there are other factors such as ambiguities in legislation, as well. The specific purpose of this chapter is to ascertain how rural women's land rights are fulfilled and whether these rights are (1) legally recognisable, (2) socially recognisable or (3) enforceable by the external

P. Eskelinen (✉)
University of Turku, Turku, Finland
e-mail: pia.j.eskelinen@utu.fi

G. Guney et al. (eds.), *Towards Gender Equality in Law*,
https://doi.org/10.1007/978-3-030-98072-6_6

authorities (Agarwal, 1994; Mehra, 1995). As part of the broader social context, these three stances affect rural women's position as independent and equal actors. This chapter presents an example of how society and its diverse practices affect rural women's contractual land rights in modern China.

Rapid urbanisation is causing problems in rural areas, as expanding cities need more land. Urbanisation puts pressure on rural people in areas close to expanding cities rather than on landholders in areas further away. For this reason, areas categorised as "rural" that surround and belong to cities are the fastest-growing regions in China. Furthermore, various agents are interested in these areas: cities are interested in expanding; builders and construction companies can see potential profit; while the people living in those areas (landholders) are left somewhere in between. This places pressure on local governments, which then expropriate lands from rural landholders, as Sect. 6.5 confirms.

To understand the problems rural women face in land contracting, it is important to understand the role of the land tenure system, which is discussed in Sect. 6.4. Another contributor is *hukou*, or the household registration system, in which citizens are registered with a certain status—namely, rural or urban—and a recorded area to live. More research on this is under way in another article that is part of a PhD thesis, which studies the position of rural women in Chinese society.[1] However, to assess the impact of land tenure on the treatment of rural women, it is necessary to understand the significance of it to Chinese society, which in turn is based on how its development is intertwined with Chinese history.

Both the controlling *hukou* or household registration and more ambiguous land tenure rights that regulate the allocation of rural land are supposedly gender-neutral, bestowing women with the same opportunities as men. However, the law in books differs from the law in action. The ambiguity of land use legislation and the dogmatic implementation of the *hukou* legislation deprive women of their chances of survival in rural China, and women become legally invisible, ignored and forgotten, as Sect. 6.5 demonstrates.

This chapter is based mainly on interviews. Previous research and official documents are also used, but they merely corroborate the research. The benefit of this approach is that it provides a better representation of the grassroots level at which rural women reside. The All-China Women

Federation (ACWF), which is the only women's organisation in China, was able to provide an important insight into the lives of rural women during the interviews. A combination of qualitative and intersectional thematic analysis was used in the data analysis.

As this chapter focuses on women in rural areas, a feminist standpoint (Hartsock, 1983) provides an interesting framework. It is easy for those at the top of social hierarchies to lose sight of real human relations and the true nature of social realities (Harding, 1987). In China, it is noticeable that the social realities of different groups, authorities and rural women are so far apart from each other that there is no real connection or understanding between them (Li & Dennis Wei, 2010). However, it is not enough to use gender as a single analytical category. Therefore, this research uses an intersectional approach to qualitative thematic analysis. It allows the simultaneous exploration of numerous intersecting themes (Hill Collins & Bilge, 2020). For example, according to my research, age, marital status, location and gender all play an important role in the situation surrounding women's equality: younger, unmarried rural women are commonly more vulnerable than women who are older or married, whether in rural or urban areas.

Of course, it is important to remember that land-rights issues are not the only challenge that women face in China. Women encounter all kinds of harassment (Srivastava & Gu, 2009) and systemic gender discrimination in employment (Dasgupta et al., 2015) and education (Ross, 2015). When lecturing at Fudan University, I was told of a professor (not Fudan-based) who categorically refused to take female students as Master's/postgraduate students because women "get pregnant and stay at home". In addition, news articles reveal the hostility from the authorities that has extended to women's rights activists over the last few years. In January 2016, Guo Jianmei, founder of the Beijing Zhongze Women's Legal Counselling and Service Centre, closed the organisation. It has been argued that the authorities ordered the closure (Zeng, 2014).

This chapter is organised in the following way. Section 6.2 introduces previous research. Section 6.3 begins by laying out the theoretical dimensions of the research and how the data have been analysed. After that, land rights are addressed to better highlight their effects on Chinese society and on rural women. Finally, a summary and discussion are provided.

6.2 Previous Research

Even though the rural population faces difficulties in land tenure practices, many previous studies have suggested that rural women experience more hardship. Also, rapid urbanisation causes difficulties because the relevant legislation does not adapt fast enough.

Long (2014) has noticed that rapid urban-rural transformation gives rise to the formulation of new policies affecting land use. However, Liu et al. (2014) point out that the overall land policy framework is still insufficient and that policy changes and their implementation have not always been positive towards rural women. These findings are parallel with Li et al. (2010, p. 432), who suggest that the "Chinese government at various levels needs to improve the system of property rights through reforming rural collective property rights".

Liu et al. (1998) highlight the fact that regional and temporal variation in rural property rights signals a pattern in which decentralised institutional innovation occurs in response to the competing interests of the nation state, of local authorities and of present and possible future individual land users. As noted by Perry and Selden (2010), the current property rights problems are complicated, because the possible conflicts of interest between individuals, local collectives and the state are far larger than the desire for clarity and equality over property rights.

It is well established that studies on land rights have mainly focused on the rural population. Peter Ho (2017) has addressed property rights, but he also sees the rural population as a coherent group of people, as do Yongjun (Zhao, 2011), Chen et al. (2014) and Samuel P.S. Ho and George C.S. Lin (2003). In addition, Weil (2008) addresses property seizures, land disputes and inadequate compensation, but from a rural male's point of view. However, he gives an excellent example of injustice towards two women that took place prior to the summer Olympic Games in Beijing in 2008: "two poor women in their 70s were sentenced to a year of 're-education through labour'… for appealing the undercompensated taking of their home" (Weil, 2008, p. 63).

There is a consensus among some researchers suggesting that land tenure and associated property rights in rural China affect the status of rural women (Li, 1993). As rural women face discrimination in all areas of land rights (Kelkar & Krishna Raj, 2013), the issue should also be addressed as a rural women's problem, not just a problem in or of rural areas.

Some analysts (e.g. Liaw, 2008) discuss how existing legislation should be used as a tool to secure women's land rights in rural China. Liaw (2008) identifies the issue as a legislative problem, as ambiguities, especially in implementation, can cause problems in land-rights disputes. Tinker and Summerfield (1999) identify women's land problems as an issue of male dominance. It seems that the social structure allows the institutional exclusion of women from decision-making processes to continue. Jacka (2006a, b) and Sargeson (2006; Jacka & Sargeson, 2011) have conducted several studies on gender relations and social change in contemporary China, women in rural-urban migration, and gender and family relations. They have briefly addressed rural women's land-rights issues, criticising the *hukou* system, which causes hardship for rural women.

Other researchers (see Li, 2003; Duncan & Li, 2001; Zhu, 2001; Li & Yin-Sheng, 2006) have confirmed that a substantial number of rural women have lost their land rights in the process of land reallocation as a result of moving from their original residential villages to a new village after marriage, divorce or being widowed.

6.3 Theory, Data and Method

China is, at least in theory, still a socialist country. However, since 1978, the Chinese Communist Party, under Deng Xiaoping's leadership, has slowly introduced the capitalist economy to Chinese society (Jiawen, 2009). Marxism no longer has a strong foothold either. In Daniel Bell's (2010, p. 8) words:

> [H]ardly anybody really believes that Marxism should provide guidelines for thinking about China's political future. The ideology has been so discredited by its misuses that it has lost almost all legitimacy in society.

Although the power of the Chinese Communist Party (CCP) is still strong, the norms that govern society at the grassroots level are anchored deeper than in the structures of state and administrative power. Even though the CCP has a significant hierarchical power structure, power does not entirely lie in the hands of one person or even the Communist Party. The Communist Party and other structures such as village committees, other authorities and courts are aware of and operate within the known power structures (Wang, 2010). These are structures in which everyone (those who exercise power and the objects of the exercise of power) is stuck, but within which they also know how to operate.

A feminist standpoint places women in the centre of the whole power structure (Hartsock, 1983; Harding, 1987). Hartsock is aware that power is an essentially contested concept and that different epistemologies are based on different theories of power (Hartsock, 2013). Hartsock also claims that it is women's unique standpoint in society that provides the justification for the truth claims of feminism while also providing it with a method with which to analyse reality (Hartsock, 1983; Harding, 1987). Social hierarchies, which are strongly present in Chinese society, lose sight of real human relations and the true nature of social reality. As Yingru Li and Dennis Wei (2010) have noticed, the social gap between the authorities and rural women is too wide to establish a real understanding.

Previously in gender studies, women were considered a standardised group with common interests, desires and problems regardless of class or ethnic connection (Mohanty, 1988; Nicholson & Seidman, 1995). Yet women's lives in a given society are shaped not by a single axis of social division (e.g. gender), but by many intersecting axes that work together and influence each other (Hill Collins & Bilge, 2020, pp. 3–30). In this chapter, age, marital status, location and gender all interact and interplay to position a rural woman within social and legal relations. These intersecting social justice problems are subclasses of topics such as gender inequality, gendered societies or gendered decision-making structures.

Several researchers have utilised government and other official documents to analyse Chinese policies. Likewise, this study utilises Chinese policy documents, but since the interest is in grassroots interaction, the specific data are interviews with personnel from the All-China Women's Federation (ACWF) and one expert on this topic. As this is a qualitative study, the idea was to produce contextual real-world knowledge about the social structures and political atmosphere in which the ACWF is currently operating, by using semi-structured interviews.[2] Even though such interviews usually produce results that cannot be generalised beyond the sample group, they provide a more in-depth understanding of participants' perceptions, motivations and emotions.

The main topic of the interviews was rural women's land-rights situation in rural areas of China. The interviews addressed the ACWF's work, the organisation's support for women on landownership and the overall situation surrounding equality in different areas. As this chapter tries to establish how land tenure legislation affects rural women's lives, the responses to the interview questions were revealing. The interviewees' responses painted a picture of various policies, practices and power relations that have a great impact on women's economic and overall independence. Also, during the interviews, it was important to pay attention on what was not mentioned, the small silences. Nevertheless, the interviewees were very responsive and willing to answer the questions.

The interviews were conducted in City A in Central China in April 2017 and in City B in Eastern China in April 2018. There were three and four participants, respectively, from the ACWF but the reference is to the group as a whole. In addition, an interview with a professor of human rights law provided insight into women's legal status, equality and society's effect on land rights. The ACWF was chosen because it is basically the only national women's organisation in China. The interviews were not recorded, but full transcripts were taken.

Intersectional thematic analysis was conducted and the interviews were closely analysed to identify common themes—topics and patterns of meaning that came up repeatedly. Both inductive and deductive approaches were used. Primarily, the inductive approach allowed the determination of the main themes. Of course, there were some preconceived themes that were expected to be found based on existing knowledge. The themes that emerged from the interviews were gender inequality, the ostensible neutrality of legislation and gendered decision-making structures. These themes seem firstly to affect the work of the ACWF. Secondly, the themes and their consequences also have effects on women, as the ACWF is not able to provide adequate support and/or guidance concerning land tenure rights.

Gopaldas and DeRoy (2015, p. 24) argue that conclusions drawn from intersectional research tend to be more inclusive, precise and somewhat radical. Furthermore, McCall (2005, p. 1780) reminds us:

> Interest in intersectionality arose out of a critique of gender-based and race-based research for failing to account for lived experience at neglected points of intersection—ones that tended to reflect multiple subordinate locations as opposed to dominant or mixed locations.

The rural women, whom the ACWF is representing, are living at such points of intersection, by and large neglected due to the Chinese political discourse.

6.4 Land Rights

Previously, when socio-economic development plans called for land development, Chinese municipal governments increased their land supply through land acquisition, a conversion of landownership from the collective to the state. In cases of land acquisition, municipal governments compensated farmers for their land. Since there were no land markets, peasants were instead compensated with a package that included job offers in which farmers would work for the enterprises established on the acquired land, housing compensation, referred to as resettlement fees, compensation for the loss of crops and belongings connected to the land, and urban *hukou*. It was common for large projects such as motorways, railways and water projects to leave farmers with no land to farm (Ding, 2004).

Nowadays, the compensation for compulsory land acquisition is primarily guided by the Land Administration Law (LAL), which was first passed in 1986 and then amended in 1998. In 1986, the LAL followed the old model used in the system to guide land acquisition compensation, which contained four main components: land compensation, resettlement subsidies, compensation for young crops and attachments on the land, and labour resettlement. Despite the positive impact of land acquisition and public land leasing for local government financing, an examination of land acquisition reveals institutional flaws that lead to socio-economic and administrative problems, which are addressed in the following sections.

In 1984, the state stipulated that land use rights should be leased to villagers for a minimum of 15 years, which was extended to 30 years in 1993. If a piece of land is leased for 30 years and the lessee receives a land-rights certificate, then land use rights should be protected during the entirety of the lease term. However, there are grey areas where basic land-rights certificates do not offer *enough* land use rights protection: pieces of land can be taken back if certain conditions are met. For example, reallocation is allowed if approved by more than two-thirds of the members of a collective. An extra layer of protection is provided by the clause "reallocation is prohibited before expiry date," if it is included on land-rights certificates.

However, in China, anything not specifically banned is considered to be acceptable. If the clause "reallocation is prohibited before expiry date" is not included on land-rights certificates, the understanding is that reallocation may be permissible (Feng et al., 2014, p. 255). This implicit but practically effective requirement captures the importance of the formality of land-rights certificates and measures the impact of the functionality of these certificates.

There have been some reforms of the land-rights legislation over the years, and the situation has improved, but not enough. When the first version of the RLCL debuted in 2002, one matter was clear: Articles 6, 30 and 54 in the law vowed to uphold women's rights to use and to manage land under tenure contracts. Also, the law banned rural collective economic organisations—which were the legally designated owners of farmland, comprising villages and village groups—from revoking their female members' access to land upon marriage, divorce or widowhood. In other words, so long as their families hold valid land tenure contracts with rural collectives, women's land rights should not be compromised by changes in marital status. What the 2002 RLCL omitted to mention, though, were the criteria necessary to determine the membership of rural collectives. In the absence of criteria defined by the state laws, rural collectives remained free to decide who could or could not enjoy membership, a question at the heart of the distribution of income and benefits based on land use. The law's silence on this matter soon proved to be highly problematic, leaving millions of women with little certainty about their standing as members of a particular community (Li, 2020).

The problem of land management and division has also been identified by Tamara Jacka and Sally Sargeson, who have long studied the problems faced by women in Chinese society. Jacka and Sargeson are concerned about the fact that women, especially those in rural areas, are often left out of decision-making and not given enough attention as full members of society (Jacka, 2006b; Jacka & Sargeson, 2011; Sargeson, 1995, 2006).

The non-transfer of new land to women is also often justified by the authorities with the fact that the land has been allocated for 30 years under Section 14 of the Land Management Act, although the same section allows for the division of land if a two-thirds majority supports it. However, the interviews revealed that most of the decision-makers are men, creating a gendered process.

During recent decades, changes in Chinese land tenure rights and practices have given incentives for rural developments, including farmer incomes and living standards (Ding, 2003; Keliang & Prosterman, 2007; ACWF, 2014, 2017). As Fan et al. (2004, p. 400) state in their article, "the well-being of many rural landowners has been improved by various indicators and factors such as human capital".

Furthermore, those improvements have benefitted the entire Chinese economy, as Bingqin Li (2014) discovers in his article. However, this positive progress does not necessarily apply to women. As Woodhams et al. (2009) note, women's status in China is far from equal to men's.[3] Rudd (2007) and Song and Dong (2017) follow Woodhams and her colleagues, arguing that women's situation is even more complicated in rural or peri-urban areas.[4]

6.4.1 *Land, Social Benefits and Hukou*

Land tenure rights constitute the most significant form of income, economic safety and social security for the rural population (H. Li et al., 2015; Liang & Burns, 2017). In other words, a farmer's land not only generates income but also acts as a means of life security.

Hukou affects the social benefits of Chinese citizens. Even though peasants' and urban residents' health insurance and other benefits have been improved,[5] peasants' insurance is still less comprehensive than that of China's elite and those living in cities with urban *hukou* (Liang & Burns, 2017, pp. 75–115). Judith Banister (1987, p. 328) notes the dichotomic social order produced by the registration system, finding that:

> [Urban] areas are essentially owned and administered by the state, and their residents are the state's direct responsibility. The state budget must supply urban areas with employment, housing, food, water, sewage disposal, transportation, medical facilities, police protection, schools, and other essentials and amenities of life.

The opposite side of the coin is that the state assumes direct responsibility for none of these services for the *countryside*. Nor does it provide rural people with any of the other vital services and welfare benefits that are routinely provided to urban residents, particularly to state sector employees, including free or subsidised healthcare, retirement benefits and subsidised food and housing. To the extent that any of these services have been available in the countryside, they have relied on the highly differentiated resources allocated by self-reliant rural communities (villages) or their collective subunits, namely production teams (Afridi et al., 2015).

It is easy to agree with Chengri Ding's (2007, p. 2) argument that, despite the benefits of the public land leasing system for local government financing, flaws and ambiguities within the legislation and implementation of land leasing policies have produced negative impacts for various sectors of society.

6.4.2 *Lack of Contracts*

The Land Contract Law for Rural Areas (Law of the People's Republic of China on the Contracting of Rural Land, 2002, RLCL) increased tenure security for rural people. Two documents are supposed to record rural people's land rights and provide them with some measure of protection: contracts and land-rights certificates (RLCL Art 21). Still, many households and individuals do not possess the required documents. According to the Summary of 2011 17-Province Survey Findings, 36.7% have both documents (contracts and land-rights certificates) as required by law and policy. However, only 20.9% of issued contracts and 40.3% of issued certificates contain all the legally required information. Women's names are generally not listed on land documents (Zimmermann, 2012, p. 1):

> rural women sometimes don't have written contracts. Their father, brother has their [rural women's] land, in contract. (ACWF, City A)

The head of the family administers the land tenure on behalf of the women in the family. This fundamental act of suppression violates rural women's freedom of contract. In addition to that, denying rural women their right to have a written land use contract has far-reaching consequences that affect more than just their social status as equals. Refusal to compensate rural women accordingly affects not only their economic and social situation but also their economic freedom. In a way, refusal constructs gender-based violence that forms a barrier to women's equal participation in society and affects their overall social and economic development and independence (García-Moreno et al., 2014; World Bank, 2014).

As selling land is usually one of the largest sources of revenue for local governments (Xiangzheng et al., 2010), economic reasons are a key factor in discriminating against rural women. Village officials might be tempted to abuse their power and dismiss the rural population so that they do not receive proper compensation for expropriated land (Ong, 2014). Rural women are subject to even more discrimination when their compensation is refused or given to someone else[6]:

> The village or the local government gets more money, but it is not given to the original landholder. (ACWF, City A)

The following case demonstrates how rural women are discriminated against in more than just one way. First, rural women do not have their name on the land use contract, and, second, the father of the household does not give the compensation to the women. It also shows how the mother of the family considers the situation of not receiving compensation to be normal and so she herself refuses the compensation:

CASE 1, source All-China Women's Federation:

> A family, 5 members. Mother, father, 2 sons, 1 daughter. Father was the head of the family. The mother's and daughter's land contract was in the father's name. The sons had their names on their contracts. The father and brothers were given compensation when their land was expropriated. The mother's and daughter's share was given to the father. The mother did not want the money, but the daughter did.

The ACWF case presented here is a normal one among the complaints they receive. After arbitration,[7] the parties decided that the father must give the compensation originally provided by the local government (RMB 16,490 yuan) to the daughter, because she was the actual proprietor of the land even though the tenure contract was not in her name. In opposition to the RLCL, which demands that everyone has a written tenure contract, this case illustrates how family relations enable discrimination and how the society surrounding the family accepts this.

It appears that women's property rights in community-based systems, such as the land tenure contracting system in China, are derived from their status as mothers, daughters, sisters or widows—rather than in their own right. Thus, women usually lose their rights to land when their status within the household changes (Cleaver & Schreiber, 1994) and if they are divorced, widowed or abandoned (Li, 2015; Kelkar & Krishna Raj, 2013; Liu & Chan, 1999). The following case is an example of a situation where a land use contract is not externally enforceable or socially recognised:

CASE 2, source All-China Women's Federation:

> A girl married and moves into a new village. She kept her [written] land contract in the original village. Her father, mother and brother grew grain on her land. All the family land was expropriated, and monetary compensation was paid. The daughter was left without compensation.

The village committee decided in this case, with the daughter's family, that because the daughter did not live in the village, there was no need to compensate her. In other words, the village committee and the family acknowledged the tenure contract but said it was void because the daughter did not live in the village. After arbitration, it was decided that the father must pay the compensation (RMB 54,684 yuan) to the actual contract holder, the daughter.

These acts of inequality underline the fact that there are discriminative legal practices and social norms. The state has failed in protecting women because there are frictions and ambiguities in the legislation. Furthermore, it seems that the state tolerates friction in land legislation and its application.

It is worth noticing that when rural women have sought help from the ACWF in arbitration situations, the organisation has been able to help. It seems that ACWF′s input in these difficult situations is vital.

6.5 Rural Women Between Men, Family and State Dominance

The issue of women losing rights to land and property at marriage, divorce and widowhood has long been regarded as a major obstacle to achieving gender equality in rural China (Liaw, 2008; Wu, 2016). In these situations, Chinese rural women are placed in a disadvantaged position, and become vulnerable and dependent on their immediate family's help (Li, 2003; Duncan & Li, 2001; Zhu, 2001).

Furthermore, it seems that the impact of society and public opinion on the functioning of village committees is greater than that of official legislation, as Rosen suggests (2017). This is the case in today's China; village committees are constantly aware of the expectations set for them (Xu & Fuller, 2018).

Even though both men and women face difficulties in rural areas, women are more vulnerable and so more at risk of facing poverty and abuse. The wording used in the legislation concerning land rights is ambiguous. This ambiguity of legislation and legal loopholes create a space for the officials to interpret legislation unequally.

This dilemma is also familiar for Nordic feminists, where attention has been drawn to the fact that formally gender-neutral legislation can mask and even prop up gender-segregated practices and ways of thinking (Lykke, 2010).

In addition, local-level officials are left with little guidance or no guidance at all. That creates a challenge: officials at the lower levels, including village councils, avoid interference or simply forbid everything in fear of doing something wrong. However, problems in implementing decisions or legislation are part of the overall system of Chinese policy-making (Shi et al., 2014). This also came up during the interviews:

> There is no interpretation guidance. …officials don't know how to interpret the law… they forbid everything so that they don't do anything wrong. (Professor of law, City A)

Furthermore, government officials making decisions at the national level do not understand life in rural areas. It can also be argued that since legislators at the national level do not understand life in rural areas, the areas do not receive the support they need.

> Most of the national legislators live in big cities. They don't know what is going on in rural areas. (Professor of law, City A)

6.5.1 *Legal and Social Recognition, and Enforceability by External Authorities*

The rights to land should not be only legally and socially recognisable but also enforceable by external authorities such as village-based institutions. However, these external authorities, which decide on the unwritten social agreements that create behavioural and gendered norms of conduct, are male-dominated (Kandiyoti, 1988; Mautner, 2011):

> Old customs are very strong; women are lower than men. (ACWF, City A)

Even though social recognition of the land tenure contract is crucial, legal recognition and external enforceability also play an important role (Agarwal, 1994; Mehra, 1995). For a land tenure contract to be externally enforceable, it must be recognised by the village council:

> village councils are powerful; they can choose [*decide who is allocated a certain piece of land*] about the land. They are decision-makers. (ACWF, City A)

Village councils do not just ignore the existing law but also use their own strong customs that ignore rural women's right to land. In this context, it can be argued that there is an obvious lack of social recognition concerning rural women's land rights.

> village committees just ignore the law sometimes. They have their own laws. (ACWF, City A)

Chinese village councils have the power to decide whether land contracts belonging to a tenant can be enforced. Local officials have created regional traditions that allow them to interpret the law in their own way. Therefore, the male-dominated village councils (Du, 2018) are engaged in social cooperation through which they together choose the principles in accordance with which rights and duties are assigned (Rawls, 1971). In this light, the law is not effective enough to protect rural women's right to landownership. Village councils have established procedures and agreements among themselves that replace the meaning of the law and discriminate against rural women. In a way, the village councils have created an informal institution within formal society by creating circumstances that tolerate their strong and selected cooperation. There is a lack of recognition and enforceability and a lack of two crucial mechanisms that create stability: predictability and, importantly, equality.

6.6 Discussion and Conclusion

The fulfilment of rural women's land tenure rights and whether these rights are (1) legally recognisable, (2) socially recognisable or (3) enforceable by external authorities is a key issue in protecting rural women's economic and social independence. At the moment, though, it seems that there are problems in accomplishing and securing rural women's land tenure rights. Since the land tenure system is a crucial institution in defining an individual's socio-economic status and opportunities in rural China, it impacts not only women's bargaining power but also their social security, economic well-being and independence.

Between the 1980s and mid-1990s, gender bias was explicit in the implementation of land tenure policies and population control, especially in rural China. Since then, explicit gender bias has been reduced, reflecting China's goals of modernisation. However, the policies are still not gender-neutral in their implementation. Women are more likely to become "landless" at some point in their lives. The greatest threat follows marriage, divorce or if they become widowed. The lack of recognition of women's land use rights deprives women of their chances of survival in rural China. Even though both men and women face difficulties in rural areas due to the land tenure system, the system has failed to protect the latter.

Although a written land tenure contract and a land use certificate are two of the most important documents that secure rural women's economic situation and land use rights in the case of expropriation, there are other key factors that contribute to the actualisation of rural women's land rights. To enhance women's ability to claim and keep control of their land, one aspect needs attention: reducing gender bias in village land tenure contracting practices and in village council rulings. Although women's rights to land in the People's Republic of China have, in theory, always been equal to those of men, the household tenure contracting and male dominance in decision-making have created a situation in which practices exist that do not involve rural women, their well-being or their equal treatment. This practice is (ab)use of power, which society enables. As was pointed out in the introduction to this chapter, the legal and social acceptance of a land tenure contract is vital for the empowerment of rural women.

It is also important to acknowledge that rural Chinese women form a distinct and significant group that needs to be addressed as such, and that rural women in China face discrimination in land-rights situations. The discrimination, however, is part of a deep-rooted gender discrimination spectrum reflected not just in rural areas but throughout Chinese society.

The implementation of relevant legislation should focus on rural women's rights to access, use and control land. Social factors and a lack of guidance prevent rural women from obtaining secure rights to land. It is crucial to ensure that legislation and land reform policies are gender-responsive and consider rural women's historically disadvantaged socio-economic position compared to rural men. Furthermore, an environment that encourages rural women's increased participation in (political) decision-making, such as village committees, should be created and maintained.

Since women make up half of the world's population, research and analysis on women is critical in understanding many forms of social stratification. Women undoubtedly face unique disadvantages and social problems because of their gender. Trends and changes in women's lives and the obstacles that women face in improving and securing their own rights are worthy of research, documentation and analysis.

Notes

1. This chapter was funded by the Academy of Finland (ASLA: Actors, Structures and Law, decision 312497); the Joel Toivola Foundation, Finland; and a NIAS-SUPRA scholarship, University of Copenhagen.
2. The interviews were a result of a wide and almost-endless flow of emails, phone calls and word-of-mouth communication. However, after reaching one core person, it was relatively easy to arrange the interviews.
3. For more information, see Riley (1997); and Rudd (2007).
4. In this study, the word "peri-urban" means areas between the city and the countryside, which are shaped by the urbanisation of formerly rural areas at the urban boundary.
5. Enrolment has increased from 20% of the population in 2000 to 95% in 2012 (Huang, 2015).
6. After expropriation, the state must compensate the original contractor; however, the compensation can be quite low in comparison to the real value. Also, the distribution of the compensation by the village collective can be discriminatory (Chan, 2003; Wu, 2016).
7. Arbitration with the help of the ACWF is equivalent to an appeal against the original decision.

References

ACWF. (2014). *Shaanxi to Boost Protection of Rural Women's Land Rights—All-China Women's Federation*. Retrieved October 9, 2017, from http://www.womenofchina.cn/womenofchina/html1/news/china/1409/594-1.htm

ACWF. (2017). *NE China Document Protects Rural Women's Rights, Interests on Land Contracts*. Retreived April 13, 2018, from https://landportal.org/node/61203

Afridi, F., Li, S. X., & Ren, Y. (2015). Social Identity and Inequality: The Impact of China's Hukou System. *Journal of Public Economics, 123*, 17–29.

Agarwal, B. (1994). *A Field of One's Own: Gender and Land Rights in South Asia*. Cambridge University Press.

Araujo, K. (2017). Rural Women Must Not be Left Behind. *Field Focus Blog*, 16 October. Retrieved March 20, 2020, from https://www.landesa.org/blog-rural-women-must-not-left-behind/

Banister, J. (1987). *China's Changing Population*. Stanford University Press.

Beijing Declaration and Platform for Action (1995). *UN Women*. Retrieved March 12, 2018, from https://www.unwomen.org/sites/default/files/Headquarters/Attachments/Sections/CSW/PFA_E_Final_WEB.pdf

Bell, D. A. (2010). *China's New Confucianism: Politics and Everyday Life in a Changing Society*. Princeton University Press.

Chan, N. (2003). Land Acquisition Compensation in China—Problems & Answers. *International Real Estate Review, 6*(1), 136–152.

Chen, J., et al. (2014). Comparing Urban Land Expansion and Its Driving Factors in Shenzhen and Dongguan, China. *Habitat International, 43*, 61.

Cleaver, K. M., & Schreiber, G. A. (1994). *Reversing the Spiral: The Population, Agriculture, and Environment Nexus in Sub-Saharan Africa*. World Bank. Retrieved July 15, 2020, from https://documents.worldbank.org/en/publication/documents-reports/documentdetail/541511468741617720/reversing-the-spiral-the-population-agriculture-and-environmental-nexus-in-sub-saharan-africa

Dasgupta, S., Matsumoto, M., & Xia, C. (2015). Women in the Labour Market in China: International Labour Organization. Retrieved January 25, 2019, from https://www.ilo.org/wcmsp5/groups/public/%2D%2D-asia/%2D%2D-ro-bangkok/documents/publication/wcms_371375.pdf

Ding, C. (2003). Land Policy Reform in China: Assessment and Prospects. *Land Use Policy, 20*(2), 109–120.

Ding, C. (2004). Effects of Land Acquisition on China's Economic Future. Retrieved March 19, 2021, from https://www.lincolninst.edu/publications/articles/effects-land-acquisition-chinas-economic-future

Ding, C. (2007). Policy and Praxis of Land Acquisition in China. *Land Use Policy, 24*, 1–13.

Du, Q. (2018). Modernization, Culture, and the Class Ceiling: Women's Political Participation in China. Retrieved August 14, 2019, from http://d-scholarship.pitt.edu/34346/

Duncan, J., & Li, P. (2001). *A Study of Women's Land Rights in Dongfang County, Hainan Province*. RDI Reports on Foreign Aid and Development #110.

Fan, S., Zhang, L., & Zhang, X. (2004). Reforms, Investment, and Poverty in Rural China. *Economic Development and Cultural Change, 52*(2), 395–421.

Feng, L., Bao, H. X. H., & Jiang, Y. (2014). Land Reallocation Reform in Rural China: A Behavioral Economics Perspective. *Land Use Policy, 41*, 246–259.

García-Moreno, C. et al. (2014). Violence Against Women and Girls, Addressing Violence Against Women: A Call to Action. *The Lancet, 385*(978). https://doi.org/10.1016/S0140-6736(14)61830-4

Gopaldas, A., & Deroy, G. (2015). An Intersectional Approach to Diversity Research. *Consumption, Markets and Culture, 18*(4), 333–364.

Harding, S. G. (1987). *Feminism and Methodology: Social Science Issues*. Open University Press.

Hartsock, N. (2013). Foucault on Power: A Theory for Women? In L. Nicholson (Ed.), *Feminism/Postmodernism*. Routledge.

Hartsock, N. C. M. (1983). The Feminist Standpoint: Developing the Ground for a Specifically Feminist Historical Materialism. In S. Harding & M. B. Hintikka (Eds.), *Discovering Reality* (pp. 283–310). Springer.

Hill Collins, P., & Bilge, S. (2020). *Intersectionality* (2nd ed.). Polity.

Ho, P. (2017). 'Who Owns China's Housing? Endogeneity as a Lens to Understand Ambiguities of Urban and Rural Property. *Cities, 65*, 66–77.

Ho, S. P. S., & Lin, G. C. S. (2003). 'Emerging Land Markets in Rural and Urban China: Policies and Practices. *The China Quarterly, 175*, 681–707.

Huang, X. (2015). Four Worlds of Welfare: Understanding Subnational Variation in Chinese Social Health Insurance. *The China Quarterly, 222*, 449–474.

Jacka, T. (2006a). *Rural Women in Urban China: Gender, Migration, and Social Change*. Routledge.

Jacka, T. (2006b). Approaches to Women and Development in Rural China. *Journal of Contemporary China, 15*(49), 585–602.

Jacka, T., & Sargeson, S. (2011). *Women, Gender and Rural Development in China*. Edward Elgar Publishing.

Jiawen, A. (2009). Two Sides of One Coin: The Party's Attitude Toward Confucianism in Contemporary China. *Journal of Contemporary China, 18*(61), 689–701.

Kandiyoti, D. (1988). Bargaining with Patriarchy. *Gender and Society, 2*(3), 274–290.

Keliang, Z., & Prosterman, R. (2007). Securing Land Rights for Chinese Farmers: A Leap Forward for Stability and Growth. *Cato Development Policy Analysis Series*, 3.

Kelkar, G., & Krishna Raj, M. (2013). *Women, Land and Power in Asia*. Routledge.

Law of the People's Republic of China on the Contracting of Rural Land. (2002). Promulgated by order no. 73 of the President of the People's Republic of China on August 29, 2002.

Li, B. (2014). Coordinating Urban and Rural Development in China, Learning from Chengdu. *Regional Studies, 48*(5), 936–937.

Li, X., Xu, X., & Li, Z. (2010). Land Property Rights and Urbanization in China. *The China Review, 10*(1), 11–38.

Li, H., et al. (2015). Changes in Farmers' Welfare from Land Requisition in the Process of Rapid Urbanization. *Land Use Policy, 42*, 635–641.

Li, J. D. (2003). Rural Land Tenure Reforms in China: Issues, Regulations and Prospects for Additional Reform. *Land Reform*, pp. 59–72. Retrieved September 15, 2020, from https://www.researchgate.net/publication/291766706_Rural_land_tenure_reforms_in_China_Issues_regulations_and_prospects_for_additional_reform

Li, K. (2015). *Divorce, Help-Seeking, and Gender Inequality in Rural China*. ProQuest Publishing, Indiana University.

Li, K. (2020). Land Dispossession and Women's Rights Contention in Rural China. *China Law and Society Review, 5*, 33–65.

Li, X., Xu, X., & Li, Z. (2010). Land Property Rights and Urbanization in China. *The China Review, 10*(1), 11–38.

Li, Y., & Dennis Wei, Y. H. (2010). The Spatial-Temporal Hierarchy of Regional Inequality of China. *Applied Geography, 30*, 303–316.

Li, Y., & Yin-Sheng, X. (2006). Married Women's Rights to Land in China's Traditional Farming Areas. *Journal of Contemporary China, 15*(49), 621–636.

Li, Z. (1993). *Changes in the Role of Rural Women Under the Household Responsibility System*. University of Wisconsin.

Liang, X., & Burns, L. R. (2017). China's Public Health System and Infrastructure. In L. R. Burns & G. G. Liu (Eds.), *China's Healthcare System and Reform* (pp. 75–118). Cambridge University Press.

Liaw, H. R. (2008). Women's Land Rights in Rural China: Transforming Existing Laws Into a Source of Property Rights. *Pacific Rim Law & Policy Journal, 17*. Retrieved January 10, 2019, from https://digitalcommons.law.uw.edu/wilj/vol17/iss1/10

Liu, M., & Chan, C. (1999). Enduring Violence and Staying in Marriage. *Violence Against Women, 5*(12), 1469–1492.

Liu, S., Carter, M. R., & Yao, Y. (1998). Dimensions and Diversity of Property Rights in Rural China: Dilemmas on the Road to Further Reform. *World Development, 26*(10), 1789–1806.

Liu, Y., et al. (2014). Implications of Land-Use Change in Rural China: A Case Study of Yucheng, Shandong Province. *Land Use Policy, 40*, 111–118.

Long, Hualu. (2014). Land use policy in China: Introduction. *Land Use Policy, 40*, 1–5.

Lykke, N. (2010). *Feminist Studies: A Guide to Intersectional Theory, Methodology and Writing*. Routledge.

Mautner, M. (2011). Three Approaches to Law and Culture. *Cornell Law Review, 96*(839), 839–868.

McCall, L. (2005). The Complexity of Intersectionality. *Signs, 30*(3), 1771–1800.

Mehra, R. (1995). *Women, Land and Sustainable Development* (pp. 1–48). International Center for Research on Women.

Mohanty, C. (1988). Under Western Eyes: Feminist Scholarship and Colonial Discourses. *Feminist Review, 30*, 61–88.

Nicholson, L. J., & Seidman, S. (1995). *Social Postmodernism: Beyond Identity Politics*. Cambridge University Press.

Ong, L. H. (2014). 'State-Led Urbanization in China: Skyscrapers, Land Revenue and "Concentrated Villages"'. *The China Quarterly, 217*, 162–179.

Perry, E. J., & Selden, M. (2010). *Chinese Society: Change, Conflict and Resistance*. Routledge.

Rawls, J. (1971). *A Theory of Justice*. Cambridge University Press.

Riley, N. E. (1997). Gender Equality in China: Two Steps Forward, One Step Back. In W. A. Joseph (Ed.), *China Briefing, 1995–1996: The Contradiction of Change*. M. E. Sharpe.

Rosen, L. (2017). *Law as Culture: An Invitation*. Princeton University Press.

Ross, H. (2015). Challenging the Gendered Dimensions of Schooling: The State, NGOs and Transnational Alliances. In G. A. Postiglione (Ed.), *Education and Social Change in China* (pp. 25–54). Routledge.

Rudd, J. E. (2007). No Change for Thirty Years: The Renewed Question of Women's Land Rights. *Development and Change, 38*(1), 689–710.

Sargeson, S. (1995). Why Women Own Less, and Why It Matters More in Rural China's Urban Transformation. *China Perspectives, 2012*(4), 35–42.

Sargeson, S. (2006). Introduction: Women and Policy and Institutional Change in Rural China. *Journal of Contemporary China, 15*(49), 575–583.

Shi, W., Markoczy, L., & Stan, C. V. (2014). The Continuing Importance of Political Ties in China. *Academy of Management Perspectives, 28*(1), 57–75.

Song, Y., & Dong, X.-Y. (2017). Domestic Violence and Women's Land Rights in Rural China: Findings from a National Survey in 2010. *The Journal of Development Studies, 53*(9), 1471–1485.

Srivastava, D. K., & Gu, M. (2009). Law and Policy Issues on Sexual Harassment in China: Comparative Perspectives. *Oregon Review of International Law, 11*(43), 43–70.

Tinker, I., & Summerfield, G. (1999). *Women's Rights to House and Land: China, Laos, Vietnam*. Lynne Rienner Publishers.

Wang, Y. (2010). *Harmony and War: Confucian Culture and Chinese Power Politics*. Columbia University Press.

Weil, R. (2008). A House Divided: China After 30 Years of "Reforms". *Economic & Political Weekly, 43*(52), 61–85.

Woodhams, C., Lupton, B., & Xian, H. (2009). The Persistence of Gender Discrimination in China—Evidence from Recruitment Advertisements. *The International Journal of Human Resource Management, 20*(10), 2084–2109.

World Bank. (2014). Voice and Agency: Empowering Women and Girls for Shared Prosperity. Retrieved January 17, 2019, from http://www.worldbank.org/en/topic/gender/publication/voice-and-agency-empowering-women-and-girls-for-shared-prosperity

Wu, Y. (2016). *Negotiating Rural Land Ownership in Southwest China: State, Village, Family*. University of Hawaii Press.

Xiangzheng, D., et al. (2010). Economic Growth and the Expansion of Urban Land in China. *Urban Studies, 47*(4), 813–843.

Xu, S., & Fuller, T. (2018). Land Transfer and the Political Sociology of Community: The Case of a Chinese Village. *Journal of Rural and Community Development, 13*(3), 38–55. Retrieved March 23, 2021, from www.jrcd.ca

Zeng, B. (2014). Women's Political Participation in China: Improved or Not? *Journal of International Women's Studies, 15*(1), 136–150.

Zhao, Y. (2011). China's Land Tenure Reform: Time for a New Direction? *The China Review, 11*(2), 125–151.

Zhu, L. (2001). The Issue of Gender Equality in Rural Land Distribution. Land Settlement and Cooperatives. Retrieved June 27, 2019, from https://www.google.com/search?q=Zhu%2C+L.+(2001)+The+issue+of+gender+equality+in+rural+land+distribution.&oq=Zhu%2C+L.+(2001)+The+issue+of+gender+equality+in+rural+land+distribution.&aqs=chrome..69i57.343972j0j9&sourceid=chrome&ie=UTF-8

Zimmermann, M. A. (2012). Summary of 2011 17-Province Survey's Findings: Insecure Land Rights. *Landesa*. Retrieved July 6, 2017, from http://zpmpd2mggwg34rgsm60didr9-wpengine.netdna-ssl.com/wp-content/uploads/Landesa_China_Survey_Report_2011.pdf

CHAPTER 7

One Step Forward, Two Steps Back: An Analysis of Turkey's Implementation of the Istanbul Convention in Addressing Gender-Based Domestic Violence

Gizem Guney

7.1 Introduction

Turkey holds a special importance in terms of its implementation of the Council of Europe Preventing and Combatting Violence against Women including Domestic Violence (the Istanbul Convention, 2014), since it was the first country that signed and ratified it. The representatives of Turkey took an active part during the drafting process of the Convention, whose efforts considerably contributed to the final text of the Convention. Turkey, on the other hand, decided to withdraw from the Convention with a presidential decree after six years of its ratification in March 2021. This move has sparked concerns about the future of the Convention in Europe, and it caused heavy criticism in both the domestic and international arena (Council of Europe, 2021; Bengisu, 2021; Stanimirova, 2021).

G. Guney (✉)
University of Portsmouth, Portsmouth, UK
e-mail: gizem.guney@port.ac.uk

G. Guney et al. (eds.), *Towards Gender Equality in Law*,
https://doi.org/10.1007/978-3-030-98072-6_7

In looking at the reasons put forward by the Turkish government in this withdrawal decision, it can be said that there were two main critiques against the Convention. First, it was argued that the Convention was challenging traditional family structures and therefore was harmful to the family unity. Secondly, it was argued that the Istanbul Convention, due to its gender definition and inclusion of sexual orientation and gender identity into its anti-discrimination provision, had an agenda to increase the scope of the LGBTQI+ rights, such as introducing same-sex gay marriage and third sex in civil laws (Guney in Torunoglu, 2020). These concerns were constantly expressed by conservative NGOs in Turkey since the ratification of the Convention and were echoed in some other Central-Eastern European countries, including Poland, Croatia, Bulgaria, Hungary, Lithuania and Slovakia. However, at the time of writing, Turkey was the first and only country who officially declared a withdrawal.

The focus of this chapter is neither on the withdrawal reasons nor on the question whether these reasons have legal validity. This chapter rather focuses on legal and political steps taken by Turkey in the period between the ratification and the withdrawal. In doing this, the chapter specifically focuses on the steps taken to address gender-based domestic violence against women. It is believed that the real reason for Turkey's abandonment of the Istanbul Convention can be discovered by looking at how Turkey has treated the Istanbul Convention from the beginning up to the point of withdrawal. This chapter argues that the withdrawal decision should not be taken as a surprise considering that, although Turkey has adopted a novel and progressive law in addressing violence against women, it has failed to recognise gender equality in its other policies. As the promotion of gender equality is one of the most prominent obligations that the Convention imposes on the states, Turkey was already failing to meet the obligations imposed by the Istanbul Convention and therefore was not committed to effectively implement the Convention.

7.2 The Istanbul Convention in a Nutshell

The Convention on Preventing and Combating Violence against Women and Domestic Violence was adopted in 2011 in Istanbul and entered into force on 1 August 2014. Following the tradition of the Council of Europe requiring treaties to be referred to by the name of city in which they were opened for signature, the Convention is commonly called the "Istanbul Convention" (Acar, 2014). The Istanbul Convention is a significant development on behalf of women victims of violence on the grounds of its unique and progressive features. It is the first legally binding instrument within Europe specifically aimed at combating violence against women, including domestic violence (Sainz-Pardo, 2014), and second in the world after the Organization of American States' Convention of Belem do Para (1995).

Thanks to its specific focus on gender-based forms of violence against women, the Convention provides the most comprehensive and holistic set of measures in the world that a state can adopt in order to address all forms of violence against women (Stanley & Devaney, 2017). In doing this, it involves a wide range of actors in the fight against violence, including law enforcement bodies, members of the judiciary, non-governmental organisations, the private sector and the media (Alwood, 2016). Furthermore, it requires states to establish institutions (Art 10(1)) that ensure that these actors work in co-ordination with each other through a holistic anti-violence policy (Art 7(1)). The Convention imposes state responsibilities through a 4Ps approach in a similar vein to the other recent conventions within the Council of Europe, that is, the (P)revention of violence, the (P)rotection of victims, the (P)rosecution of perpetrators and the adoption of gender-sensitive (P)olicies. Under each of these (P) pillars, the Convention brings detailed and multidimensional responsibilities to be fulfilled by the state parties.

The Istanbul Convention has been signed by 45 out of 47 member states of the Council of Europe and ratified by 33 of them as of the time of writing. It is also important to note that the Istanbul Convention has been signed by the European Union in 2017, and this can be considered as an indicator of the widely acknowledged nature of the Istanbul Convention at a European level. For these and more reasons, many scholars, journalists and human rights practitioners have described the adoption of the Istanbul Convention as a milestone development and a "defining moment" in the struggle against violence against women (Human Rights Watch, 2014; Simonovic, 2014; Amnesty International, 2011; Meyersfeld, 2012).

7.3 The Picture of Gender-Based Domestic Violence Against Women in Turkey and Turkish Law: Pre- and Post-Ratification of the Istanbul Convention

Following the ratification of the Convention, the Turkish government made several statements underlining the way in which the Istanbul Convention was being taken seriously by the state, specifically since it had been the first signatory and ratifying country among all Council of Europe member states (Tok, 2017). In contrary to these political promises of the government, however, we can observe increasing media coverage on the incidence of domestic violence against women (Boyacıoğlu, 2016)[1] and on state officials' controversial declarations on gender equality in general. At the same time, Turkey did enact a new law and developed new policies in order to comply with the provisions of the Istanbul Convention aiming to eliminate violence against women (the *6284 numbered Law on the Protection of Family and Prevention of Violence against Women (hereinafter 6284 Law), 2012*). At the face of this clash between Turkey's legal promises and the concerning number of gender-based violence incidents occurring, Turkey presents an interesting case study. Considering that the Turkish Constitution openly supersedes international agreements on human rights and individual freedoms over the Turkish laws in the case of an incompatibility between them (Art 90 of *the 2709 Numbered Constitution of Turkish Republic, 1982*), to analyse the legal steps taken as a consequence to the ratification of the Istanbul Convention becomes vital.

Turkey presents a unique case study for one other reason too. Turkey has always remained in the double bind between its modernised Western laws on the one hand and its own eastern-originated culture and traditions on the other, and women's rights have been one of the issues that have been affected most from this tension. In fact, with the foundation of the Turkish Republic, the country has found itself in a rapid modernisation process leading to a secular Western legal framework prevailing over the non-secular laws and eastern and Muslim identity of its predecessor, the Ottoman Empire (Silverstein, 2003; Gökariksel & Gündoğdu, 2007).[2] This separates Turkey from many of the other state parties to the Istanbul Convention.[3] While conducting analysis on Turkey, it is important to take these unique cultural dynamics of the country into consideration.

Unsurprisingly, Turkey is not an exception to the outrageous prevalence of gender-based domestic violence against women, perpetrated by their male partners all over the world (WHO, 2017).[4] Again, in a parallel vein to the global picture of the issue, women are predominantly the victims of domestic violence in Turkey (Akın, 2013).[5] Becoming aware of the disproportionate effects of domestic violence on women took long in Turkey, since up until quite recently there had been neither comprehensive research in the field nor the collection of data with regards to the problem. There are two far-reaching studies presenting the qualitative data on the rates, types and reasons for domestic violence against women across the whole country, which were conducted in 2008 and 2014 (Hacettepe University Institute of Population Studies, 2009, 2014). According to the study of 2014, in Turkey, 36% of women are subject to physical violence, 12% to sexual violence, 38% to both sexual and physical violence, 44% to emotional violence, and 30% to economic violence from their husbands, male partners or ex-partners. On the basis of research analysing the rates of domestic violence against women across the European Union countries, the average of all European women suffering from male partner violence is 22% (EU Agency for Fundamental Rights, 2014). Therefore, the rate of domestic violence against women in Turkey supersedes the one in Europe.

Turkey is also familiar with gendered practices stemming from its own traditional and cultural values, such as arranged marriages, marriages following elope, polygamy and religious marriages, which are increasing the risk of domestic violence against women, unlike many European countries (Boyacıoğlu, 2016). In fact, within these practices, women lose the agency to take decisions and therefore become more restricted within family structures. These practices originate primarily from the *honour culture* that is dominant within the country and which promotes the patriarchal structure. Men are perceived as the protector of family honour, thus having control on the sexual behaviours of women. When women act in contrast to those structures, men are perceived to be entitled to react in violent manners (Boyacıoğlu, 2016). Comparing the data collected in 2014 and 2008, we cannot reach the conclusion that the rates of domestic violence have increased during the last decade. However, it is evident in this comparison that the type of male violence that women have been subjected to is more violent and harmful than before. At this point, it should be reiterated that these two analyses cannot be taken as the mere basis of information, since there are various other surveys pointing out different amounts of gender-based domestic violence in Turkey, sometimes in far higher levels (Akın, 2013; Harcar et al., 2008).

Before the ratification of the Istanbul Convention, Turkey had been exposed to various criticisms from the CEDAW Committee (the monitoring body of the *UN Convention on the Elimination of All Forms of Discrimination against Women (CEDAW), 1981*) with regards to its regulations on gender-based domestic violence. The CEDAW Committee (2005, 2010) consistently criticised Turkey on the grounds that the patriarchal attitudes and deep-rooted traditional and cultural stereotypes regarding the roles and responsibilities of women were pervasive, and these behaviours contributed to the perpetuation of violence against women. It was also underlined that no sufficient protection services such as shelters for battered women had been provided (CEDAW Committee, 2005), and that discriminatory provisions against women were still present within the legal framework (CEDAW Committee, 2010). It is noteworthy to mention that in its last state report, the CEDAW Committee expressed its concerns on the potential negative effects of the policies developed following the attempted coup on women's rights, and the rise of patriarchal attitudes within state authorities and society (CEDAW Committee, 2016). It particularly underlined discriminatory and offensive statements made by high-level representatives of the government against women who did not adhere to the stereotypical traditional roles (CEDAW Committee, 2016). It should also be noted that Turkey was ranked as 131st among 144 states in terms of gender equality in the survey conducted by the World Economic Forum (2017).

Following the ratification of the Istanbul Convention, as mentioned above, Turkey adopted the 6284 Law in 2012 in order to comply with its obligations imposed by the Convention. It is a common practice that a particular international human rights law instrument on which a Turkish law is based upon is referred in the explanatory report of that domestic law (Uğur, 2009). However, it is interesting that the Istanbul Convention is cited as the basis for the 6284 Law within the law itself (Art 1). Therefore, it is beyond doubt that the 6284 Law was adopted as the main tool to be used for the effective implementation of the Istanbul Convention in the Turkish context. For this reason, the next section focuses on the 6284 Law and analyses the steps taken by the Turkish government therein to address gender-based domestic violence.

7.4 The 6284 Law: A New Ray of Hope to Address Gender-Based Domestic Violence?

The 6284 Law has improved the legal framework concerning gender-based domestic violence in Turkey in three distinct ways. First of all, it brought a woman-centred approach in addressing gender-based violence for the first time as required by the Istanbul Convention. Before the 6284 Law came into force, the 4320 Numbered Law (*The Law on the Protection of Family (hereinafter 4320 Law), 1998*) was the primary law applicable to domestic violence cases. Enacted in 1998 and abolished by the 6284 Law, the 4320 Law was a law devoted to all form of violence within family, and it was the first legal instrument in this regard in Turkey. Those protected within the scope of this law were determined as "one of the married partners, children or the other family members living in the same residence" (Art 1), and in the rest of the law no specific attention on women was given at any point. In other words, this law took a gender-neutral path towards violence that occurs in an intimate setting. Considering the disproportionate and gendered impacts of domestic violence on women, this gender-insensitive approach was problematic and had been subject to critiques.

In 6284 Law, on the other hand, there is no provision explicitly declaring that women victims of violence, including domestic violence, are a central concern of the legislation. However, it is evident in the title of the law, which is 'the law on the protection of family and prevention of violence against women,' that when violence is at stake, it is women whom the law primarily aims to protect. Furthermore, the 6284 Law makes it clear that its purpose is to protect four groups of people, women, children, family members and the victims of stalking, who are subjected to violence or potentially at risk of being subjected to violence (Art 1).

This being the case, women are protected within the scope of law purely because they are women. In other words, women are protected outside the realm of family or domestic violence and are protected under any circumstance. Children are granted the same protection as women. However, men can benefit from the protection of the law only if they legally identify as family members or the victims of stalking who are subjected to or under the risk of being subjected to violence. Therefore, it could be easily argued that women are ensured a broader and more explicit protection from violence within the framework of the 6284 Law. In this context, it is clear that the 6284 Law is far more progressive than the previous 4320 Law due its prioritisation of women's protection.

Secondly, the 6284 Law broadens application and scope of legal protection when compared to the former 4320 Law. During the time when the previous 4320 Law was in force, whether women having an *imam* marriage, women cohabiting with their partners without any form of marriage or divorced, women were entitled to protection from violence had been contentious (Kırbaş-Canikoğlu, 2015; Uğur, 2009). *Imam marriage* is a type of religious marriage conducted by an *imam* (the name of the religious priest in Islam) and is not recognised as a marriage before the law and official bodies in Turkey. However, such a marriage is still a common religious ritual in the country. The 4320 Law required women to be officially married in order to be included within the protection scope (Art 1). Even though in 2007, the 4320 Law was amended to broaden the scope of the protection and to remove the requirement that family members had to be living together in order to be protected, the requirement of "official marriage" was nevertheless kept for the victims of violence. In the application of the law, there had been inconsistency in the protection of such women; while in some cases protection orders were issued for women cohabiting with their partners without marriage or *imam* marriage, or divorced women, in others, the injunction was rejected (Karınca, 2008).

However, in the 6284 Law, although the domestic violence definition does not include "former or current spouses or partners", as contained in the definition of the Convention, there is a consensus in the literature that the 6284 Law applies to all partners, regardless of their marital status. Thus, it includes couples married solely by an *imam*, those who live together outside marriage, and even ex-partners (Kırbaş-Canikoğlu, 2015; Uğur, 2009). In fact, the Justice Commission confirmed this approach in its report that the main purpose of the law is the protection of women from any type of violence; whether or not the marriage is conducted through official or in other ways or, whether or not there is any declared commitment to marriage between partners, women are going to be protected from violence within the borders of the 6284 Law. It can, therefore, be argued that Turkey took a positive step with its adoption of the 6284 Law on inclusion of women who are not officially married, even though the Law does not explicitly include the words of "former or current spouses or *partners*".

Thirdly, in accordance with the Convention, the 6284 Law provides a wide array of preventive and protective orders. The Istanbul Convention requires state parties to strike a fair balance between their criminal and special civil law measures while addressing domestic violence. In other words, the Convention does not only oblige states to criminalise domestic violence, it also explicitly imposes an obligation to ensure special civil law measures including emergency barring orders (Art 52), and restriction and protection orders. In looking at the 6284 Law, it can be seen that this law is predominantly devoted to the regulation of these orders and authorises the family courts to issue such orders, when women are subjected to violence or are at risk of being subjected to violence (Arts 3, 4, 5).

These orders have been categorised under two different titles, as prevention orders and protection orders. The protection orders include providing suitable accommodation for victims and their children (Art 3(1)(a)), provisional financial assistance (Art 3(1)(b)), guidance and counselling on psychological, occupational and legal matters (Art 3(1)(c)), changing the victim's workplace (Art 4(a)), locating a separate settlement than the family settlement, if the victim is married to or cohabiting with the abuser (Art 4(b)), and changing the identity documents of the victim when necessary (Art 4(d)). The prevention orders, on the other hand, include the prevention of the perpetrator to humiliate and insult victim in words or behaviour (Art 5(1)(a)), immediate removal of the perpetrator from the settlement of the victim (Art 5(1)(b)), prohibiting the perpetrator to approach the settlement, school or workplace of the victim (Art 5(1)(c)), restriction on the relationship between children and perpetrator (Art 5(1)(ç)), prohibiting the perpetrator to disturb victim through communication instruments (Art 5(1)(f)), treatment for perpetrator if he is an alcohol or drug addict in a health centre and so on (Art 5(1)(h)). Thus, it becomes clear that the 6284 Law provides a comprehensive array of prevention and protection orders in line with the Convention's requirements. It is important that GREVIO, the monitoring body of the Istanbul Convention, expressed its appreciation in this regard in its first evaluation report on Turkey (GREVIO, 2018, para 296).

In the light of the analysis of the 6284 Law that was specifically enacted to implement the Convention, Turkey has taken progressive steps to improve its measures to address gender-based violence against women including domestic violence. These measures included bringing a more woman-centred approach towards violence against women, including more women into the scope of protection regardless of their official marital status and adopting comprehensive civil measures. This demonstrates that the impact of the Istanbul Convention has been wide, on taking all these measures in such a short time. In the next parts of the chapter, I will demonstrate how Turkish government deployed problematic policies towards gender equality despite all these positive developments in the special context of gender-based violence. Before doing this, the equality approach of the Istanbul Convention should be unpacked.

7.5 The Istanbul Convention and Its Approach to Equality

The Convention, in its entirety, is established on the understanding that gender-based violence against women and the inequality of women are two issues that are strictly related to each other through an organic and structural link (Guney, 2020). Therefore, it is not possible to address one (gender-based violence against women) without responding to the other (gender inequality against women) and vice versa (Alwood, 2016). To put it differently, the Convention confirms that violence and inequality are two phenomena that protect and promote each other in a vicious cycle. For this reason, it explicitly recognises all forms of violence against women as a form of discrimination against women (Art 3(a)). For the drafters, gender-based violence is simply a structural problem that stems from historical power inequalities between women and men (Peroni, 2016). In fact, the drafters confirmed in the preamble that women and girls were exposed to a higher risk of gender-based violence than men. By confirming the structural and gendered nature of violence, the preamble makes it clear that the realisation of *de jure* and *de facto* equality is the key element in the prevention of violence against women.

It is *de facto* equality that the Convention particularly emphasises in eliminating violence. As the Convention considers gender inequality as the main reason of gender-based violence, it obliges states to address not only legal but also socio-economic and cultural inequalities that women suffer from. For this reason, as a significant step, the Convention requires state parties to condemn all forms of discrimination against women, *whether or not related to violence against women*. In Article 1, the Convention proposes two separate but interrelated aims. While one is the eradication of violence against women, the other one is the "contribution to the elimination of all forms of discrimination against women and promotion of substantive equality between women and men, by empowering women". As the Convention obliges states to provide equality beyond the violence context, it is argued that the Istanbul Convention has a dual character in being both an anti-discrimination and anti-violence instrument (Acar, 2017).

The purpose of the Convention, "to contribute to substantive equality between women and men, including by empowering women", needs to be highlighted (Art 1). The Convention's reference to substantive equality implies that such equality does not consist only of formal equality, and thus the eradication of direct discrimination would not satisfy the expectations of the Convention. In Article 4, the Convention enumerates the legal and other measures to be taken for this purpose, namely that of providing the right to equality in national laws, the abolishment of discriminative laws and the prohibition of discrimination through effective sanctions. All these measures refer to a rather formal, namely *de jure*, equality understanding (Facio & Morgan, 2009). However, through the requirement of the "practical realisation" of these legislative measures, the Convention points out that, unless states' laws and their application result in equality in a practical sense on behalf of women, the equality would not be achieved in its substantial terms. This refers to substantive equality (Saksena, 2007) and is directly borrowed from CEDAW.[6]

In providing this *de facto* equality, one essential responsibility that the Convention imposes on states is "to promote changes in the social and cultural patterns of the behaviour of women and men" that are based on the idea of the inferiority of women (Art 12(1)). The drafters explained this provision by arguing that present behaviour patterns of women and men are often shaped by prejudices, stereotypes and gender-based customs or traditions, and unless the states actively attempt to change such mentalities and attitudes, it would not be possible to prevent gender-based violence against women (Explanatory Report, 2011, para 85). In the same article, the Convention ensures that states cannot invoke culture, religion, tradition or the so-called honour as justification for any acts of violence within its scope (Art 12(5)).

It can be seen in these regulations that the Istanbul Convention holds a firm stance against any potential cultural or traditional arguments which could be harmful to women and women's equality. In the next part, Turkey's approaches towards women's equality and its interpretation of culture in the context of violence against women will be discussed.

7.6 A Cultural Uprising: A Threat to Women's Equality

As explained above, the Istanbul Convention, in its own wording, requires states to promote changes in the social and cultural patterns of behaviour of women and men, in a way that eradicates the customs and traditions leading to the subordination of women. In the respective article, states are obliged not only to take legal measures to this end but also to take all measures beyond law that could be effective (Art 12(2)). This aspect of the Convention is particularly vital considering the unique cultural position of Turkey and its recent gender policies.

Turkey's attitude on culture and its relation to women's equality seems more concerning than ever been before, on both legal and political grounds. Particularly in last few years, the controversial statements of public officials serving to strengthening the gender roles of women on traditional grounds, and therefore endangering women's equality, are broadly being reflected in the media. These examples include, but are not limited to, the then health minister's declaration that the only career for women can be the motherhood; the then prime minister Erdoğan's statement that women are half women if they are not mothers, because of working; one minister's argument that Turkish women are the accessory of their house and the honour of their husbands; and the then deputy prime minister's claim that women's laughing loudly in public space is equivalent to unchastity, and so on. This situation was subjected to the criticism of the CEDAW Committee in its last report of Turkey:

> [The persistence of deep-rooted discriminatory stereotypes against women] overemphasise the traditional roles and responsibilities of women as mothers and wives, thereby (…) constituting an underlying cause of gender-based violence against women. The Committee also notes with concern that high-level representatives of government have, on several occasions, made discriminatory and demeaning statements about women who do not adhere to traditional roles. (CEDAW Committee, 2016)

The same issue was also criticised by GREVIO, the monitoring body of the Istanbul Convention, in its first Turkey report which argued that public statements of statesmen and leading public professionals that blamed women victims of violence had amounted to hate speech in some instances and called these speeches "disquieting" considering the opinion-shaping role of these individuals (GREVIO, 2018, para 104).

As complementary to this part of the Convention requiring the dismissal of traditions that are harmful to women, the Convention has another subsection requiring states to ensure that culture, custom, religion, tradition or the so-called honour shall not be considered as justification for any acts of violence (Art 12(5)). The Convention also asks states to ensure that any of these factors shall not be regarded as justification in criminal proceedings (Art 42(1)). This is a very crucial part of the Convention since one of the most prominent types of violence against women in Turkey is custom (*töre*) murders and honour (*namus*) killings.[7] In fact, in the cases of women getting married or having a romantic relationship without permission of their family, losing their virginity in extramarital relationships, being raped and so on, women are being murdered by males in their families, such as their brothers, fathers, husbands or ex-husbands (Karınca, 2011). In some circumstances, women are murdered on the basis of honour, due to their dressing styles, talking to foreign men or wanting to divorce their partners (Karınca, 2011). Looking at the Turkish legal framework in this regard, in the previous Turkish Criminal Law, *namus* (honour) and *töre* (custom) were considered as a reason for the application of unjust provocation, and therefore the perpetrators were issued a reduced sentence (*The 765 Numbered Turkish Criminal Law (abrogated), 1926*). However, in 2005 the law was amended to exclude *töre* (custom) as a legitimate reason for unjust provocation. In contrast, this amendment required the perpetrator to receive an increased sentence (*The 5234 Numbered Turkish Criminal Law, 2004*).

Although this amendment made in 2004 is a positive development in accordance with the respective provisions of the Istanbul Convention, it needs to be highlighted that the new law does not refer to *namus* (honour) as a forbidden ground for unjust provocation. It only refers to *töre cinayetleri* (custom murders [direct translation]). It is important to underline that custom and honour killings in the Turkish context hold differences. *Töre cinayeti* (custom murder) refers to the case in which a family council decides on the killing of the woman who arguably dishonoured the family due to her inappropriate sexual or non-sexual behaviours, and one male member of the family is selected to execute the murder. This tradition is particularly unique to the eastern part of the country.[8] *Namus cinayetleri* (honour killings) are, however, the murders of women due to the personal interpretation of honour of the males and does not require the involvement of a family council or anything as such. In other words, these murders are being prosecuted on a wider spectrum of honour-related reasons, and they are murders having an individual character (Karınca, 2011). Considering that honour killings are one of the most prominent types of domestic violence against women, the failure of the Turkish law to include honour as a forbidden ground for the unjust provocation is concerning in terms of Turkey's compliance with the Istanbul Convention (Akbulut, 2014). What is more concerning is that, as noted by GREVIO, the unjust provocation is still being considered as applicable to honour killings before Turkish courts (GREVIO, 2018, para 254). In this regard, "honour" arises as a loophole that the government, law enforcers and judiciary can fill by grounding it on cultural factors, in line with their own political desire to suppress women.

Besides controversial political statements and judicial interpretations, chastity, religion and traditions also formed ground for some controversial attempts of legal reform such as prohibiting abortion and re-criminalising adultery. The recent law authorising *imams* to legally validate the marriage is another example. These legal steps are in contradiction with the earlier era, when progressive legal reforms took place to annul some laws having discriminatory effects on women, as a result of strong women lobbying and feminist movements. For example, in the 1990s, the provision binding women's work to the permission of their husband was abolished by the Constitutional Court. By 1997, women were allowed to officially use their maiden name and the husband's surname together, and, by 1998, the adultery of women was decriminalised. Yet, the most essential and holistic change among these was the mass of amendments to both Criminal and Civil Law by the beginning of the 2000s, so as to abolish the inequality between women and men in family structures and to perceive the sexuality of women as a part of their personal integrity, rather than a component of morality and family order (Altınay & Arat, 2008).

In the light of these, the Turkish government seems to have been jeopardising women's equality in its policies, and it has been doing this by relying on the so-called cultural, traditional and religious norms and values. As revealed above, this has been confirmed by the CEDAW Committee in its recent country report. This constitutes an example for how *culture* can be instrumentalised by a state to imperil women's social and political equality, bodily integrity and freedom. As confirmed by GREVIO, these practices are in stark contradiction with the spirit of the Convention as well as its specific provisions on women's equality explained above.

7.7 Conclusion

Turkey has been the first state to withdraw from the Istanbul Convention with a recent presidential decree. Instead of analysing the reasoning behind this withdrawal and its legal validity, this chapter studied the legal and political steps taken by the Turkish government in addressing gender-based domestic violence between its ratification of the Convention and withdrawal from it.

The chapter demonstrated that, in implementing the Convention, Turkey took effective steps by adopting the 6284 Law which provided a more efficient response to gender-based domestic violence. In this law, Turkey took a woman-centred approach in its legal measures for domestic violence, it included more women into protection scope compared to its previous laws (by including women who are not officially married), and it guaranteed a wide range of prevention and protection orders to the extent that it was never done before and the Convention's requirements were fully satisfied.

Alongside these developments, however, as this chapter has demonstrated, the Turkish government took legal and political initiatives which seriously jeopardised women's equality, and it did this by relying on the so-called cultural and traditional norms of the country. To put it differently, it became visible that on the one hand the government enacted a very new law specifically devoted to tackling violence against women (the 6284 Law) through promising features and on the other it took legal and political steps endangering women's both *de facto* and *de jure* equality.

This signified a worrying turn in terms of the effective implementation of the Istanbul Convention. As explained above, the concept of violence and women's inequality are conceptualised as two sides of the same coin in the Istanbul Convention. For this reason, the Istanbul Convention made it clear that, without empowering women from all aspects, including legal, the elimination of violence was an impossible project. However, Turkey egregiously failed to establish this link between women's equality and eliminating violence against women, threatened the former and, therefore, failed to implement the Convention effectively altogether.

This makes it clear that Turkey's sincerity in its political commitment to address gender-based domestic violence was suspicious from the beginning. This tells a lot about Turkey's withdrawal decision, regardless of whatever reasoning was put forward by the government (which is the subject of another study). Considering this conservative approach positioning women as secondary and subordinate positions within in society, on the top of withdrawal from the Convention, it would not be wrong to expect a rise in all types of gender-based violence against women, including domestic violence, in Turkey in the forthcoming years. As one author stated, Turkey has already turned into a *laboratory of violence* requiring more research and comprehensive policies towards gender equality (Boyacıoğlu, 2016).

Notes

1. According to the research conducted by the Branch Office of Prevention of Violence against Women and Children in 2014, the number of women injured in male violence cases in 2013 was 36% more than 2012.
2. Silverstein explains how the religion has been privatised since the Republican Revolution in 1923. Gökariksel and Gündoğdu underline the fact that the Islamist politics and culture is gaining significant ground in the last decades, and they analyse the impacts of this shift on women through headscarf example under the concept of Islamic modernism.
3. As a component of cultural difference, religious difference of Turkey to the other members of Council of Europe should be mentioned: The state parties that are non-European Union members are Albania, Andorra, Bosnia and Herzegovina, Georgia, Monaco, Montenegro, San Marino and Turkey. Among these, only Albania and Bosnia and Herzegovina have more Muslim citizens than the other religions (almost 58% and approximately 45%, respectively.)
4. According to the WHO, almost one-third (30%) of women who have been in a relationship report that they have experienced some form of physical and/or sexual violence by their intimate partner in their lifetime.
5. In Turkey, 90% of domestic violence victims are argued to be women and children. Women constitute the majority of victims in the context of each type of domestic violence, including physical, sexual, psychological and economic violence.
6. CEDAW Article 2(a) is worded in an almost exactly same manner, with Article 4(2) of the Istanbul Convention. CEDAW also specifically refers to the "practical realisation".
7. The first official data with regards to the prevalence and risk factors of custom and honour killings in Turkey was collected by research conducted by the Parliamentary Research Commission and released in 2005. This report revealed that between 2000 and 2005, 29% of all women's murders were committed to preserve honour. The report also showed that these forms of violence are still prevalent in Turkey and being experienced in every region,

albeit at different rates (the largest portion being Marmara Region hosting 19% of all honour and custom killings). The report also underlined that much of the deaths which were reported as "suicide" are likely to result from the pressure on women on the basis of honour and customs. See "The Report of the Parliamentary Research Commission on the Causes of Honour and Custom Killings of Women and Children" (22th term, 4th Legislative Year), para. 1140.

8. In fact, the Courts require the presence of a decision to murder from a family council in order to classify it as a custom murder.

References

Acar, F. (2014). CEDAW'dan İstanbul Sözleşmesine: Kadınların İnsan Hakları ve Kadınlara Karşı Şiddete İlişkin Uluslararası Standartların Evrimi. In F. Kaya, N. Özdemir, & G. Uygur (Eds.), *Kadına Yönelik Şiddet ve Ev- İçi Şiddet.* Savaş Yayınevi.

Acar, F. (2017). Linking Gender Inequality and Violence Against Women: Istanbul Convention. Retrieved June 24, 2021, from https://rm.coe.int/1680631cab

Akbulut, B. (2014). 6284 Sayılı Kanunda Şiddet ve İstanbul Sözleşmesi'nin TCK Açısından Değerlendirilmesi. *TAAD, 5*(16), 141.

Akın, M. (2013). Aile içi Şiddet. *İUHFM, 71*(1), 27.

Altınay, A. G., & Arat, Y. (2008). *Türkiye'de Kadına Yönelik Şiddet.* Punto Yayınları.

Alwood, G. (2016). Gender-Based Violence Against Women in Contemporary France: Domestic Violence and Forced Marriage Policy since the Istanbul Convention. *Modern& Contemporary France, 24*(4), 377.

Amnesty International. (2011). Time to Take a Stand: Amnesty International Opposes Amendments That Will Weaken the Council of Europe Treaty on Violence against Women. AI Index: IOR 61/004/2011.

Bengisu, I. (2021). Turkey's Withdrawal from the Istanbul Convention: A Step in the Wrong Direction. *LSE Blogs*, 5 May. Retrieved June 23, 2021, from https://blogs.lse.ac.uk/wps/2021/05/05/turkeys-withdrawal-from-the-istanbul-convention-a-step-in-the-wrong-direction/

Boyacıoğlu, İ. (2016). Dünden Bugüne Türkiye'de Kadına Yönelik Şiddet ve Ulusal Kadın Çalışmaları: Psikolojik Araştırmalara Davet. *Türk Psikoloji Yazıları, 19*, 126.

CEDAW. (2005). *Consideration of Reports Submitted by States Parties Under Article 18 of the Convention on the Elimination of All Forms of Discrimination Against Women: Combined 4th and 5th Periodic Report of States Parties –* Turkey, 8 July 2004. New York: Committee on the Elimination of Discrimination against Women.

CEDAW. (2010). *Responses to the List of Issues and Questions with Regard to the Consideration of the Sixth Periodic Report* – Turkey, 12 February 2010, CEDAW/C/TUR/Q/6/Add.1.
CEDAW. (2016). Concluding observations on the 7th periodic report of Turkey. CEDAW/C/TUR/CO/7. New York: Committee on the Elimination of Discrimination against Women.
Council of Europe. (2011). Explanatory Report to the Council of Europe Convention on preventing and combating violence against women and domestic violence. Istanbul, 11.V.2011. Available at: https://www.istat.it/it/files/2017/11/ExplanatoryreporttoIstanbulConvention.pdf
Council of Europe. (2014, August 1). Council of Europe Convention on preventing and combating violence against women and domestic violence.
Council of Europe. (2021, March 21). Council of Europe Leaders React to Turkey's Announced Withdrawal from the Istanbul Convention. Retrieved June 23, 2021, from https://www.coe.int/en/web/portal/-/council-of-europe-leaders-react-to-turkey-s-announced-withdrawal-from-the-istanbul-conventi-1
European Union Agency for Fundamental Rights (FRA). (2014, March 5). Violence Against Women: An EU-Wide Survey. Retrieved May 23, 2021, from http://fra.europa.eu/en/publication/2014/violence-against-women-eu-wide-survey-main-results-report
Facio, A., & Morgan, M. I. (2009). Equity or Equality for Women: Understanding CEDAW's Equality Principles. *Alabama Law Review, 60*(5), 1133.
Gökariksel, B., & Gündoğdu, A. (2007). Review of Modernity, Islam and Secularism in Turkey: Bodies, Places, and Time by Alev Cinar. *Environment and Planning D: Society and Space, 25*, 581.
GREVIO. (2018). GREVIO Baseline Evaluation Report: Turkey, GREVIO/Inf(2018)6, 15 October 2018. Strasbourg: Council of Europe.
Guney, G. (2020). Istanbul Convention: A Genuine Confirmation of the Structural Nature of Domestic Violence Against Women Within Human Rights Law Framework? In S. Kewley & C. Barlow (Eds.), *Preventing Sexual Violence*. The Policy Press and University of Bristol.
Hacettepe University Institute of Population Studies. (2009). National Research on Domestic Violence against Women in Turkey. Ankara.
Hacettepe University Institute of Population Studies. (2014). National Research on Domestic Violence against Women in Turkey. Ankara.
Harcar, T., et al. (2008). Kadına Yönelik Siddet ve Türkiye'de Kadına Yönelik Siddetin Durumu. *Toplum ve Demokrasi, 2*(4), 51.
Human Rights Watch. (2014). Europe Treaty on Violence Against Women to Take Effect: "Defining Moment" for Women Facing Domestic Violence. Retrieved March 27, 2021, from https://www.hrw.org/news/2014/04/24/europe-treaty-violence-against-women-take-effect
Karınca, E. (2008). *Kadına Yönelik Aile İçi Şiddete İlişkin Hukuksal Durum ve Uygulama Örnekleri*. TC Başbakanlık Kadının Statüsü Genel Müdürlüğü.

Karınca, E. (2011). *Sorularla Kadına Yönelik Aile İçi Şiddet*. Ankara Barosu Yayımı.

Kırbaş-Canikoğlu, S. (2015). Kadınlara Yönelik Şiddetin ve Ev İçi Şiddetin Önlenmesine Dair Ulusal ve Uluslararası Mevzuat: İstanbul Sözleşmesi ve 6284 Sayılı Kanun. *Ankara Barosu Dergisi, 3*, 357.

Meyersfeld, B. (2012). Introductory Note to the Council of Europe Convention on Preventing and Combating Violence against Women and Domestic Violence. *International Legal Materials, 51*, 106.

Organization of American States (OAS). (1995, 5 March). Inter-American Convention on the Prevention, Punishment and Eradication of Violence against Women ("Convention of Belem do Para").

Peroni, L. (2016). Violence Against Migrant Women: The Istanbul Convention Through a Postcolonial Feminist Lens. *Feminist Legal Studies, 24*(1), 49.

Sainz-Pardo, P. W. (2014). Women and Children versus Domestic Violence: Legal Reflections, Needs and Challenges in Spain Today. *The International Journal of Human Rights, 18*(6), 660.

Saksena, A. (2007). CEDAW: Mandate for Substantive Equality. *Indian Journal of Gender Studies, 14*(3), 481.

Silverstein, B. (2003). Islam and Modernity in Turkey: Power, Tradition and Historicity in the European Provinces of the Muslim World. *Anthropological Quarterly, 76*(3), 497.

Simonovic, D. (2014). Global and Regional Standards on Violence against Women: The Evolution and Synergy of the CEDAW and Istanbul Conventions. *Human Rights Quarterly, 36*(3), 590.

Stanimirova, G. (2021). The Domino Effect of Normalizing Violence Against Women: Why Turkey's Withdrawal from the Istanbul Convention Has Become the Norm Rather Than the Exception. *Global Risk Insights*, 21 May. Retrieved June 23, 2021, from https://globalriskinsights.com/2021/05/the-domino-effect-of-normalizing-violence-against-women-why-turkeys-withdrawal-from-the-istanbul-convention-has-become-the-norm-rather-than-the-exception/

Stanley, N., & Devaney, D. (2017). Gender-Based Violence: Evidence From Europe. *Psychology of Violence, 7*(3), 329.

Tok, H. (2017). Türkiye, övündüğü İstanbul sözleşmesine ne kadar uydu?' *Evrensel*, 1 August. Retrieved June 10, 2021, from https://www.evrensel.net/haber/328136/turkiye-ovundugu-istanbul-sozlesmesine-ne-kadar-uydu

Torunoglu, G. (2020). "Peyniri Deri Korur, Kadını Eri": İstanbul Sözleşmesi üzerinde mutabakat eksikliği. *T24*, 6 August. Retrieved June 20, 2021, from https://t24.com.tr/k24/yazi/peyniri-deri-korur-kadini-eri-gunahiyla-sevabiyla-istanbul-sozlesmesi,2795

Uğur, H. (2009). Uluslararası Sözleşmeler ve AİHM Kararları Işığında Ailenin Korunmasına Dair Kanun ve Gayrıresmi Evlilikler Hakkında Yargıtay Kararı. *Terazi Hukuk Dergisi, 24*(4), 155.

WHO. (2017, November 29). 'Violence Against Women: Key Facts. Retrieved February 3, 2021, from https://www.who.int//mediacentre/factsheets/fs239/en

World Economic Forum. (2017). The Global Gender Gap Report. Geneva: World Economic Forum. Available at: https://www3.weforum.org/docs/WEF_GGGR_2017.pdf

CHAPTER 8

Hate Speech Law and Equality: A Cautionary Tale for Advocates of "Stirring up Gender Hatred" Offences

Jen Neller

8.1 Introduction: Beyond the Free Speech Clash

Debates about hate speech and the law are dominated by an unavoidable and seemingly interminable conflict between the need to address the harms of hate speech on the one side and the right to freedom of expression on the other. While this chapter does not entirely escape from the so-called free speech dilemma, it questions this confrontational framing of issues and identity groups and seeks to look beyond it. The conflict is often presented in the abstract as though two equal forces slam together and where they meet in the middle is where the objective "balance" between them lies. Indeed, the need to strike "the correct balance" between rights is widely asserted and rarely questioned in discussions on hate speech. But are the two sides always so evenly weighted? Can a fair or neutral balance be struck when interests in regulating speech are presented as "minority rights" and interests in free speech are exalted as universal

J. Neller (✉)
Manchester Metropolitan University, Manchester, UK
e-mail: j.neller@mmu.ac.uk

G. Guney et al. (eds.), *Towards Gender Equality in Law*,
https://doi.org/10.1007/978-3-030-98072-6_8

and fundamental? To what extent does this representation of distinct and inherently opposing interests obscure complex realities? What other issues might this abstract binary distract us from?

This chapter draws on the parliamentary debates that preceded the enactment of the stirring up hatred offences of England and Wales to flag a number of important considerations beyond the free speech dilemma for introducing stirring up gender hatred offences. The aim, therefore, is not to evaluate proposals and criticisms relating to the enactment of stirring up gender hatred offences, but rather to draw insights from research into the *existing* offences that can be used to contextualise and inform such evaluations. Currently, the use of threatening, abusive or insulting words or behaviour to stir up racial hatred is prohibited under Part III of the Public Order Act 1986 (POA86), and the use of threatening words or behaviour to stir up hatred on grounds of religion or sexual orientation is prohibited under Part IIIA of the same Act. In 2014, the Law Commission conducted a consultation on the possibility of extending these offences through the addition of hatred on grounds of disability and transgender identity but concluded that there was insufficient evidence that such offences were necessary. In this consultation, which also examined other areas of hate crime law, the issue of gender hatred was conspicuously absent. However, in 2018 the Law Commission commenced a new review of hate crime law, with consideration of gender hatred explicitly within its terms of reference. The remit of this review is considerably wider than its predecessor and includes not only whether the stirring up hatred provisions should be extended to include more types of hatred, including gender hatred, but also whether and how they might be reformed, and whether the scattered provisions of anti-hate law should be consolidated within a single Hate Crime Act.[1]

Free speech has been a prominent concern in the Law Commission's consultation, alongside various other issues primarily relating to the overall coherence of the provisions. These issues are briefly mapped out in relation to the stirring up hatred offences in the first section of this chapter so as to establish the legal context within which an offence of stirring gender hatred would be situated. The relationship between the stirring up hatred provisions and other areas of law that are premised on identity categories—hate crime law and anti-discrimination law—is also considered. Having established the uneven legal terrain of the existing offences, we then turn to their logics. Here, we question how the justifications advanced for the existing stirring up hatred offences might apply to gender hatred offences, including how they might fit within the logics of public order law. Through this analysis, another conflict is revealed: that between the preservation of public order and the pursuit of equality. Ultimately, I argue that this conflict and other underlying tensions need to be exposed and confronted in order for stirring up gender hatred offences to challenge—rather than reproduce—forms of inequality.

8.2 The Current Stirring up Hatred Offences

The offence of stirring up racial hatred was first enacted by the Race Relations Act (1965), under the subheading of "Public Order". Although it was criticised for its limited scope and enforcement mechanisms, this act was groundbreaking as the first legal instrument of England and Wales that sought to address racism. An offence under Section 6 of the Race Relations Act (1965) required the publication, distribution or use in a public place of threatening, abusive or insulting words that were both intended and likely to stir up racial hatred.[2] The Race Relations Act (1976) relocated this offence to Section 5A of the Public Order Act (1936) and removed the requirement for intent to be proved. Then, Part III of the Public Order Act (1986, hereafter "POA86") introduced intent as an alternative, rather than an additional requirement, to proving that racial hatred was likely to be stirred up and replicated the offence across a range of media, including publications, plays, recordings and broadcasting. I refer to this suite of offences (Sections 18-22 POA86) as the "stirring up racial hatred offences". The first of these offences reads as follows:

> A person who uses threatening, abusive or insulting words or behaviour, or displays any written material which is threatening abusive or insulting, is guilty of an offence if–
>
> a) he intends thereby to stir up racial hatred, or
> b) having regard to all the circumstances racial hatred is likely to be stirred up thereby. (Section 18(1) POA86)

Important features of these offences, which have not changed since 1986, are as follows: (1) they are inchoate (i.e. there is no requirement to prove that racial hatred has actually been stirred up), (2) they concern speech addressed to third parties who might be incited to hate, rather than speech addressed directly to its targets, and (3) they concern speech that targets a group of people defined by reference to their race, rather than individuals. These features are often overlooked or confused but are important for understanding the particular conduct that the offences prohibit and, therefore, how they are distinct from other provisions.

The Racial and Religious Hatred Act (2006) added offences of stirring up religious hatred to the POA86. Such an addition had been discussed for decades. Prior to the twentieth century, attempts to introduce a religious hatred provision tended to be in the form of a proposed amendment to a bill or a private members bill. Conversely, in the twentieth century the government sought to amend Part III of the POA86 so that the racial hatred provisions would be extended to include religious hatred. However, parity between the two offences was rejected by the House of Lords. Race and religion were distinct and should be treated as such, it was argued, because race is immutable, and it makes no sense to persuade someone to change their race, while religion is chosen and proselytising is often viewed as a religious duty (see Wintemute, 2002, pp. 137–138).[3] Consequently, the Lords imposed changes to the Racial and Religious Hatred Bill, with the effect that the religious hatred offences differ from the racial hatred offences in four ways:

- The religious hatred offences were enacted within a new Part IIIA of the POA86, instead of being incorporated within Part III.
- They encompass only words or material that are threatening, and not also that which is abusive or insulting.
- They require both intent to stir up religious hatred and the likelihood that religious hatred would be stirred up to be proved, rather than either.
- They include an additional free speech provision.[4]

The religious hatred offences are therefore considerably narrower and more difficult to prosecute than the racial hatred provisions. Indeed, the necessity of proving intent was removed from the racial hatred offences by the Race Relations Act (1976) precisely because it was an excessively difficult criterion to meet (see Scarman, 1975, p. 35).

While different types of hatred might well require different responses (Goodall, 2009, p. 219), the discrepancies between the racial and religious hatred provisions is problematic due to the difficulty in meaningfully distinguishing between the two sentiments in practice and the particular approach that parliament has taken in its attempts to do so. Racial hatred is defined in the current provisions as "hatred against a group of persons defined by reference to colour, race, nationality (including citizenship) or ethnic or national origins" (Section 17, POA86). When the racial hatred offence was first enacted in 1965, in the shadow of the Holocaust, there was concern to ensure that antisemitism would be encompassed. It was claimed that explicit language in the text of the provision to clarify the matter was unnecessary and that Jews would of course, one way or another, be deemed a group of persons defined by the abovementioned criteria (see HC Deb 3 May 1965). The question of the scope of "race" was then considered in the 1983 case of *Mandla v Dowell Lee*. This case before the House of Lords concerned whether Sikhs could benefit from racial discrimination legislation. The Lords' nuanced examination of the issue resulted in the establishment of seven criteria for ethnicity, including shared religion, and Lord Fraser explicitly ruled out the necessity of being "drawn from what in biological terms was common racial stock" (pp. 549 and 564). However, in subsequent debates on the stirring up hatred offences (e.g. Ramsay and Mackay, HL Deb 14 Mar 2005; Khan and Harris, HC Deb 21 June 2005), this judgement was reduced to the assertion that Sikhs (and Jews) benefit from racial hatred provisions because they are "mono-ethnic" religions, but other religious groups such as Muslims, Hindus and Christians do not because they are "multi-ethnic".

There are two important things to note about the distinction between purportedly "mono-ethnic" and multi-ethnic religions (aside from the circularity of using ethnicity to classify religious groups when religion is a criterion for identifying ethnicity). Firstly, this distinction means that hatred against some religious groups can be prosecuted under the wider racial hatred provisions, while identical hatred against other religious groups can only be prosecuted under the narrower religious hatred provisions.[5] Secondly, the approach to determining the scope of the offences has focused on classifying the groups targeted by the hatred, rather than classifying the hatred. Thus, rather than considering whether a particular group is racialised within the speech at issue, it has been deemed appropriate to instead assess whether that group *is* racial, as though race is something that can be objectively and apolitically ascertained. This approach was demonstrated not only in relation to the distinction between mono- and multi-ethnic religions but also in a discussion in the Lords (HL Deb 23 October 1986) on the extent to which the stirring up of hatred against gypsies might fall within the scope of the racial hatred offence. Here, it was concluded that only hatred against "genuine" gypsies would be caught. In this way, the law racialises by asserting which groups are and are not "defined by reference to race" and distributes protections accordingly. There is therefore some contradiction within measures that are ostensibly enacted to facilitate integration and inclusion but that reproduce practices of differentiation and classification.

The provisions on stirring up hatred on grounds of sexual orientation ("SO hatred offences"[6]) were enacted by the Criminal Justice and Immigration Act (2008), which amended Part IIIA of the POA86 to include SO hatred alongside religious hatred. Even though it was generally (although not unanimously) agreed that sexual orientation is, like race, an immutable characteristic, the inclusion of the SO hatred offences at the narrower threshold of the religious hatred offences was not questioned. Rather than any particular property of sexual orientation, the establishment of the SO hatred offences at the stricter threshold seems to reflect the extent to which homosexuality was viewed as a controversial and contestable topic. For example, Liberal Democrat MP Evan Harris rationalised the stricter threshold for SO hatred as follows:

> it perhaps requires less protection because there is a great deal of sincerely held, often religious, opinion that extends to sexual orientation that does not—generally speaking, in this country, thank goodness—extend to race. (HC Deb 6 May 2008)

There is also a separate free speech provision in relation to the SO hatred offences, to which a second paragraph was added by the Marriage (Same Sex Couples) Act (2013).[7] Ignoring the fact that no such free speech provision exists in relation to the racial hatred offences, advocates of an SO free speech provision argued that it was necessary for consistency with the religious hatred provisions, while opponents argued that it was a "wrecking amendment" (Bercow, HC Deb 26 Jan 2009) that neutered the SO hatred offences. After a decade of being in force, there has been only one prosecution for stirring up hatred on grounds of sexual orientation (*R v Ali, Ahmed and Javed*, 2012).

8.3 Stirring up Gender Hatred

Consideration of the current law on stirring up hatred demonstrates that there is no straightforward option to simply add gender to the existing offences. It would need to be decided if gender hatred offences should be enacted at the wider or the narrower threshold, that is, should intent be a necessary element of the offences and should they encompass language that is abusive and insulting as well as that which is threatening? Also, could an argument for an explicit free speech provision be made in relation to gender hatred offences and to what extent might this undermine them? Furthermore, if the scope of the current offences was replicated for gender hatred, there is a risk that this could lead to problematic classificatory decisions regarding what counts as "a group defined by reference to gender". For example, might threatening speech against feminists escape from the offences on the basis that not all feminists are women? While these considerations would apply to the addition of any identity category to the stirring up hatred provisions, this section briefly sets out some further considerations and contexts that are specific to gender hatred.

8.3.1 Gender Hatred and Misogyny

Technically, the stirring up hatred provisions do not protect particular identity groups. Despite being enacted with certain minority groups in mind (Jews, Commonwealth immigrants, Muslims, homosexuals), the stirring up hatred offences address hatred on grounds of characteristics that may be common to either a minority or a majority group (Bell, 2002, p. 181). For example, a person may not stir up hatred against a group defined by reference to race, regardless of whether their race is black, white, British, Pakistani, Welsh and so on. Nevertheless, protection on certain grounds is likely to be far more important to persons who comprise a minority in relation to that characteristic and where there is a history of that minority being oppressed and persecuted (Neller, 2018, p. 77). This is reflected in advocacy of the stirring up hatred provisions that emphasises the need to protect particularly victimised groups. There is therefore some discrepancy between the justification of a provision and the text of the enacted legislation, where the former recognises structural inequalities and the latter does not (Mason, 2014b, p. 166). Thus, there is considerable debate as to whether the incorporation of gender within anti-hate legislation should replicate this veil of neutrality or should refer specifically to misogyny (see Campbell, 2018, p. 34; Mullany & Trickett, 2018, pp. 28–30; Sloan Rainbow, 2017, pp. 63–64). I refer throughout this chapter to prospective "stirring up gender hatred offences", not to advocate the former approach, but to draw attention to this feature of the existing offences.

However, while several scholars have pointed to the ways in which misogyny, like racial hatred, aims to reinforce the structural dominance of one group over another (see Gill and Mason-Bish, 2013, p. 4), the notion of gender hatred nevertheless "questions our conception of hate crime victims as a minority group" (Mason-Bish, 2014, p. 178). This could be a double-edged sword: on the one hand, it may be more difficult to evoke the required levels of group vulnerability, deservingness and sympathy for half the population (Mason, 2014a, pp. 83–84); on the other hand, misogyny cannot so easily be marginalised or deprioritised as a "minority" interest. Here, understandings of how gender intersects with other identity categories can add important nuance that has often been lacking in parliamentary debates. Femaleness, like other characteristics, should not be viewed as a uniform marker of vulnerability, thereby allowing the existence of successful and powerful women to be touted as evidence that misogyny is not a problem. Equally, the existence of misogyny—evidence of which abounds, from domestic violence and femicide to "pick-up artists" and the "manosphere" (e.g. Ging, 2017)—should not be used to attach fearfulness and risk to femaleness. Rather, gender hatred should be seen as an element that accumulates unevenly, combining with and exacerbating other forms of hatred, disadvantage and exclusion (Williams Crenshaw, 1993; Mason-Bish, 2014, p. 177; Sloan Rainbow, 2017, p. 73). Indeed, Hannah Mason-Bish (2014, p. 173) suggests that attention to gender within the hate crime paradigm might illuminate a need to move away from approaches that focus on membership of one identity group at a time (see also Mason, 2005; Moran & Sharpe, 2004).

8.3.2 *The Absence of Gender in UK Anti-Hate Law*

In her examination of how federal hate crime laws were constructed in US Congress, Valerie Jenness (1999) argues that sex was incorporated within US hate crime law relatively easily. In the US, gender was incorporated within federal hate crime law by the Violence Against Women Act 1994, with advocacy of this law presenting violence against women as a civil rights issue. Additionally, violence against women was found to fit within the logic of hate crime law through the notion that acts of gender-based violence are acts of discrimination, the effects of which extend beyond the individual victim and are seen to disadvantage women as a group (ibid., p. 562). While there were debates in the US about how feasible it would be to include violence against women within hate crime law, Jenness states:

> There was no debate about the legitimacy of sex as a status in need of protection and legal consideration, in large part because the legitimacy of 'sex' as a line of stratification resulting in discrimination had long since gained legal and extralegal currency. (Ibid., p. 563–564)

However, the acceptance of sex as a prohibited ground for discrimination has not led to the category's smooth incorporation into either hate crime law or hate speech law in England and Wales. Ten years after the Race Relations Act (1965), parliament passed the Sex Discrimination Act (1975). This Act drew upon the racial discrimination provisions but sought "to avoid a number of weaknesses which experience had revealed in the enforcement provisions of the race relations legislation" (Home Office, 1975, p. 11). Then, in the drafting of the Race Relations Act (1976), the government (ibid.) aimed to harmonise the legislation on racial and gender equality but, as noted above, ousted the stirring up racial hatred provision to the Public Order Act (1936). Thus, the commensurability of the categories of race and sex as prohibited grounds of discrimination was well established in UK law, but stirring up hatred was excluded from this frame; there was no discussion of the possibility of including a stirring up hatred provision within the Sex Discrimination Act (1975).

Hate crime law was enacted in the UK with the introduction of racially and religiously aggravated offences under the Crime and Disorder Act (1998, as amended by the Anti-Terrorism, Crime and Security Act, 2001) and the requirement to enhance sentences where an offence is motivated by hostility on grounds of race, religion, sexual orientation, disability or transgender identity under the Criminal Justice Act (2003, as amended by the Legal Aid, Sentencing and Punishment of Offenders Act, 2012). Again, the read-across from anti-discrimination law to anti-hate legislation described by Jenness in the US context has not occurred in England and Wales. Whereas in the US the rationales of hate crime law were used to introduce provisions on violence against women, in the UK provisions on violence against women preceded the enactment of hate crime law. Thus, gender hatred was already afforded "special" protections (Mason-Bish, 2014). Indeed, difficulties in the passage of the stirring up religious and SO hatred provisions demonstrate the need to clearly articulate the legal gap which new offences will fill, along with the difficulty of grasping and effectively communicating the intricate legal specificities of such a gap in an area of law that developed in an uneven and piecemeal fashion (Law Commission, 2020, p. 170).

8.4 Rationalising the Addition of a New Category

So, without a consensus that characteristics protected from discrimination should be protected from hatred, how might gender hatred be deemed to fit within the logics of the existing stirring up hatred provisions? In Chap. 10 of the 2020 consultation paper, the Law Commission has comprehensively reviewed approaches established by academics, stakeholders and other jurisdictions for determining which categories should be included in anti-hate legislation. The Law Commission concluded that three criteria *should* be used in the selection of categories for protection: demonstrable need, additional harm and suitability (Law Commission, 2020, p. 208). A greater understanding of these criteria and how they *have* operated in practice can be gained by looking back at the arguments made around the addition of hatred on grounds of religion and sexual orientation to the stirring up hatred offences.

Firstly, as might be expected, demonstrable need has indeed been essential to the justification of previous expansions. The question of need was at the heart of previous debates on extending the stirring up hatred offences and, as noted above, the Law Commission recommended in 2014 that the offences should not be extended to encompass hatred on grounds of disability or transgender identity due to a lack of evidence that such problems were sufficiently pressing. Secondly, additional harm requires "evidence that criminal targeting based on hostility or prejudice towards the characteristic causes additional harm to the victim, members of the targeted group, and society more widely" (Law Commission, 2020, p. 208). The notion of *additional* harms reflects the situation in relation to hate crime law, which provides for aggravated offences or enhanced sentences for existing crimes, rather than the situation of the stirring up hatred provisions, which create entirely new offences. However, the last aspect of this criterion that requires harm to be caused to "society more widely" has proved problematic in relation to the stirring up offences: this framing draws an all-too-common distinction between targeted groups and society, suggesting that their interests are separate and that harm caused to some groups somehow does not constitute harm to society. Thus, only those harms capable of being framed as a threat to the interests of legislators, and not only as a "minority rights" issue, have been deemed sufficient to warrant a legislative response. In other words, there must be a degree of "interest convergence" (Bell, 1980), which ultimately ensures that existing power relations are maintained.[8] Finally, the third criterion, suitability, appears to be so broad that it undermines any point in specifying criteria: any proposed characteristic will undoubtedly face objections on the grounds that it is "unsuitable", a poor fit with the existing offences, a poor use of criminal justice resources and inconsistent with the rights of others.

These criteria will now be considered in relation to their potential to justify the addition of gender to the stirring up hatred offences by examining how they were deployed in the justification and shaping of the racial and religious hatred offences and in the addition of sexual orientation.

8.4.1 Fitting Gender Hatred into the Logics of the Racial and Religious Hatred Offences

The stirring up racial hatred offence was presented as embroiled within a conflict between minority interests in the amelioration of hatred on the one side and universal interests in freedom of expression on the other. However, the original racial hatred provisions, their later amendments and the religious hatred provisions were also enacted amidst concerns about "race riots" and the segregation and "ghettoization" of communities. Indeed, the public order framing of the provisions belies concerns not only to protect "victims" but also to prevent their retaliation and to facilitate their integration. For example, in presenting the original Race Relations Bill, Home Secretary Frank Soskice stated:

> Basically, the Bill is concerned with public order. Overt acts of discrimination in public places, intensely wounding to the feelings of those against whom these acts are practised, perhaps in the presence of many onlookers, breed the ill will which, as the accumulative result of several such actions over a period, may disturb the peace. (HC Deb 3 May 1965)

This concern with public order and "the peace" provides the interest convergence element for justifying the provisions: racial hatred is a "minority" problem until it threatens the peace of wider (whiter) society. The conflict that carried greater weight in the impetus to legislate was therefore between free speech and public order—the Hobbesian clash between freedom and security—with the sense that the racial hatred legislation was not so much required to protect vulnerable minorities as to mitigate a "clash of civilizations".

In contrast, gender hatred presents no such risk of inter-communal conflict and violent retaliation; there is no territorial divide between genders, and cumulative acts of misogyny are unlikely to lead women to breach the peace.[9] Therefore, public order, as it was conceived in relation to racial hatred, does not seem to provide adequate justification for a stirring up gender hatred offence. Indeed, we might question whether it is desirable to include a stirring up gender hatred offence under the auspices of public order law, not least due to the extent to which the protection of public order has been associated with pacification and the protection of the status quo, rather than the promotion of a more just and equal society (Neocleous, 2000, p. 110).

A more helpful precedent for advocating stirring up gender hatred offences can be found in relation to another, albeit interconnected, justification for the racial hatred offences: the symbolic function of legislating. Here, the argument in relation to racial hatred (and later religious hatred) was that enacting stirring up hatred legislation would reassure racialised groups that their concerns were recognised and taken seriously by the government. This rationale was apparent in the extent to which the Race Relations Act (1965) was presented as a counterbalance to measures designed to increase restrictions on immigration from the Commonwealth nations. For example, a 1965 Government White Paper set out the approach to race relations as follows:

> This policy has two aspects: one relating to control on the entry of immigrants so that it does not outrun Britain's capacity to absorb them; the other relating to positive measures designed to secure for the immigrants and their children their rightful place in our society.[10]

This technique of counterbalancing measures that disproportionately disadvantage minorities with the enactment of "minority rights" legislation in order to ameliorate any backlash was also evident decades later in discussions on introducing hate crime legislation. In a letter to the Lord Privy Seal regarding the police powers to stop and search that became Section 60 of the Criminal Justice and Public Order Act (1994), Home Secretary Michael Howard wrote:

> The proposed new powers are already being described in the minority press as recreating the discredited 'sus' law and there are serious implications for both community relations and to public order if we are unable to present any positive counter-balance. It is therefore important that the Government take the initiative on racial crimes if it is to counteract the belief amongst

> ethnic minority communities that we do not take their concerns equally seriously. (Cited by Ruddock, HC Deb 12 April 1994)

This fits with the public order rationale that racial hatred provisions will reduce the likelihood of inter-communal conflict (and conflict between racialised communities and the police). However, rather than viewing the law as effective to the extent to which it is enforced against those who breach it, this approach also locates the efficacy of the law in its communication of "a message" to both potential perpetrators and victims. This function was also clearly endorsed by advocates of stirring up religious hatred provisions in the twenty-first century. For example, Labour MP Chris Mullin referred to a religious hatred clause as "a small step, but it will send a signal that we take seriously the kind of abuses to which some of our constituents are being subjected" (HC Deb 26 November 2001; see also Whitaker, HL Deb 27 November 2001), and Labour MP Frank Dobson stated: "If we do not take this opportunity to declare that incitement to hatred of people on the grounds of their religion is wrong, we will declare that we tolerate its continued existence" (HC Deb 21 June 2005).

Thus, while there is no pressing risk of rioting or outbreaks of mass violence stemming from gender hatred, advocates of a stirring up gender hatred offence could easily argue that it is necessary in order to send a clear message that such hatred is wrong and is taken seriously. Such an argument can be supported by evidence from a trial by Nottinghamshire Police of recording incidents of misogyny. While the incidents recorded here predominantly involve behaviour targeted at an individual, and therefore would not qualify as stirring up hatred, research into the trial concludes that the policy was valued for challenging the normalisation of misogynistic behaviour and empowering victims (Mullany & Trickett, 2018, pp. 24–26). It therefore seems reasonable to suggest that the enactment of national stirring up gender hatred offences could have a similar declarative and de-normalising effect. This corresponds with academic work on the moralising effect of criminal law (Mason, 2014a; Bottoms, 2002, pp. 25–26) and the importance of legal recognition for self-esteem (Thompson, 2012). However, it is an unfortunate irony that the discrepancies between the racial and religious hatred provisions currently undermine their capacity to communicate a commitment to equality. While the Law Commission (2020) has proposed equalising these provisions, the full scope of what they communicate and whether a declarative function is sufficient should be carefully considered.

8.4.2 Fitting Gender Hatred into the Logics of the Sexual Orientation Offences

Like gender hatred, hatred on grounds of sexual orientation does not present a risk to public order in the conventional sense. While gay and queer spaces have materialised and references are made to "the gay community", sexual orientation lacks the aspects of heredity, segregation and foreignness that have been recognised as producing risks to public order and "the peace": as with gender hatred, there is little risk that victims of SO hatred will seek violent retribution. So how were the SO hatred offences understood as belonging alongside the racial and religious hatred offences within the Public Order Act 1986?

Firstly, the argument that sexual orientation is commensurate to race was easier to make and more widely accepted than the argument that religion is commensurate to race. In the extensive debates on stirring up religious hatred, it was repeatedly argued, as noted above, that race is an immutable characteristic, whereas religion is not, and that this distinction warrants differential treatment. Advocacy of enacting SO hatred offences was therefore aided by a broad consensus that stirring up hatred against an immutable characteristic is morally wrong. The same substantive argument could be applied in advocacy of enacting gender hatred offences. However, the claim that special protections are required to combat hatred on grounds of immutable characteristics permits no space for understandings of race, sexual orientation or gender as socially constructed or variable phenomena; there is no space for understanding processes of racialisation, sexual discovery, gendering or any kind of fluidity in identification. Such an argument would therefore leverage "the law's propensity to classify" (Grabham, 2009, p. 186) and replicate assumptions about "true" identities as fixed, distinct and discernible. Thus, if the enactment of stirring up gender hatred offences is to pursue an equality agenda, advocacy based on the parity of gender with identity categories that are afforded protection under the existing offences may first need to challenge how those protected categories are conceptualised.

Arguments about the symbolic importance of legislating also played a role in the passage of the SO hatred offences. However, the need to reassure sexual minorities that hatred against them was taken seriously and to utilise the declarative power of the law to affirm their status in society was far less prominent in the debates preceding the enactment of the SO hatred offences than it was in those preceding the enactment of the religious hatred offences. Presumably, this again reflects the fact that the reassurance of sexual minorities was not deemed important for the maintenance of public order. This calls into question the extent to which advocacy of stirring up gender hatred offences might succeed through a justification based on the need to empower women and affirm the principle of gender equality. While such objectives seem undeniably worthwhile, could gender hatred offences lack the necessary interest convergence to render such legislation not only desirable but also essential in the eyes of legislators?

The question of interest convergence in relation to the SO hatred offences provides insight into how stirring up hatred can be viewed as a public order issue where there are no discernible risks of riots. First, however, it is relevant to consider the interest *divergence* that produced considerable opposition to the SO hatred offences. Whereas the debates on the racial and religious hatred provisions pitched "minority interests" against the universal value of free speech, but were lent support by public order concerns, opponents of the SO hatred offences pitched "minority interests" in stymying expressions of homophobia against both the universal value of free speech *and* the particular rights of Christians to express their religious beliefs. Essentially, it was suggested that the message communicated by the SO hatred offences could not affirm the valued status of homosexual and bisexual persons without simultaneously denouncing Christians who expressed their belief that homosexuality is a sin. Thus, while sexual orientation was likened to race as an immutable identity category, it was differentiated through a distinction between being homosexual—which should not be disparaged—and engaging in same-sex sexual activities—which is fair game for moral judgement. This distinction, which is expressed explicitly in the SO hatred free speech provision (Section 29JA, POA86), creates a tension between the right of religious groups not to have hatred stirred up against them on the basis of their religious practices (e.g. wearing religious attire) and the absence of such a right for groups who might have hatred stirred up against them on the basis of their sexual practices.

Yet, in the representation in parliament of a clash between the interests of homosexuals and Christians, the issue was depoliticised as an unfortunate conflict between discrete, fixed and relatively homogeneous identity groups.[11] However, the side of Christianity was bolstered by associations with both free speech and "tradition", from which homosexuals were implicitly excluded by their history of being criminalised.[12] While homosexuals were surely able to stand up for themselves (HL Deb 22 January 2008), persons who might be criminalised by the SO hatred offences were repeatedly described as fearful pensioners, who were merely expressing their "legitimate" and "sincere" beliefs. Lord Waddington expressed this Christian exceptionalism particularly clearly in his statement that "it should be clear in the Bill … that a Christian expressing strong views will not be caught" (HL Deb 3 March 2008). Despite such special dispensation, speakers presented the whole of Christianity as under attack from a new "orthodoxy" that was using law to assert itself (Johnson & Vanderbeck, 2014). In the framing of a conflict between minorities, then, Christianity benefited from a revered history of moral authority and valued traditions (which were never associated with the persecution and oppression of homosexuals), while homosexuals were supposedly representatives of a new orthodoxy that threatened vulnerable Christians. Such a framing can hardly be deemed conducive to a "neutral" balancing of interests.

Despite this, a form of interest convergence was achieved and the SO hatred provisions were passed into law (albeit at the narrow threshold of the religious hatred provisions). The extra ingredient that made this possible was the invocation of a more familiar and less revered type of perpetrator: black rap artists, whose violently homophobic lyrics were cited as evidence in support of the SO hatred offences. In contrast to the "sincere" beliefs of Christians, freedom of expression and sincerity of belief were not raised in relation to the criminalisation of homophobic lyrics (Johnson & Vanderbeck, 2014, p. 163). Significantly, the lyrics were all in Jamaican patois and were therefore recognisably "non-British": the image of the young, black, Caribbean rapper is opposite in almost every way to the white, British, Christian, middle-class pensioner, and provided a means of locating homophobia outside of what is conventionally considered "respectable" society. The lyrics

> emerge from a culture, mostly in the Caribbean, that is deeply homophobic and where violence and murders on such grounds are commonplace. (Turner, HL Deb 9 July 2009)

Thus, hatred was again presented as a public order issue through the representation of a "clash of civilisations". A "righteous white moralising" (Williams Crenshaw, 2017, p. 57) narrative of good versus evil, wherein respectable, tolerant society is at risk from uncivilised, intolerant others, provided the interest convergence that transformed minority interests into societal interests.

In order for the stirring up SO hatred offences to make sense within public order law, public order needed to be reconceptualised beyond risks of riots and intercommunal violence. However, the achievement of this through the image of the tolerant society that must be protected from foreign vulgarity reinforced the existing privileges and exclusions of society. Homosexuals were "folded into" (Puar, 2007) this society through a narrative that affirmed simultaneously the virtuous status of white Christians and the familiar "problem status" of black youth (Hall et al., 1987, pp. 200–201). The risk that the fight against gender hatred could be similarly co-opted to reinforce such narratives and differentiations should be taken seriously. Comparable evidence of violent misogyny in rap lyrics abounds and tropes about how "they" treat "their" women are a well-worn means of differentiating and subordinating racialised minorities (see Farris, 2017; Spivak, 1988). Questions should therefore be asked about who it is anticipated that stirring up gender hatred offences would criminalise and the extent to which such offences are justified—and may therefore be implemented—on the basis of the supposed deviance of racialised and already-marginalised groups.

8.5 Conclusion: Pursuing Gender Equality

This chapter sets out the ways in which adding gender hatred offences to the Public Order Act (1986), as it currently stands, could replicate several problematic dynamics and cannot be assumed to represent a straightforward advancement towards equality. The passage of the current stirring up hatred offences suggests that the free speech objection can only be overcome where interests in stymying a particular type of hatred converge with interests in protecting public order. However, the public order that is to be protected has been conceptualised as the status quo, complete with contemporary biases and exclusions. Uninterested in change, a public order framing erases histories of oppression to produce depoliticised "clashes of civilisations" that require appeasement and pacification (Jackson, 2013), rather than the redress of structural biases (Spade, 2011). Protecting public order and pursuing equality therefore appear as incompatible objectives, such that the capacity of stirring up gender hatred offences to challenge the existing order may be curtailed by their enactment under the auspices of public order law. Alternatively, the foregrounding of an equality agenda could be used to reformulate the minority/majority dynamics of the free speech dilemma. By prioritising equality over "order", ameliorating expressions of hatred can be viewed as a universal interest, and interests in propagating such hatred can be viewed as minority interests. Here, the burden of proof is reversed so that it is the "free speech" interests of those who would stir up hatred that must demonstrate convergence with the universal value of promoting a fair and equal society in order to be taken seriously.

Moreover, care should be taken to look beyond these dramatic, binarising conflicts and to listen to the persistent dissonance that surrounds the law's approach to identity, not least because such dissonance could significantly distort the desired symbolic function of the offences: to present the stirring up hatred offences as a desirable model to be replicated in regard to gender could be to endorse the ways in which they currently stratify and circumscribe identity. If the offences continue to be stratified, adding gender hatred offences alongside either race in Part III of the POA86 or religion and sexual orientation in Part IIIA would affirm a hierarchy of victims that requires different criteria to be met depending on who the hatred targets. Additionally, the inflexible, taxonomic understanding of identity has enabled identity groups to be pitched against each other and their interests to be treated as zero sum. Advocates of stirring up gender hatred offences should therefore make a case for a clear break from this approach, unless they also advocate legal pronouncements on who does and does not count as a group defined by reference to gender and unless they are willing to risk essentialising representations of women's interests.

To meaningfully pursue gender equality—for all diverse, fluid and intersecting identity groups who are disadvantaged by gender hatred—a holistic approach is required. In an area of law that addresses hatred against groups, rather individuals, it is essential that basic third-wave feminist precepts do not get drowned out in the clamour for legal recognition. The empowerment of women cannot be complete until prejudices and hatreds on grounds of race, religion, sexual orientation, disability, transgender identity, class and all other such grounds are eradicated alongside sexism and misogyny. This is not to say that the law should never address any one of these issues singularly, but that legislation should be formulated in such a way that recognises rather than negates intersections and fluidities. The law cannot effectively address inequality if the inequalities of the law are not confronted.

Notes

1. Hate speech legislation is often talked about as a type of hate crime legislation, but here I treat them as distinct to enable clear analysis of how they differ. I use the term "anti-hate legislation" to refer to both.
2. The "threatening, abusive or insulting" criteria were derived from earlier public order legislation, which prohibited the use of such language to provoke a breach of the peace (Public Order Act (1936), Section 5).
3. The extent to which religion is necessarily chosen was contested, but the extent to which race is immutable was not.
4. The free speech provision (Section 29A) provides as follows:

   > Nothing in this Part shall be read or given effect in a way which prohibits or restricts discussion, criticism or expressions of antipathy, dislike, ridicule, insult or abuse of particular religions or the beliefs or practices of their adherents, or any other belief system or the beliefs or practices of its adherents, or proselytising or urging adherents of a different religion or belief system to cease practising their religion or belief system.

5. In the field of anti-discrimination legislation, the need to determine which religious groups classify as racial groups was erased by the enactment of commensurate protections from discrimination on the grounds of religion.
6. Throughout this chapter, hatred on grounds of sexual orientation is abbreviated to "SO hatred." While the phrase "sexual orientation hatred" was never used in parliamentary debates, and indeed seems awkward and off-key, "SO hatred" acts as a useful shorthand that replicates the form of "racial hatred" and "religious hatred". The term "homophobia" is also used in this chapter to reflect its common usage in the debates, even though it does not encompass the full range of hatreds that are technically addressed by the provisions.
7. The SO hatred free speech rider (Section 29JA) provides as follows:

   > In this Part, for the avoidance of doubt, the discussion or criticism of sexual conduct or practices or the urging of persons to refrain from or modify such conduct or practices shall not be taken or itself to be threatening or intended to stir up hatred.
   >
   > In this Part, for the avoidance of doubt, any discussion or criticism of marriage which concerns the sex of the parties to marriage shall not be taken of itself to be threatening or intended to stir up hatred.

8. Derrick Bell established this term to describe the desegregation of schools in the US: "this principle of 'interest convergence' provides: the interest of blacks in achieving racial equality will be accommodated only when it converges with the interests of whites" (Bell, 1980, p. 532).

9. Or at least, police and politicians have a harder time presenting protesting women as violent and volatile threats to society, as demonstrated by the backlash against the policing of the Sarah Everard vigil in Clapham, March 2021.
10. It is notable here that their rightful place in our society is not specified: "rightful" is not defined as equal and immigrants—which were generally assumed to be "non-white"—were not presented as constituent members of British society.
11. The possibility of being both gay and Christian was only briefly acknowledged by one speaker in the debates preceding the enactment of the SO hatred offences (Turner, HL Deb 21 April 2008).
12. In relation to both same-sex sexual activities up until the Sexual Offences Act (1967) and "intentionally promoting" homosexuality up until the Local Government Act (2003).

References

Bell, D. (1980). *Brown v. Board of Education* and the Interest-Convergence Dilemma. *Harvard Law Review, 93*(3), 518–533.

Bell, J. (2002). *Policing Hatred: Law Enforcement, Civil Rights, and Hate Crime.* New York University Press.

Bottoms, A. (2002). Morality, Crime, Compliance and Public Policy. In A. Bottoms & M. Tonry (Eds.), *Ideology, Crime and Criminal Justice: A Symposium in Honour of Sir Leon Radzinowicz.* Willan.

Campbell, A. (2018). *Independent Review of Hate Crime Legislation in Scotland: Final Report.* Retrieved February 27, 2020, from https://www.gov.scot/publications/independent-review-hate-crime-legislation-scotland-final-report/.

Department of Economic Affairs. (1965). *Immigration from the Commonwealth.* HMSO (Cm 2739).

Farris, S. (2017). *In the Name of Women's Rights: The Rise of Femonationalism.* Duke University Press.

Gill, A., & Mason-Bish, H. (2013). Adressing Violence against Women as a Form of Hate Crime: Limitations and Possibilities. *Feminist Review, 105*, 1–20.

Ging, D. (2017). Alphas, Betas, and Incels: Theorizing the Masculinities of the Manosphere. *Men and Masculinities.* Retrieved February 27, 2020, from https://doi.org/10.1177/1097184X17706401.

Goodall, K. (2009). Challenging Hate Speech: Incitement to hatred on grounds of sexual orientation in England, Wales and Northern Ireland. *International Journal of Human Rights, 13*(2-3), 211–232.

Grabham, E. (2009). Intersectionality: Traumatic Impressions. In E. Grabham, D. Cooper, J. Krishnadas, & D. Herman (Eds.), *Intersectionality and Beyond: Law, Power and the Politics of Location.* Abingdon and New York.

Hall, S., Critcher, C., Jefferson, T., Clarke, J., & Roberts, B. (1987). *Policing the Crisis: Mugging, the State and Law and Order*. Macmillan Press.
Home Office. (1975). *Racial Discrimination*. HMSO (Cm 6234).
Jackson, W. (2013). Securitization as Depoliticization: Depoliticization as Pacification. *Socialist Studies, 9*(2), 146–166.
Jenness, V. (1999). Managing Differences and Making Legislation: Social Movements and the Racialization, Sexualization, and Gendering of Federal Hate Crime Law in the U.S., 1985-1998. *Social Problems, 46*(4), 548–571.
Johnson, P., & Vanderbeck, R. (2014). *Law, Religion and Homosexuality*. Routledge.
Law Commission. (2014). *Hate Crime: Should the Current Offences Be Extended?* Retrieved February 16, 2020, from https://www.lawcom.gov.uk/project/hate-crime-completed-report-2014/.
Law Commission. (2018). *Law Commission Review into Hate Crime Announced*. Retrieved February 16, 2020, from https://www.lawcom.gov.uk/law-commission-review-into-hate-crime-announced/.
Law Commission. (2020). *Hate Crime Laws: A Consultation Paper*. Retrived April 14, 2022, from https://www.lawcom.gov.uk/project/hate-crime/
Mason, G. (2005). Hate Crime and the Image of the Stranger. *British Journal of Criminology, 45*(6), 837–859.
Mason, G. (2014a). The Symbolic Purpose of Hate Crime Law: Ideal Victims and Emotion. *Theoretical Criminology, 18*(1), 75–92.
Mason, G. (2014b). Victim Attributes in Hate Crime Law. *British Journal of Criminology, 54*, 161–179.
Mason-Bish, H. (2014). We Need to Talk about Women: Examining the Place of Gender in Hate Crime Policy. In N. Chakraborti and J. Garland (Eds.), *Responding to Hate Crime*. Policy Press.
Moran, L., & Sharpe, A. (2004). Violence, Identity and Policing: The Case of Violence Against Transgender People. *Criminal Justice, 4*(4), 395–417.
Mullany, L., & Trickett, L. (2018). *Misogyny Hate Crime Evaluation Report*. Retrieved February 27, 2020, from http://www.nottinghamwomenscentre.com/wp-content/uploads/2018/07/Misogyny-Hate-Crime-Evaluation-Report-June-2018.pdf.
Neller, J. (2018). The Need for New Tools to Break the Silos: Identity Categories in Hate Speech Legislation. *International Journal for Crime, Justice and Social Democracy, 7*(2), 75–90.
Neocleous, M. (2000). *The Fabrication of Social Order: A Critical Theory of Police Power*. Pluto Press.
Puar, J. (2007). *Terrorist Assemblages: Homonationalism in Queer Times*. Oxford University Press.
Scarman, L. (1975). *Red Lion Square Disorders of 15 June 1974*. HMSO (Cm 5919).

Sloan Rainbow, J. (2017). Sex Doesn't Matter? The Problematic Status of Sex, Misogyny, and Hate. *Journal of Language and Discrimination.*, *1*(1), 61–82.
Spade, D. (2011). *Normal Life: Administrative Violence, Critical Trans Politics, and the Limits of Law*. South End Press.
Spivak, G. C. (1988). *Can the Subaltern Speak?* Macmillan.
Thompson, S. (2012). Freedom of Expression and Hatred of Religion. *Ethnicities, 12*(2), 215–232.
Williams Crenshaw, K. (1993). Beyond Racism and Misogyny: Black Feminism and 2 Live Crew. In M. Matsuda, C. Lawrence, R. Delgado, & K. Williams Crenshaw (Eds.), *Words that Wound: Critical Race Theory, Assaultive Speech and the First Amendment*. Westview Press.
Williams Crenshaw, K. (2017). Race to the Bottom: How the Post-Race Revolution Became a Whitewash. *The Baffler.*, *35*, 40–57.
Wintemute, R. (2002). Religion vs. Sexual Orientation: A Clash of Human Rights? *Journal of Law and Equality.*, *1*(2), 125–154.

PART III

Law Is Practical?

CHAPTER 9

Towards Gender Equality in the Solicitors' Profession in England and Wales A Practical, Intersectional, Socio-legal Approach

Julia Winstone

9.1 Background

At the time of writing, it is almost 100 years since Carrie Morrison was admitted as the first woman solicitor in England, on 18 December 2022, so it is an opportune moment to reflect on how far women have advanced as solicitors since then. This chapter, which confines its subject matter to the jurisdiction of England and Wales, uses a socio-legal perspective to interrogate the position of women solicitors in private practice and thus provides a critical analysis of relevant equality law, policy, practice and research. Since the 1970s, equality laws in statute have made it illegal to discriminate on the basis of gender in terms of work and pay. Yet, despite their legal entitlements, these measures have failed to translate into equality for women who practise as solicitors.

More recently, the Equality Act 2010 (2010 Act), which came into force on 1 October 2010, sought to simplify and strengthen equality law,

J. Winstone (✉)
University of Sussex, Brighton, UK
e-mail: J.Winstone@sussex.ac.uk

G. Guney et al. (eds.), *Towards Gender Equality in Law*,
https://doi.org/10.1007/978-3-030-98072-6_9

giving greater protection to individuals against discrimination on several grounds, including race, sex, age, being pregnant or having a child[1] (Ministry of Justice, 2010). Law firms have duties as service providers and employers under the 2010 Act (Equality Act 2010, Chapter 1; Law Society, 2020a). The Law Society, Solicitors Regulation Authority (SRA) and Legal Services Board (LSB) also have duties to meet their obligations under the 2010 Act in respect of equality and diversity (Law Society, 2012, 2020a; LSB, 2021; SRA, 2014, 2017, 2021). Many initiatives were introduced to implement the 2010 Act, including collecting data on workforce diversity. Nevertheless, regardless of legal duty and supporting strategies, the burden of enforcing the 2010 act, falls on the individual facing discrimination.

For the past 50 years, significant numbers of women in England and Wales have entered the solicitors' profession and remained at junior levels. In 1970, women comprised 10% of people admitted to the profession by registering on the Roll of solicitors. This figure increased to 51.1% in 1992–1993, rising to 60% in 2004–2006, and by 2018–2019, 63.4% of new admissions were women (Aulack et al., 2017; Cole, 1998; Law Society, 1988, 2015, 2019). Since 31 July 2017, women who hold practising certificates[2] have outnumbered men (Law Society, 2018). There is, however, a gap, between the participation rates of men and women holding practising certificates, which steadily increases as solicitors grow older: Over time, the numbers of women practising reduces with age and experience (2019a Law Society, 2015, 2019a). This gap between men and women solicitors is not a new phenomenon, socio-legal studies have observed this for years, although predictions of a "trickle up" process towards full equality have not materialised (Sommerlad & Sanderson, 1998, p. 106; Law Society, 2019a).

This chapter highlights discrepancies between the substantive law on equality enacted by Parliament and the failure to achieve equality in practice in the solicitors' profession in England and Wales.

Barriers to career progression and equal pay faced by women solicitors include law firm cultures (Sommerlad, 2016; Sommerlad et al., 2013) work–life balance (Nicolson, 2005; Webley & Duff, 2007) and childcare issues (Bacik et al., 2003; Nicolson, 2005; Sommerlad, 2002; Sommerlad & Sanderson, 1998). As documented by the First 100 Years Project (Acland & Broomfield, 2019), a small number of women have made significant progress reaching senior positions; however, the Law Society's report on women in leadership confirms that men dominate the senior levels of the profession (Law Society, 2019a). During her time as Law Society president, 2018–2019, Christina Blacklaws initiated and led the *Women in Leadership in Law* project that was designed to better understand why men continue to lead the solicitors' profession, regardless of the numbers of women who have entered the profession since the 1990s. The subsequent report found that contributing factors included unconscious bias, a gender pay gap and the need for flexible working practices (Law Society, 2019a). Blacklaws not only drew attention to the dominance of male leaders in a profession populated mostly by women, she also highlighted further conditions of under-representation:

> Women from minority ethnic communities or who have disabilities face further barriers in their careers and continue to be significantly under-represented in positions of leadership in the sector. (Law Society, 2019a, p. 4)

The current Law Society president, I. Stephanie Boyce, is the Society's first ever Black office holder, the first person of colour, and only the second in-house lawyer to hold the post in nearly 50 years. She has an agenda to bring about change and hopes that when she leaves office, it will be a more diverse and inclusive profession. Her objectives include the promotion of genuine equal opportunities and equal treatment in the profession and the judiciary (Law Society, 2021a & 2021c). Increasing diversity, inclusion and social mobility is a presidential priority, and there is a focus on overcoming mid-career and progression and retention gaps to accommodate a more diverse range of solicitors. In her inaugural presidential address, Boyce stated (Law Society, 2021b, p. 2):

> Solicitors with disabilities, solicitors with caring responsibilities and solicitors from minority ethnic backgrounds continue to face obstacles. Personal characteristics or an individual's socio-economic background should not determine how far people can go.

Boyce's position reflects themes from socio-legal studies and is found in research commissioned by the Law Society, SRA and LSB, and it reminds us that significant diversity issues still need to be addressed within the solicitors' profession. Given the parliamentary intention behind equality legislation, serious reflection is required about the amount of work which needs to be accomplished to ensure that women achieve, in practice, the same equality that they have been legally entitled to, in statute, for so many years.

I will argue that making inequality history requires urgent action and must incorporate an intersectional and practical strategy within a socio-legal framework. I term the approach "practical, intersectional, socio-legal approach", to address how the combined diversity characteristics of individuals affects their progression, advancement and exit from the solicitors' profession. The approach engages with quantitative and qualitative methods to develop a range of practical initiatives based on issues identified by practising solicitors (on the Roll and with a current certificate of practice), non-practising solicitors (on the Roll without the certificate of practice) and solicitors who have left the profession (no longer on the Roll or with a certificate of practice).

This chapter represents a bridge between collating existing research and outlining elements of my current research. The juxtaposition exemplifies the argument, for instance, I use a wider range of participants than those included in recent Law Society (2019a) and SRA commissioned research (Aulack et al., 2017) whose inquiry was focused on practising solicitors. The aim of my research is to close the highlighted equality gaps and enable solicitors to stay in the profession, make career progress or return to practise after a spell away from work. These subsequent proposals compliment those developed by the Law Society and the SRA; furthermore, they include examples of good practice and offer practical toolkits to facilitate career progress for a more diverse profession.

9.2 Practical, Intersectional, Socio-legal Research: Law in Action

The term "socio-legal" is difficult to define and is a contested concept often used as an "umbrella term" rather than falling within clearly defined boundaries (Cownie & Bradney, 2013, p. 35). Banakar and Travers (2005) also view the open-endedness of socio-legal research design as a mark of interdisciplinary strength within the discourse of the sociology of law. The unclear parameters of socio-legal research also provide space to consider transformative approaches to diverse legal issues, particularly in interdisciplinary research (Moran, 2002).

For the purposes of the practical, intersectional, socio-legal research discussed in this chapter, I follow Pound's (1910) original description of "socio-legal" as representative of "law in action", in other words a way of examining how the law is applied in practice rather than how it appears in books (Banakar & Travers, 2013). Sommerlad argues that, for a long time, socio-legal studies have focused on law as a cultural practice and so develops our understanding of the relationship between the law and the social. Such a framework, therefore, applies well to this examination of gendered inequalities among solicitors' (Sommerlad, 2013) because it allows an understanding about the operation of law and legal institutions as embedded in other social processes and institutions (Menkel-Meadow, 2019).

Recent research commissioned by the SRA assessed individual experiences of the legal profession. The researchers argued that it would be impossible to capture the data by focusing on singular variables, which would measure only gender or ethnicity, and, instead, they adopted an intersectional approach (Aulack et al., 2017). The concept of intersectionality was codified by Crenshaw (1991), and is now used to examine how social characteristics are critical to understanding the complexity of human relations in societies and organisations. Originating in Black feminist research, intersectionality emphasised how black and white women had different experiences of gender-based discrimination. The lens of intersectionality stressed that gender is not the only focus of inequality, because race and class are also arenas of inequality; moreover, these social characteristics co-construct each other (Crenshaw, 1989; Hill-Collins, 1998). An intersectional approach is applied in this research to develop an understanding of the complexity of women's experiences within the solicitors' profession.

9.2.1 *Mixed Methods Approach*

A mixed methods approach is taken that follows Banakar and Travers' (2005, p. 5) view to "transcend some of the theoretical and methodological limitations" of past socio-legal research. Quantitative data from the Law Society and the SRA, cited earlier, is used to identify issues that need resolution. My research triangulates data obtained from surveys and qualitative methods (following a constructivist approach) that provide data from round tables and semi-structured interviews. My ongoing investigations capture the professional perspectives of practising, non-practising and former women solicitors.

9.2.2 *Positionality*

My research has been developed from my perspective as a non-practising solicitor and is, therefore, "insider research". I am adopting a reflexive approach to this research, commenting on my positionality throughout to demonstrate the complex relationship between processes of knowledge production and the contexts of these processes. This disclosure includes my involvement as a reflective and interpretative knowledge producer (Alvesson & Skoldberg, 2009). Following Bourdieu and Wacquant (1992), I also include knowledge associated with my membership and position in the field as a non-practising solicitor.

9.3 Equality Legislation

The *Sex Disqualification (Removal) Act* 1919 enabled women to qualify as solicitors (and barristers) for the first time, by removing the legal barriers that prevented them from entering the professions because they were women or married. This was not a case of overnight success; indeed, the change in the status quo followed years of campaigning (Acland & Broomfield, 2019; Sommerlad, 2016; Sommerlad & Sanderson, 1998).

9.3.1 *Equal Pay*

Fifty years after the 1919 act and after a similarly long campaign, enactment of the *Equal Pay Act* 1970 (which came into force on 29 December 1975) meant that, legally, on the basis of gender, women could no longer be paid less than men for the same work or work of equal value. Today, nearly 50 years after it came into force, the 1970 act has still has not translated into equal pay for women solicitors in private practice in the twenty-first century, or, indeed for most women, wherever they work. Recent gender pay gap reporting from the Office for National Statistics in June 2019 indicates that women solicitors hold 54% of these jobs and earn 13.1% per hour less than men, at £21.89 per median hourly earnings compared with £25.19 per median hourly earnings for men solicitors (Office for National Statistics, 2019).

9.3.2 *Equality in Law*

Since the enactment of the *Sex Discrimination Act* 1975, it has also been illegal to treat women and men less favourably at work because of their gender or marital status. The current *Equality Act* 2010, which came into force on 1 October 2010, aimed to simplify and strengthen equality law and introduced a public sector duty of equality. The act gives greater protection to individuals against discrimination on grounds including sex, sexual orientation, gender reassignment, pregnancy and maternity, marriage and civil partnership, race, religion or belief, disability and age (Ministry of Justice, 2010). Law firms have duties as service providers and employers under the 2010 act and are subject to SRA requirements on equality and diversity (SRA, 2014 & 2021). The public sector duty of equality applies to the SRA and the LSB, requiring them to have due regard for the need to eliminate unlawful discrimination, harassment and victimisation. It also requires them to advance equality of opportunity and good relations between people with and without protected characteristics under the act.

Despite these equality provisions, there are ongoing, long-term issues with retention, progression, promotion and equal pay for women solicitors (Law Society, 2019a) that indicate discrepancies between equality legislation and its implementation in practice, which will be discussed below alongside recent initiatives by the Law Society and the SRA.

Currently, individuals facing discrimination must bring individual claims to combat this through the courts. This burden has long been criticised by socio-legal scholars (Bacik et al., 2003; Sommerlad, 2016). The House of Commons Women and Equalities Committee investigated how both the Equality Act 2010 and the role of the Equality and Human Rights Commission (EHRC) were being enforced. Their inquiry found that the current individual approach to enforcement was "not fit for purpose", and proposed a change in approach so that individual challenges to alleged discrimination through the courts would become an exception rather than the rule. The Committee envisaged a "fundamental shift" in the way the act is thought about and implemented. They wanted to create a model that not only acts as a "sustainable deterrent" but also tackles "institutional and systemic discrimination" through system-wide transformation. The committee recommended that the EHRC should engage more in enforcement activity to deter discrimination, suggesting more action is taken by, inter alia, regulators, inspectorates and ombudsmen

(Women and Equalities Committee (2019) *Enforcing the Equality Act: The Law and the Role of the Equality and Human Rights Commission* (HC) Tenth Report of Session 2017–2019, 1470, p. 3). Further proactive participation by the Law Society, SRA and LSB will help facilitate these changes, and my proposed research is designed to contribute towards the same goals.

9.4 Women Solicitors: Retention and Progression in Private Practice

In 2014, women solicitors made up around 60% of practising certificate holders *under* the age of 35 years. By contrast, men solicitors represented 60% of practising certificate holders *over* the age of 35 years (Law Society, 2015). The participation rate for solicitors is the percentage of solicitors on the Roll of Solicitors holding practising certificates, which is higher for men than women aged 26 years and above. This gap increases as solicitors grow older, with the number of women reducing with age and experience (Law Society, 2015, 2019, 2019a, 2020b). Figures from July 2018 show 60% of solicitors (0–9 years since admission) were women, with similar proportions of women spread across private practice and in-house. Women who are practising certificate holders continue to be younger on average than men, with the difference currently being over five years. In 2017, the difference in median ages of male and female practising certificate holders was greater at seven years since admission, with the distribution of female solicitors remaining "skewed to those under 40" (Law Society, 2018, p. 13).[3] Mid-career solicitors (10–29 years since admission) were spilt fairly evenly between men and women, with a larger proportion of men in private practice compared to in-house (Law Society, 2018, 2020b).

The Chambers Student Guide (2021) examines how, between 2014 and 2020, law firms recruited, trained and promoted women solicitors in UK law firms. The "retention gap", which measures the percentage difference between women partners and trainees, is the core issue of the report. The study shows that during the six-year period against a backdrop of women making up 63% of law school graduates, women partners and trainees grew by 5% and women associates by 2%. Meanwhile, the retention gap remained flat. Chambers acknowledges that their measurement of the retention gap is a "blunt" instrument because it does not track women solicitors hired and their actual promotion histories. Their research does, however, find that law firms across the UK "are doing little to change the working cultures that cause attrition" and are narrowly approaching the "diversity problem by hiring more women at graduate level" (Chambers, 2021, p. 2).

Recent research commissioned by the SRA, which adopts an intersectional approach, has begun to identify how the combined diversity characteristics of individuals may affect solicitors' progression, advancement and exit from the legal profession. The SRA looked at records of individual solicitors on the Roll of Solicitors in England and Wales between 2006 and 2016, and their key findings demonstrated that white men are most likely to become partners than any other groups (Aulack et al., 2017).

In 2019, 49% of women solicitors were working in private practice compared with 29% in 1994, women partners in private practice increased to 31% compared to 14% in 1994 (Aulack et al., 2017), but only 18% of women solicitors in private practice were partners, compared to 40% of men (Law Society, 2020c). Analysis of SRA data indicates that women are four times less likely to obtain partnership than men (Tomlinson et al., 2019). Law Society statistics show that a smaller number of women in private practice, with 10 to 19 years post-qualification experience, were partners or partner equivalents as sole practitioners in 2009 (47%) and 2019 (31%). This suggests that the progression gap is not a reflection of the age profile of women solicitors. Women are likely to leave private practice or work in-house (Law Society, 2019a & 2020c).

The statistics indicate there are major differences between the law in statute and the law in practice.

9.5 Law Society Research

The Law Society's *Women in Leadership in Law Project* used round tables to help identify gender equality needs in the legal profession. Issues that arose included unconscious bias, the gender pay gap and flexible working issues (Law Society, 2019a). In a 2017–2018 Law Society survey, unconscious bias in the profession was cited by 52% of respondents as the most common reason why few women reach senior positions in law firms (Law Society, 2019a, pp.13–14). Sixty per cent of respondents were aware of a gender pay gap in their organisation (Law Society, 2019a), with women often being paid less than men (Law Society 2015, 2019a & 2020c). Ninety-one per cent of respondents believed that a flexible working culture was critical to improving diversity in the legal profession. Although in the five years leading up to the survey there had been improvements in this area and flexible working was embedded in some organisations, a long-hours culture in the legal profession which valued "presenteeism" remained, which the report challenged (Law Society, 2019a, p. 25).

Recommendations were made to address unconscious bias, the gender pay gap and flexible working conditions (Law Society, 2019a, pp. 26–27). Men were recommended as champions for change and catalysts for increasing diversity in the profession. This resulted in a series of round tables for men who proposed making flexible working available to everyone, using clear policies and encouraging men to take paternity and shared parental leave. Distributing work evenly, regardless of working arrangements, and encouraging regular monitoring of policies and practice were also suggested. Developing returners programmes were advised, together with improving retention of senior women solicitors and offering "alternative sourcing" to clients for skilled, experienced lawyers to work on fixed periods of contract work if they preferred not to work full time (Law Society, 2019b, pp. 14–15).

At the time of writing, research on the career experiences of Black, Asian and other ethnic groups of solicitors is currently being conducted by the Law Society, which notes that some of the barriers faced by these groups are "largely societal and as such not wholly within the gift of law firms to influence and change" (Law Society, 2020c, p. 19). Despite this view, some law firms have worked alongside client networks to provide career development opportunities for students from these groups.

My ongoing practical, intersectional, socio-legal research will highlight good practice, developing additional toolkits and approaches to facilitate women's progress in practice from the research data, using a wider range of participants than have been involved to date and similarly address issues of ethnicity.

9.6 Making Inequality History through Practical, Intersectional, Socio-legal Research

To make inequality history in the legal profession in England and Wales, I argue that new practical, intersectional, socio-legal research based on additional quantitative surveys and qualitative information obtained from research participants will assist in developing practical approaches to flexible working, developing job shares, career breaks and returnships.

Additionally, taking advice from leaders in these approaches will assist in developing realistic strategies and practical toolkits to help overcome barriers, for instance, on previously reported matters like childcare issues (Sommerlad, 2016; Sommerlad & Sanderson, 1998). This study will highlight examples of good practice within the profession and in other fields to develop best practice practical guidelines to develop equality in this area. Part of this approach will use models of good practice abroad, for example in France and Scandinavian countries (Glancy, 2021; Shieldgeo, 2021), to develop alternative national strategies for maternity/paternity and parental leave.

Tomlinson et al. (2013) argued that a detailed socio-legal study of solicitors who had left the profession is required to better facilitate initiatives designed to fortify their retention. Sommerlad (2016, p. 61) suggests that although a rhetorical commitment to diversity is "almost universally espoused" across the legal profession, its working conditions continue to require "a professional identity unencumbered by responsibility for social reproduction", which suggests that equality and a corresponding work–life balance "appears remote". Therefore, efforts must be concentrated on practical measures to develop retention, progression, partnership and equal pay and to overcome childcare related issues.

9.7 Conclusion

It has been argued that as the first centenary arrives since the first woman was admitted as a solicitor in December 1922, a new socio-legal approach is required to address ongoing inequalities in the legal profession. This approach would complement recent initiatives by the Law Society, the SRA and the LSB. It is further argued that representative voices across practising, non-practising solicitors and solicitors who have left the profession must be heard. Accordingly, this practical, intersectional, socio-legal approach will develop strategies to assist women solicitors, by involving a wider range of participants covered by recent research and Law Society and SRA initiatives. Given the issues identified in terms of retention, progression, partnership and equal pay as well as maternity and childcare, it is envisaged that some of the measures considered will include flexible working, job sharing, career breaks, returnships, appropriate work–life balance strategies and measures to facilitate working practices around childcare responsibilities.

Approaches routinely used outside the legal profession will also be incorporated. The Covid-19 pandemic has demonstrated that flexible working and other initiatives can be a highly productive approach to legal working practices and other arenas of employment that previously centred on office-based working. If the proposed improvements do not translate to major changes within a limited time frame, as suggested by the House of Commons Women and Equalities Committee (Women and Equalities Committee (2019) *Enforcing the Equality Act: The Law and the Role of the Equality and Human Rights Commission* (HC) Tenth Report of Session 2017–2019, 1470), it is envisaged that practical strategies will be introduced whilst additional national strategies to strengthen equality legislation and its enforcement are developed. Finally, it is suggested that the proposed practical opportunities should not only apply to those women currently in the profession but also extend to those who have left so that, if they choose, they can readily find avenues to return to the profession. In short, the proposed approaches have an underlying ethos to maximise the opportunities available for all.

Notes

1. Equality Act 2010, Chapter 1: Protected characteristics also include disability, gender reassignment, marriage and civil partnership, religion, belief and sexual orientation.
2. Practising certificates are issued annually by the Law Society to individual solicitors before a solicitor may practice in the profession. The practising certificate renewal fee for 2021/22 for an individual solicitor is £306, which includes £266 for the regulatory fee and a £40 contribution towards the Solicitors' Compensation Fund. Reduced fees are payable by solicitors on statutory maternity leave or who started this during the current practising year. Crown Prosecution Solicitors are exempt from paying the Compensation Fund contribution. Firms also pay mandatory annual periodic fees based on turnover. Detailed information is available at https://www.sra.org.uk/mysra/fees/current-fees/.
3. Once a person is admitted to the Roll of solicitors, they are automatically a member of the Law Society and are entitled to apply for a practising certificate to practise as a solicitor. Until 2015, the keeping of the Law Society's Roll of solicitors was conducted annually. Since 2015, solicitors can remove themselves from the Roll at any time, or may wait until the next roll-keeping exercise.

References

Acland, L., & Broomfield, K. (2019). *First 100 Years of Women in Law*. Scala Arts and Heritage Publishers Ltd.

Alvesson and Skoldberg. (2009). *Reflexive Methodology* (3rd ed.). SAGE.

Aulack, S., Charlswood, A., Muzio, D., Tomlinson, J., & Valizade, D. (2017). *Mapping Advantages and Disadvantages: Diversity in the Legal Profession in England and Wales*. Solicitors Regulation Authority.

Bacik, I., Costello, C., & Drew, E. (2003). *Gender InJustice: Feminising the Legal Profession*. Trinity College Dublin Law School.

Banakar, R., & Travers, M. (Eds.). (2005). *Theory and Method in Socio-Legal Research*. Hart Publishing.

Banakar, R., & Travers, M. (2013). Law in Action. In R. Banakar & M. Travers (Eds.), *Law and Social Theory* (2nd ed., pp. 161–164). Hart.

Bourdieu and Wacquant. (1992). *An Invitation to Reflexive Sociology*. Chicago University Press.

Chambers Student Guide. (2021). *Women in Law 2021*. Retrieved June 1, 2021, from www.chambersstudent.co.uk/where-to-start/commercial-awareness-info/diversity-and-inclusion/women-in-law-2021

Cole, B. (1998). *Trends in the Solicitors Profession—Annual Statistical Report 1997*. The Law Society.

Cownie, F., & Bradney, A. (2013). Socio-Legal Studies: A Challenge to the Doctrinal Approach. In D. Watkins & M. Burton (Eds.), *Research Methods in Law*. Routledge.

Crenshaw, K. (1989). Demarginalizing the Intersection of Race and Sex: A Black Feminist Critique of Antidiscrimination Doctrine, Feminist Theory and Antiracist Politics. *University of Chicago Legal Forum, 14*, 538–554.

Crenshaw, K. (1991). Mapping the Margins: Intersectionality, Identity Politics and Violence Against Women of Colour. *Stanford Law Review, 43*, 2141–2199.

Glancy, J. (2021). Our Pathetic Paternity Leave System Works Just Fine for the Patriarchy, *The Sunday Times*, 18 April 2021. Retrieved April 20, 2021, from www.thetimes.co.uk/article/josh-glancy-our-pathetic-paternity-leave-system-works-just-fine-for-the-patriarchy-hjfl6rt2k?shareToken=a255fe235b6a76cdd85462bd402834b5

Hill-Collins, P. (1998). It's all in the family: Intersections of Gender, Race and Nation. *Hypatia, 13*(3), 62–87.

Law Society. (1988). *Equal in the Law*. The Law Society.

Law Society. (2012). Equality Act 2010: Practice Note, London, The Law Society. Retrieved April 22, 2021, from www.lawsociety.org.uk/support-services/advice/practice-notes/equality-act-2010/

Law Society. (2015). *Trends in the Solicitors' Profession: Annual Statistics Report 2014*. The Law Society.

Law Society. (2018). *Trends in the Solicitors' Profession: Annual Statistics Report 2017.* The Law Society.
Law Society. (2019). *Trends in the Solicitors' Profession: Annual Statistics Report 2018.* The Law Society.
Law Society. (2019a). *Influencing for Impact: The Need for Gender Equality in the Legal Profession: Women in Leadership in Law Report.* The Law Society.
Law Society. (2019b). *Male Champions for Change: The Case for Gender Equality in the Legal Profession Report.* The Law Society.
Law Society. (2020a). *Business Case for Equality, Diversity, Inclusion within the Legal Profession.* The Law Society. www.lawsociety.org.uk/en/topics/hr-and-people-management/equality-diversity-and-inclusion-a-business-case. Accessed: 9 June 2021
Law Society. (2020b). *Trends in the Solicitors' Profession: Annual Statistics Report 2019.* The Law Society.
Law Society. (2020c). *Diversity Profile of the Solicitors' Profession 2019*, London, The Law Society. Retrieved April 30, 2021, from www.lawsociety.org.uk/en/topics/research/diversity-profile-of-the-solicitors-profession-2019
Law Society. (2021a). *Our Strategy and Business Plan*, London, The Law Society. Retrieved June 9, 2021, from www.lawsociety.org.uk/about-us/our-strategy-and-business-plan.
Law Society. (2021b). *"The trail is ready to be blazed": New Law Society President Sets Out Ambitious Agenda for Change.* , The Law Society. Retrieved April 30, 2021, from www.lawsociety.org.uk/topics/news-articles/new%2D%2Dlaw-society-president-sets-out-ambitious-agenda-for-change
Law Society. (2021c). *Presidential Year Plan 2021 to 2022.* London, The Law Society. Retrieved June 9, 2021, from www.lawsociety.org.uk/about-us/our-governance/chief-executive-and-office-holders/presidential-year-plan-2021-2022.
Legal Services Board. (2021). *Final Business Plan 2021.* Retrieved June 9, 2021, from https://legalservicesboard.org.uk/our-work/ongoing-work/business-plan-2021-22
Menkel-Meadow, C. (2019). Uses and Abuses of Socio-Legal Studies. In N. Creutzfeldt, M. Mason, & K. McConnachie (Eds.), *Routledge Handbook of Socio-Legal Theory and Methods* (pp. 35–57). Routledge.
Ministry of Justice. (2010). *Equality Codes of Practice and Technical Guidance.* Ministry of Justice. www.gov.uk/discrimination-your-rights/print. (Accessed: 7 May 2020)
Moran, J. (2002). *Interdisciplinarity.* Routledge.
Nicolson, D. (2005). Demography, Discrimination and Diversity: A New Dawn for the British Legal Profession? *International Journal of the Legal Profession, 12*(2), 201–228.

Office for National Statistics. (2019). *Gender Pay Gap Explorer Statistics*, Office for National Statistics. Retrieved August 25, 2020, from www.ons.gov.uk/emplymentandlabourmarket/peopleinwork/earningsandworkinghours/articles/genderpaygapexplorer/2019-06-07.

Pound, R. (1910). Law in Books and Law in Action. *American Law Review*, 12–36.

Shieldgeo. (2021). *Maternity and Paternity Leave in France: A Guide for Overseas Employers.* Retrieved May 11, 2021, from https://shieldgeo.com/maternity-and-paternity-leave-in-france-a-guide-for-overseas-employers/

Solicitors Regulation Authority. (2014). *SRA Meeting the Public Sector Equality Duty.* SRA.

Solicitors Regulation Authority. (2017). *SRA Unlocking the Benefits of Diversity.* SRA.

Solicitors Regulation Authority. (2021). *SRA Standards & Regulations 2021.* SRA.

Sommerlad, H., & Sanderson, P. (1998). *Gender, Choice and Commitment: Women Solicitors in England and Wales and the Struggle for Equal status.* Dartmouth Publishing Company.

Sommerlad, H. (2002). Women Solicitors in a Fractured Profession: Intersections of Gender Professionalism in England and Wales. *International Journal of the Legal Profession, 9*(3), 213–234.

Sommerlad, H. (2013). Socio-Legal Studies and the Cultural Practice of Lawyering. In D. Feenan (Ed.), *Exploring the 'Socio' of Socio-Legal Studies* (pp. 181–202). Palgrave Macmillan.

Sommerlad, H. (2016). A Pit to Put Women in: Professionalism, Work Intensification, Sexualisation and Work-life Balance in the Legal Profession in England & Wales. *International Journal of the Legal Profession, 23*(1), 61–82.

Sommerlad, H., Webley, L., Duff, L., Muzio, D., & Tomlinson, J. (2013). *Diversity in the Legal Profession in England and Wales: A Qualitative Study of Barriers and Individual Choices.* Legal Services Board.

Tomlinson, J., Muzio, D., Sommerlad, H., Webley, L., & Duff, L. (2013). Structure, Agency and Career Strategies of White Women and Black Minority Ethnic Individuals in the Legal Profession. *Human Relations, 66*(2), 245–269.

Tomlinson, J., Valizade, D., Muzion, D., Charlwood, A., & Aulakh, S. (2019). Privileges and Penalties in the Legal Profession: An Intersectional Analysis of Career Progression. *The British Journal of Sociology, 70*(3), 1043–1066.

Webley, L., & Duff, L. (2007). Women Solicitors as a Barometer for Problems within the Legal Profession—Time to Put values Before Profit? *Journal of Law and Society, 34*(3), 1–23.

Women and Equalities Committee. House of Commons (2019) *Enforcing the Equality Act: the law and the role of the Equality and Human Rights Commission, Tenth Report of Session 2017—19.* (HC 2019 1470). London: The Stationery Office.

CHAPTER 10

Exploring Barriers in the Enjoyment of Sexual and Reproductive Health and Rights in Kenya: A Case Study of Sex Workers

MaryFrances Lukera

10.1 Introduction

Kenya has a strong record of ratifying major international and regional human rights treaties such as the International Covenant on Economic, Social and Cultural Rights (ICESCR, 1966), Convention on the Elimination of All Forms of Discrimination against Women (CEDAW, 1979) and the Protocol to the African Charter on Human and Peoples' Rights on the Rights of Women in Africa (commonly known as Maputo Protocol, 2003). The Vienna Convention on the Law of Treaties (1969, Art. 2) defines a treaty as "an international agreement concluded between states in written form and governed by international law, whether embodied in a single instrument or in two or more related instruments and whatever its particular designation". Hamm (2001, p. 1014) points out that

M. Lukera (✉)
University of Sussex, Brighton, UK
e-mail: M.Lukera@sussex.ac.uk

G. Guney et al. (eds.), *Towards Gender Equality in Law*,
https://doi.org/10.1007/978-3-030-98072-6_10

the commitment to human rights treaties means that "the realisation of human rights becomes an interest in itself" and that states parties "not only are obliged not to violate human rights but also to contribute to political and socio-economic conditions favourable to respect, protect, and fulfil human rights on the national and international level". Sexual and reproductive health and rights are essential components of human rights (Freid & Landsberg-Lewis, 2001, p. 109; Leary, 1994, p. 39). Sexual and reproductive health was recognised at the International Conference and Population Development (ICPD) in 1994 and reaffirmed in the Fourth World Conference on Women in 1995 (Oronje, 2013). ICPD (1994, para 7.2) defined reproductive health as "a state of complete physical, mental and social well-being and not merely the absence of disease or infirmity", and WHO (2002, p. 5) has provided a definition of sexual health as "a state of physical, emotional, mental and social well-being in relation to sexuality; it is not merely the absence of disease, dysfunction or infirmity".

The enforcement of sexual and reproductive health and rights also engages a right to information, a right to life, a right to dignity, a right to privacy, a right to education and a right to non-discrimination (Freid & Landsberg-Lewis, 2001; Gruskin et al., 2010; Tamale, 2008; Durojaye & Ayankogbe, 2005). Violating the right to sexual and reproductive health may impair the enjoyment of other human rights and vice versa (Office of the United Nations High Commissioner for Human Rights and World Health Organisation, 2008). At the domestic level, these rights are embodied in the Constitution of Kenya 2010 and in the Health Act of 2017 to ensure rights-based approach to sexual and reproductive health. In this chapter, I explore four barriers that hinder the enjoyment of sexual and reproductive health and rights. I argue that for women in sex work to enjoy sexual and reproductive health and rights in the country, barriers must be dismantled and the state held accountable (Stefiszyn, 2005) to promote equality and non-discriminatory practices.

10.2 Methodology

The chapter is based on a qualitative study conducted in 2015 to interrogate whether a human rights-based approach (HRBA) could guarantee sexual and reproductive health of sex workers. It focused on the potential of HRBA laws and policies to improve the right to health leading to greater empowerment of sex workers (Hunt et al., 2015, pp. 2–3). I obtained the data in Kenya between May and July for my PhD research

(Lukera, 2019). The research was subject to ethical review process and approved by ethics committee at the University of Sussex. The ethical considerations were subject to the Data Protection Act 1998.

To reach the participants engaged in sex work, I used the Bar Hostess Empowerment and Support Programme (BHESP), a local non-governmental organisation (NGO) working directly with sex workers to recruit them for the study. Given the sensitivity of the topic, which involved discussion of sexual activity and that the interviews, especially with sex workers, could potentially provoke emotional experiences, particularly when sex workers had to relive their difficult experiences (Mitchell & Irvine, 2008, p. 35), I used BHESP, which already had offered counselling services to sex workers, to provide counselling to any of the sex workers who felt distressed, including any delayed reactions of distress (ibid., p. 39), if necessary.

It was important that all the participants in the in-depth interviews and focus group discussion (FGD) give their informed consent. I obtained informed consent by the participants signing the consent forms. To ensure confidentiality in the focus group, the consent form contained information requiring participants to respect the confidentiality of other participants. The participation of participants was voluntary, and I explained to them that they had the right to withdraw at any stage of the interview or focus group without giving reasons. For confidentiality purposes for all the participants including professionals, I used anonymised quotes.

I conducted 1 focus group and 18 key informant interviews. They included ten sex workers, someone from the Division of Reproductive Health in the Ministry of Health, one police officer and four people from NGOs. The selection criteria targeted females 18 years and older and self-identified as sex workers. Purposive sampling was used to select the participants, transcription and thematic analysis conducted. I identified the mobilising organisation together with other key informants through my personal and professional networks (Rapley, 2004, p. 17; Sinha et al., 2007, p. 425; Kristensen & Ravn, 2015, p. 726).

10.3 Findings

10.3.1 The Ambiguous and Confusing Policies

Coherent laws and policies play a significant role in the enjoyment of sexual and reproductive health and rights. The inconsistency of laws and policies in Kenya merits some discussion. In a human rights-based approach, sexual and reproductive health rights-related laws and policies need to be transparent as well as easy to understand and the government has to be accountable in implementation. In situations where the law is not clear, implementation is equally a problem:

> I think a good policy is a policy that is responsive to the needs of the people. We have blanket policies. They are too general in the way they have been framed. They are not specific. They do not highlight specific issues they are addressing. They are just blanket policies, in the sense that they are misinterpreted, misused, misapplied and depend on the prevailing environment in terms of application, which is also a danger because it puts a lot of fear in the general population. They [laws] contradict each other. While one will appear to be pro a certain issue there is always another law in place that counters that. So you will find that in terms of actualising these laws and providing services, there is no clear path regarding which direction we are supposed to go, literally, as service providers, programmers or people in the development field. (Representative 1, Family Health Options Kenya, field notes, 23 June 2015)

Participants in this study were concerned with the way reproductive health policies were passed and shelved, and that the public in general, more so women, including the police had very little information regarding, for example, the circumstances under which abortion was allowed in Kenya under the 2010 Constitution.:

> The government is just putting them on the shelf ... they are not effective ... Reproductive Health Policy, Adolescent Health Policy, all those policies are there, but they are not followed... The public is not aware, law enforcers are not aware of the provisions of the Constitution and so ... most of the health workers are harassed by police and there is a lot of stigma because of lack of information and misinterpretation of the Constitution because some people feel that provision of abortion services is illegal in Kenya, which is not true. (Healthcare professional, field notes, 25 June 2015)

This does not only suggest that sex workers are in a dilemma with the confusion in implementation of the 2010 Constitution and the reproductive health policies in place, but that the colonial abortion laws as stipulated in the Penal Code (ss. 158–160) have had a significant impact in practice. The healthcare providers' lives are threatened. They fear police arrests, and, at times, their clinics are vandalised or even burnt down. To deal with the threats, a group of organisations under reproductive health and rights alliance established a legal support network to support providers of reproductive health by, for instance, representing them in court. Citing a 2013–2014 study, the healthcare provider pointed out that approximately 465,000 unsafe abortions occurred in Kenya and that the most affected are poor women who go to quacks, while the rich women can afford good reproductive health services including safe abortion. The Kenya Health Policy (2012–2030) acknowledges unsafe abortion as a major cause of maternal mortality, and at the time of the study some efforts were underway to prevent all these unsafe abortions, as the healthcare provider stated:

> We are trying to work on medical abortion whereby women can manage themselves without necessarily going to hospitals. We call it community-based access to misoprostol and there are some organisations which are also training community nurses to distribute misoprostol to women. (Healthcare professional, field notes, 25 June 2015)

This harm reduction model, as the healthcare provider informed this study, discourages women from using sticks or hangers to perform life-threatening abortions because:

> They can go buy those medicines in the chemists and they swallow them and then start bleeding. If the pregnancy does not come out they can go to the hospital…We are trying to educate women so that they can do that before nine weeks, that is, one or two months…that is the safest…the bleeding is minimal. (Healthcare Professional, field notes, 25 June 2015)

The Kenyan government has the responsibility to domesticate international and regional human rights commitments into local laws and policies to ensure all women enjoy sexual and reproductive health and rights. The laws need to be clear and transparent even for accountability (Gruskin et al., 2010, p. 139). Where clarity is lacking, there will be confusion and misunderstanding in their interpretation. When this happens, the marginalised groups such as sex workers will suffer the consequences.

10.3.2 The Criminalised Sex Workers

The right to the highest attainable standard of physical and mental health is often frustrated with the enforcement of criminal law against sex workers. In Kenya, sex workers are criminalised under the Penal Code. The law criminalises living on the earnings of prostitution and distinctively targets women (Penal Code, s. 154). In so doing, their sexual and reproductive health and rights are compromised. They are often arrested by police, and some are arraigned in court, although in some instances police ask them for bribes on the spot or in custody to buy their freedom. The situation is exacerbated when sex workers barely understand the legal status of sex work in their own countries (Overs, 2014). It increases fear, anxiety and uncertainty in the lives of sex workers and inherently affects the enjoyment of sexual and reproductive health and rights. In Ethiopia, for example:

> Some suggested that sex work could not be illegal because, if it was, it could not be practised openly without police interference. Some incorrectly thought that conducting another trade alongside sex work, such as waitressing, means that the laws against prostitution do not apply. Others said that they had been told that there are licences that exempt some venues from laws concerning brothel keeping and living off immoral earnings (there are no such licences). However, many participants had an accurate understanding that there are some laws against soliciting and brothel keeping. Most said they were aware that it is illegal for minors to sell sex and for others to exploit children sexually. (Overs, 2014, p. 18)

My research in Kenya supports Overs' study and clearly demonstrates the need for a better understanding of the law on sex work for greater empowerment of sex workers and to enjoy their sexual and reproductive health and rights. Some sex workers in the focus group suggested that it was the money that they are paid by their clients that make the police "jealous" and hence arrest them. They were convinced with this view for the reasons that they are not arrested because they have been found exchanging money with clients, and also not because they have been caught in the sexual act. The arrest is often when standing at the bus stop, in their neighbourhood or on the streets. The police tend to "judge from dressing" (Sex workers, FGD, field notes, 9 July 2015). Some participants said that "when you walk in town without a man you are [labelled] a prostitute" (ibid.) and that "when a man walks with two women he is asked, which one [of them] is yours? The other one is arrested" (ibid.). Sex workers are harassed for free sex and, in most instances, without a condom. To be released from police custody, "a police officer will want to have sex with you standing in that corner without a condom" (ibid.). Even "when you are found carrying condoms you are [said to be] a prostitute" (ibid.). Sex workers wanted the police to stop arresting them for carrying condoms because "we have a right to protect ourselves because the moment I will go out there and get AIDS, it [would] still [be] the government's duty to [provide] for me the medication that I would take" (Sex Worker 2, field notes, 15 July 2015). At the time of this research, the sex workers said that the rate of those arrests had gone down but they were still happening.

In Mlolongo, less than 15 miles from Nairobi, the experience of sex workers with the police is different. There are no street-based sex workers over there. There is a sex den. It was described as one building that has 50 rooms typically for sex. Sex workers hire the whole building, and they contribute about 200 Kenya Shillings each (approximately £1.50), and anyone who goes there goes for sex. It is likely that sex workers do not encounter harassment from Mlolongo sites, probably because they do not have street-based sex workers in the area. It is a well-known fact that the police are around the corner from the sex den but they do not go over there to arrest them. According to the representative of the Highway Community Health Resource Centre, an organisation that targets truck drivers but by proxy facilitates healthcare services to sex workers "being a sex worker is not a problem today because even the people who are arresting them are their clients" (Representative, Highway Community Health Resource Centre, field notes, 23 July 2015). The kind of violence and harassment that sex workers encounter on their sites is from clients, particularly those who refuse to wear condoms as discussed below, but not necessarily from the police. When clients fail to use condoms, they expose sex workers to HIV and other sexually transmitted infections that are a threat to their sexual and reproductive health and rights.

When I asked the policymaker why sex workers in Mlolongo operated freely in the sex den even with the police around the corner while those in Nairobi were often arrested, the response showed the lack of legal clarity, discussed above, in even the people who are tasked to make policies in the country:

> I am very unclear about the law on sex work. I know when I see the police rounding up the sex workers they make it sound illegal which is also part of

> the reason that they say they are a vulnerable population. But then a lot of groups promote the health of sex workers, which is … the legal part that I have not really understood. But as health workers we are not there to judge, you know … In terms of legal, I am also just as confused. I am not sure about the legal aspect. I think … a lot of people leave alone the sex workers don't know their rights. A lot of us even who are educated don't know our rights. And that's why I was asking what the legal aspect is because at some point the police will round up the [sex workers]… You know the very people … are violating the rights of the sex workers then we expect that the sex workers will complain about sexual assault? You know those are the things that are such grey areas … One thing we could do and … if we could do it perfectly it would be, advocacy and ensuring information is out there for both the police—the law enforcement, the sex workers and the community. I really feel if we could get that information out and get some interactive forum that to me would be the epitome of achieving a lot of things in Kenya because civic education, understanding of the rights … not just for health almost everything, is still a bit shaky, It's one of our gaps. I know we have a communication strategy as a government but now we haven't addressed a lot of things like the legal rights. (Representative, Division of Reproductive Health, Ministry of Health, field notes, 24 June 2015)

Intriguingly, sex workers have a hidden "criminal informant" role. They are treated as criminals as discussed, but they are considered by the police as useful informers of the whereabouts of criminals or thugs in the city. The agenda of having an improved relationship between police and sex workers is different. It is seen as a good "crime-control strategy". The study found that "when it comes to the police, they [sex workers] can be of great help. These people are friends to the thugs, to criminals, and if you are close with them they will always tell you information about these people [criminals] … and that makes the environment safe" (Inspector of Police, field notes, 10 July 2015). I would argue that care should be taken with such views as they do not serve the interest of sex workers and suggest instead that sex workers are linked to criminals. This has its implications; it makes women in sex work susceptible to further abuse and other negative consequences to sexual and reproductive health.

10.3.3 Violence Against Sex Workers

Violence against women in sex work remain a barrier to the enjoyment of sexual and reproductive health and rights. Studies have shown that women, especially women doing sex work in Africa and other parts of the world are vulnerable to violence (Fawole & Dagunduro, 2014). The United Nations Declaration on the Elimination of Violence against Women (United Nations, 1988, Art 1) defines violence against women as “any act of gender-based violence that results in, or is likely to result in, physical, sexual or psychological harm or suffering to women, including threats of such acts, coercion or arbitrary deprivation of liberty, whether occurring in public or in private life”. Most of the violence is experienced from clients and partners of sex workers including pimps. Others include bar managers, DJs, bouncers, taxi drivers, the general public and family members (Representative, BHESP, field notes, 1 July 2015). When asked what violations they encountered from clients, the focus group said:

FGD: Assault.
FGD: You find a person refuses to pay you.
FGD: Gives you fake money.
FGD: Sleeps with you and snatches the money including the one you already had and still beat you.
FGD: Another one wants to use all styles on you because he’s paying you.
FGD: or maybe you have agreed to use the penis and him he wants your buttocks also breasts.
FGD: Another one—I got into his car we talked and we did not agree I just heard loud sound on the automatic car doors. Me I didn’t see him open the door but I just heard a sound ‘gudum’. He just did this [demonstrates the way the car door was opened] and threw me outside the car while it was moving on Peponi Road in Westlands. I was found by police. (Sex Workers, FGD, field notes, 9 July 2015)

Clients assault sex workers when they refuse to engage in sexual activities without condoms. A participant in the focus group narrated how a client once threw her out of a moving car at 2 am on a lonely road because she refused to do a “blow job” for him without a condom. Sex workers said that some clients have big penis and that they would beat them if they refused to have sex. Some clients subjected sex workers to group sex without condoms. They said, “you get into a place [client’s house] and find about fifteen fellow sex workers, what will you do and [yet] you want that money?” “He gets into this one and out” and “ejaculates in the last person” or in the “one he felt was sweeter than the rest” (Sex Workers, FGD, field notes, 9 July 2015). It is important to state that the sex workers noted that some of the violations happened to them before they knew their rights. They referred to these as "those days". After such experience, sex workers said they would rush for post-exposure prophylaxis treatment at clinics such as the Sex Workers Outreach Programme to prevent HIV infection. Prior to HIV prevention treatment, sex workers said, "we used to buy lemon you squeeze it in water … and you use to wash your vagina. Imagine that lemon is what you want to put inside there to remove the germs" (Sex Workers, FGD, field notes, 9 July 2015).

To avoid getting into the hands of abusive clients and risking their lives, sex workers came up with strategies for their safety. One safety measure was not to go to clients' houses or hotels or other places the clients chose. Where one ended up in this scenario, they would send a text to a fellow sex worker to notify them of their whereabouts. Another measure is that sex workers pay security guards at different lodges or hotels to ensure that when they go into a room with a client, the client does not walk out alone, or if security guard heard a sex worker scream in the room, the guard would rush to check on her. It was vital to come up with these measures because "our friend was killed and then we saw this is serious and because … the police are not on our side" (Sex Worker 3, field notes, 15 July 2015). Having regular clients is not totally safe either. They may even murder sex workers, especially if they are relied upon for school fees and different bills which make them think they are the only ones in the relationship (Representative, BHESP, field notes, 1 July 2015).

To ensure sexual and reproductive health and rights are respected, protected and fulfilled, the Kenyan government has a duty to ensure women including sex workers are protected against violence from the public or private individuals. These commitments are stipulated in the regional and international human rights treaties earlier mentioned and in the Kenyan Constitution including the law on the protection from domestic violence (Protection Against Domestic Violence, 2015) and the Penal Code.

10.3.4 Stigma and Discrimination of Sex Workers

The stigma and discrimination surrounding sex workers is well documented (Wong et al., 2011). Studies show that societal discrimination and lack of respect of fundamental human rights directly affect the health status of women (Leary, 1994, p. 38). African women engaged in sex work experience deep societal stigma and discrimination that affect their ability to advocate their own human rights (Mgbako & Smith, 2010, p. 1180) including sexual and reproductive health rights. Sex workers apply what Bandewar and others have referred to as a "clandestine approach" to safeguard their sex work secrets (Bandewar et al., 2010). They suggest that sex workers use this approach to shield their families, more so their children, from stigmatisation as well as embarrassment (ibid.).

Hostile Healthcare Providers

Sex workers are stigmatised and discriminated against even in health facilities. The healthcare providers judge them. Sex workers refer these providers as "hostile healthcare providers", and they can easily identify them (Representative 2, FHOK, field notes, 23 July 2015). I would refer to them as "blockers of quality health". The fear of being judged damages the relationship between these two groups: the healthcare providers and sex workers. The elements of mistrust develop. While stigma is associated with public health facilities, the shadow report by sex workers in Kenya to CEDAW reveal that NGO-based clinics are more associated with humane treatment even when they do not always have medication in their facilities as they rely on donor funds (Kenya Sex Worker Alliance and Bar Hostess Empowerment and Support Program, 2017). They listen to the sex workers and their needs over there.

> I do not go to the government [hospital] because in the first place they handle us badly. First thing if you go there with STIs [sexually transmitted infections], they will ask [loudly], "where have you gotten these prostitute diseases from?" In the first place if a person talks to you like that you will fear to open your heart and tell them all the problems you have or what you are undergoing. (Sex Worker 2, field notes, 15 July 2015)

> But many at times we do not go to those ones of the government because they abuse us and they harass us very much … So now there are our own hospitals [NGO clinics]. Like now Bar Hostess have its own clinic. SWOP has a clinic. So you go to those clinics where you will not be asked questions. You are known as a member and you have a card. So when you go there you won't be asked questions about who you are… You will just say I met with a client … and we did it without a condom. (Sex worker 3, field notes, 15 July 2015)

Alicia Yamin (2016) cautions focusing on individual health practitioners' conduct, divorced from context. Doing so gives a rights-based approach a bad name and makes little headway, argues Yamin (2016, p. 136). Nevertheless, Yamin contends that it should not be an excuse to condone negligence and abuse or malfeasance due to the individual actions of healthcare providers (ibid.). Leslie London (2008, p. 68) sets out three ways in which responsibility falling on health professionals may be construed in a rights-based framework. First, according to London, if employed by the government, a health professional may become the instrument through which the government violates the right to health and should therefore guard against involvement in such violations. Second, certain human rights obligations may have horizontal applicability among individuals, for example the obligation not to discriminate against other people. Lastly, human rights may be viewed as an essential part of one's professional conduct (ibid.). London argues that while the first two carry a possibility of legal sanctions, she notes that professional conduct basically rests almost entirely on professional self-regulation and ethical compliance (ibid.).

It is important to understand how complaints against health professionals are dealt with especially in Kenya. When I asked how the complaints were handled, the policymaker told me that the Ministry of Health received reports against individual health professionals and "a lot of those complaints are directed to specific regulatory bodies—the Kenya Medical Practitioners and Dentist Board or the Nursing Council or the Clinical Officers Council" (Representative, Division of Reproductive Health, Ministry of Health, field notes, 24 July 2015). In addition:

> We now take that [complaints] as feedback and try to tailor our training including behavioural change and communication strategy that target care givers … [on] things like post abortion care and sexual and gender-based violence [and] just to address how to interact with patients. We try to instil dignified care in caregivers. (ibid.)

In a human rights-based approach, privacy and confidentiality in the enjoyment of sexual and reproductive health rights are crucial. Nevertheless, the experience of sex workers in terms of protection of their sexual and reproductive healthcare information is different. Healthcare providers often ignore, while sex workers want to be assured of, their privacy considering the stigma and discrimination they experience. For example, sex worker would explain her health-related issue to the healthcare provider and the provider would then call a colleague to "advertise" the sex worker's problem. The healthcare providers call them names. In fact, participants in the focus group said that in some public health facilities patients are called out loudly using the names of their diseases. This is problematic and raises fundamental ethical issues. The shaming attitude from the people with responsibility to provide dignified care pushes sex workers further away from the services they so much need.

> They [healthcare providers] classify you. People with "kaswende" (sexually transmitted infections) this side and ringworms that side. Even if it is you with that "kaswende", will you get up and go to that side? ...And yet, that is the person who is supposed to examine you and know if you have STI. (Sex Workers, FGD, field notes, 9 July 2015)

Where this happens, "you will get up without treatment and go home" (ibid.). Such encounters were mainly with the female healthcare providers. Expressing their concern, one sex worker remarked, "I never understand if the women in those hospitals were born together. They usually have the same attitude" (ibid.). Stigma impacts on sex workers in several ways. Some brush it off and move on, while others do not. In the focus group, they said it makes "you feel ashamed" and also that "you see yourself as useless" and "not worthy".

Notably, sex workers in the study pointed out that private clinics were helpful but they were expensive; they, however, reiterated that they could not afford their health services because they are expensive. The clinics run by NGOs are different—they are friendlier to sex workers. When they are sexually assaulted or in need of contraception, sex workers prefer to seek help from NGO clinics because they are treated over there like human beings unlike in the public health facilities.

> Me as a sex worker, I can't go to government clinics. I will have to go to a [private] hospital, I feel it's friendly. If I go to a place that is private, it is costly, but they will treat me ... or I'll go to these clinics that NGOs have started for us. They are free. They are so much friendlier, and they understand us. They are there for us, us as sex workers. (Sex Worker 2, field notes, 15 July 2015)

> Sex workers' clinics help. They help because when I come here [referring to the BHESP office] everyone knows that I am a prostitute; even if I carry a condom or this whole box [pointing at a condom box], they will not be surprised. [But] when I go to a health centre [at the City Council] and I

> want even ten condoms they call each other and say this one has taken lots of condoms, looks like she is fucked all the time [laughter] … She is a prostitute. (Sex Workers, FGD, field notes, 9 July 2015)

As a provider of sexual and reproductive health services, Family Health Options Kenya's (FHOK) representative explained that sex workers go to their facility because they found them "accommodating" (Representative 2, FHOK, field notes, 23 June 2015). Their health providers had created a rapport with sex workers, and this meant that

> They can say anything to the healthcare provider attending to them without being judged. They go to specific doctors who may not have necessarily been trained but they have embraced sex workers and other key populations. When the particular doctor is not there, they will not go for treatment. Some doctors are taking the initiative to mentor other doctors to understand the health needs of key populations. (ibid.)

In the community, the situation is not different either. Sex workers are socially excluded. They hide to do sex work. They hide from their neighbours. They leave their houses at night for fear of being seen and operate like "thieves". This operation makes them question if they have any rights. Churches frown upon them and so do the women in the women groups who are indifferent towards them. Similarly, the children of sex workers are mocked by the neighbours or the neighbours' children, or at school including by teachers, once information about their sex-worker mothers gets there.

10.4 Conclusion

The chapter has shown that sexual and reproductive health and rights are essential elements of human rights for women in sex work. They intersect and include a wide spectrum of rights. In Kenya, these rights are embodied in the Constitution of 2010 and in the Health Act of 2017. In spite of these constitutional and legislative changes in the country, the chapter has highlighted the challenges sex workers face. From ambiguous policies to discriminatory treatment in health facilities. The enjoyment of these rights at the domestic level calls upon the government of Kenya to honour its regional and international human rights commitments to advance sex workers' health leading to their greater empowerment. A rights-based approach creates an enabling environment to deal with human rights challenges. It requires the Kenyan government to provide equal and non-discriminatory sexual and reproductive health services.

References

African Union. (2003). *Protocol to the African Charter on Human and Peoples' Rights on the Rights of Women in Africa.* AU.

Bandewar, S. V. S., Kimani, J., & Lavery, J. V. (2010). The Origins of a Research Community in the Majengo Observational Cohort Study, Nairobi, Kenya. *BMC Public Health, 10*(1), 630.

Durojaye, E., & Ayankogbe, O. (2005). A Rights-Based Approach to Access to HIV Treatment in Nigeria. *African Human Rights Law Journal, 5*(2), 287.

Fawole, O. I., & Dagunduro, A. T. (2014). Prevalence and Correlates of Violence Against Female Sex Workers in Abuja, Nigeria. *Africa Health Science, 14*(2), 299.

Freid, S. T., & Landsberg-Lewis, I. (2001). Sexual Rights: From Concept to Strategy. In K. D. Askin & D. M. Koenig (Eds.), *Women and International Human Rights Law* (p. 91). Transnational Publishers Inc.

Government of Kenya. *Constitution of Kenya, 2010.* Retrieved June 27, 2021 from http://kenyalaw.org:8181/exist/kenyalex/index.xql

Government of Kenya. *Health Act No 21 of 2017.* Retrieved June 27, 2021 from http://kenyalaw.org:8181/exist/kenyalex/index.xql

Government of Kenya. *Penal Code, 1963.* Retrieved June 27, 2021 from http://kenyalaw.org:8181/exist/kenyalex/index.xql

Government of Kenya. *Protection Against Domestic Violence Act No 2 of 2015.* Retrieved June 27, 2021 from http://kenyalaw.org:8181/exist/kenyalex/index.xql

Gruskin, S., Bogecho, D., & Ferguson, L. (2010). Rights-Based Approaches' to Health Policies and Programs: Articulations, Ambiguities and Assessment. *Journal of Public Health Policy, 31*(2), 139.

Hamm, B. I. (2001). A Human Rights Approach to Development. *Human Rights Quarterly, 23*(4), 1005.

Hunt, P., Yamin, A. E., & Bustreo, F. (2015). Making the Case: What Is the Evidence of Impact Applying Human Rights-Based Approached to Health? *Health and Human Rights, 17*(2), 1.

Kenya Sex Worker Alliance and Bar Hostess Empowerment and Support Program. (2017). Kenya Sex Workers' Shadow Report Submission to the United Nations Committee on the Elimination of Discrimination against Women 68th Session. KESWA and BHESP.

Kristensen, G. K., & Ravn, M. N. (2015). The Voices Heard and the Voices Silenced: Recruitment Processes in Qualitative Interview Studies. *Qualitative Research, 15*(6), 726.

Leary, V. A. (1994). The Right to Health in International Human Rights Law. *Health and Human Rights, 1*(1), 24.

London, L. (2008). What Is a Human-Rights Based Approach to Health and Does It Matter? *Health and Human Rights, 10*(1), 65.

Lukera, M. A. (2019). *Promoting Sexual and Reproductive Health of Sex Workers in Kenya: A Human Rights Approach.* PhD Thesis, University of Sussex. https://sro.sussex.ac.uk/id/eprint/85320/.

Mgbako, C., & Smith, L. A. (2010). Sex Work and Human Rights in Africa. *Fordham International Law Journal, 33*(4), 1178.

Ministry of Health. *Kenya Health Policy 2012–2030.* Retrieved June 27, 2021 from http://publications.universalhealth2030.org/uploads/kenya_health_policy_2014_to_2030.pdf

Ministry of Health. *National Reproductive Health Policy 2007-Kenya.* Retrieved June 27, 2021 from http://guidelines.health.go.ke:8000/media/National_Reproductive_Health_Policy.Enhancing_Reproductive_Health_Status_for_all_Kenyans.pdf

Mitchell, W., & Irvine, A. (2008). I'm Okay, You're Okay?: Reflections on the Well-Being and Ethical Requirements of Researchers and Research Participants in Conducting Qualitative Fieldwork Interviews. *International Journal of Qualitative Methods, 7*(4), 31.

Office of the United Nations High Commissioner for Human Rights and World Health Organisation. (2008). *The Right to Health.* p. 6. Retrieved April 28, 2022 from https://www.ohchr.org/Documents/Publications/Factsheet31.pdf

Oronje, R. N. (2013). The Kenyan National Response to Internationally Agreed Sexual and Reproductive Health and Rights Goals: A Case Study of Three Policies. *Reproductive Health Matters, 21*(42), 151–160.

Overs, C. (2014). *Sex Workers, Empowerment and Poverty Alleviation in Ethiopia.* Institute of Development Studies.

Rapley, T. (2004). Interviews. In C. Seale, G. Gobo, J. F. Gubrium, & D. Silverman (Eds.), *Qualitative Research Practice* (p. 17). Sage.

Sinha, S., Curtis, K., Jayakody, A., Viner, R., & Roberts, H. (2007). People Make Assumptions About Our Communities': Sexual Health Amongst Teenagers from Black and Minority Ethnic Backgrounds in East London. *Ethnicity and Health, 12*(5), 423.

Stefiszyn, K. (2005). The African Union: Challenges and Opportunities for Women. *African Human Rights Law Journal, 5*(2), 358.

Tamale, S. (2008). The Right to Culture and the Culture of Rights: A Critical Perspective on Women's Sexual Rights in Africa. *Feminist Legal Studies, 16*(1), 47.

United Nations. (1966). *International Covenant on Economic, Social and Cultural Rights*. GA Res 2200A (XXI).

United Nations. (1969). Vienna Convention on the Law of Treaties. *Treaty Series, 1155*, 331.

United Nations. (1979). *Convention on the Elimination of All Forms of Discrimination Against Women*. GA Res 34/180.

United Nations. (1988). *Convention on the Elimination of All Forms of Discrimination against Women*. A/RES/48/104.

United Nations. (1994). *Report of the International Conference on Population and Development* UN Doc A/CONF.171/13. Retrieved June 23, 2020, from https://www.unfpa.org/sites/default/files/event-pdf/icpd_eng_2.pdf.

Wong, W. C. W., Holroyd. E., & Blingham, A. (2011). Stigma and Sex Work from the Perspective of Female Sex Workers in Hong Kong. *Sociology of Health and Illness, 33*, 50–65.

World Health Organisation. (2002). *Defining Sexual Health: Report of a Technical Consultation on Sexual Health. WHO* (p. 5).

Yamin, A. E. (2016). *Power, Suffering and the Struggle for Dignity: Human Rights Frameworks for Health and Why They Matter*. University of Pennsylvania Press.

CHAPTER 11

Eradicating Gender Stereotypes in Advertising in Spain

David Davies

11.1 Introduction

Since the introduction of the Organic Act on Integrated Protection Measures Against Gender Violence (2004) (from now on "The Gender Violence Act") and subsequent egalitarian laws of the Zapatero era, Spain is often held up as a pioneer in combatting violence against women (Cubells & Calsamiglia, 2018; Lopez-Zafra & Garcia-Retamero, 2021). The act has shaped Spain's policy and legislation on proactively protecting women's rights, and one overlooked tributary from the act is the inclusion of prohibiting gender stereotypes and misogyny in advertising. Rather than utilising the de rigueur soft law option of self-regulation organisation of advertising (SROs) or the "market-driven democracy freedom of expression" (Svensson & Edström, 2016), the legislation renders gender stereotypes and misogyny in advertising unlawful (Martin-Llaguno, 2016). The repercussions of this act are finally seeing fruition with less complaints about misogynistic or sexist content in adverts and a broader reduction of gender stereotypes in advertising (Lopez-Zafra &

D. Davies (✉)
University of Sussex, Brighton, UK
e-mail: D.Davies@sussex.ac.uk

G. Guney et al. (eds.), *Towards Gender Equality in Law*,
https://doi.org/10.1007/978-3-030-98072-6_11

Garcia-Retamero, 2021). Amongst the EU27, where most states opt for self-regulation and SROs, this is an unorthodox approach. This chapter discusses how, when using feminist perspectives, legislation on prohibiting gender stereotypes in advertising can complement self-regulation. Moreover, as Spain equates sexist advertising to violence against the woman, I argue why it might be a lesson for other states that are looking to move beyond self-regulation. I begin this chapter by providing a historical backdrop of Spain's shift from dictatorship to democracy contextualising Spain's transference tacking gender-based violence as well as the politics of "la nueva via" (the new way) that led to the adoption of the legislation in 2004. I then provide analysis of the legislation and the test cases of RyanAir and Cillit Bang, which have derived from both the legislation and Spain's SRO, "Autocontrol".

11.2 From Dictatorship to Democracy

The blueprints of the unlawful use of gender stereotypes in advertising can be found in the original constitution, *La Pepa*, of 1812. It is worth briefly highlighting the original liberal democracy-driven freedom of expression that underpinned of *La Pepa* is regarded by Spanish constitutional lawyers (Villiers, 1999) and comparative lawyers (Roberts & Sharman, 2013) as a liberal use of free press and expression principles. The relatively modern Spanish legal system and constitution begins after the death of General Francisco Franco Bahamonde in 1975. After Franco's death and dictatorship, the constitution rapidly took shape with an election in 1977 and establishment of *Constituent Cortes* (National Parliament). On 6 December 1978, the Spanish Constitution was ratified. These swift three years of constitutional change were shaped by numerous actors but the most important are the *padres de la constitucion* (fathers of the constitution) representing the different autonomous regions of Spain. The fathers supposedly represent—at least symbolically—the political spectrum as well as autonomous region of Spain, and therefore the constitution is also the result of consensus building amongst political parties and autonomies of the time. The constitution, amongst other principles, ensures equality between citizens, and thus has secured the sex discrimination agenda of the early 2000s set by President Zapatero's government.

The Spanish constitution replaced Franco's complex *leyes fundamentals* with a simpler constitution based on popular sovereignty and the creation of bicameralist parliament: that is, a congress and senate. The constitution is influenced by Western European constitutions—predominantly West Germany and Italy (Villiers, 1999)—due in part to the reunification similarities but also Spain's distinct efforts to respect its own quasi-independent regions. The constitution is in stark contrast to the four decades of Franco's regime that had preceded it, and the constitutional character reflects the nation's shift to a more human rights-based approach. Principles such as gender equality, freedom of expression and political freedoms such as the right to form a political party and freedom of assembly echo the bad times of the past. Political freedoms, such as the right to form political parties and freedom of assembly rights have led to some problems; for example, the Basque region was not represented in the constitutional negotiations, and this ultimately led to separatist disputes, the ETA resurgence and deadliest period of killings from 1976 to 1980. This consensus-building regionalist approach to the constitution has also led to division within the legal system, which will be addressed later in the chapter. The structure of the constitution is complex; therefore, I will summarise only those elements that are important for the creation of legislation in the field of sex discrimination in advertising.

As a starting point, it was clear from 1976 that Spain wished to join the European Economic Community (EEC) (Wallace, 1976; Barbé, 2000) and therefore wished to aim for—and present itself as—a liberal democracy with a legal system that protects fundamental human rights, particularly the rights of women. Balfour and Quiroga (2007, pp. 122–123) have argued that the rewriting of the Spanish constitution was an opportunity—as with reunified Germany—to start afresh and provide a constitution that could heal old wounds and protects all citizens. This is certainly true on the surface: from constitution's preamble, there are principles on the protection of rule of law, human rights, rights of minorities and equality between men and women.[1] However, it was during the early years of Spain accession to the European Economic Community that the development of Spanish discrimination policy fully emerged. Since joining the EEC in 1986, Spain was fraught with EU supremacy issues due to the Spain's promise to protect and respect the autonomous regions of Spain (Juste & Sío-López, 2016). Therefore, the autonomous communities within Spain are another important element of the constitution and quirk of the Spanish legal system. This is a significant factor as the RyanAir test case for sex discrimination, the *reification* of women and their bodies in advertising took place in the regional court in Malaga, which receives autonomous protection. The autonomous regions and courts of Spain are the most intriguing and important factors of the country's constitution and political make-up (Villiers, 1999). Prior to the civil war in 1936, Spain recognised just three regions that had developed comprehensive forms of autonomy: the Basque, Cataluña and Galicia. Although Spain had operated as a unitary state for the previous 150 years, these regions were important post-Franco and received special attention due to the fact that the regime had crushed all notions of autonomy through suppression of cultural difference. Moreover, these regions suffered the most in terms of torture, murders and political persecution. The efforts by the founding fathers resulted in the creation of *Stado de las Autonomías* (state of autonomies), which is found in Article 2 of the constitution. This article seeks to balance unitary state "centralismo" and self-governance. As Villiers states, Spain is "a form of federalism characterised more by interdependence, concurrence or cooperation than by independence" (Villiers, p. 81). There are numerous problems with the *Stado de las Autonomías*—primarily (in)flexibility which has led to confusion and uncertainty over legal precedence—which is significant for the RyanAir test case, where the conflict seen hinged on whether or not federal legislation could be interpreted by a regional court (autonomous court). From a technical angle, the constitution does not provide a definition for what an autonomy means, nor what powers a region or what does not. The decentralised structure is also complex and often confusing: there are now 19 *autonomías* (including the autonomous cities), which provides for less cohesion but more importantly provides for political diversity. Article 137 of the constitution goes some way in explaining the principle of co-existence of legal systems and how the duality of state and region can operate. Since 1978, the legal system(s) have developed a parallel body of law: the regions and state co-exist with the constitution acting as a bond between the two. The *autonomías* can be considered as a "mini state" (Villiers, 1999) with its own president, government, administration and subsequently its own legal personality.

Therefore, one might perceive that the *autonomías* have their own legislative powers and character. However, the *autonomías* can be limited or even modified by *ley organicas* (substantive or fundamental laws) if a regional law is seen to be *ultra vires* or falling below the standard of national legislation. *Ley organicas* are central to the state powers held within the constitution and usually relate to laws surrounding fundamental rights or civil liberties. *Ley organicas* can be separated from *ley ordinaras* in that the former requires an absolute majority from congress members, whereas the latter requires just one-third of the vote.

11.3 Towards Gender Equality and the Politics of "La Nueva Via"

Spain under the Socialist Party (PSOE) progressed dramatically during the 2000s, particularly with gender equality legislation and policy. President Rodriguez Zapatero's government had adopted a similar position (*Nueva Via*) to Tony Blair and Bill Clinton's *third way* and ran the Socialist Party's election campaign on the promise to tackle the wider social justice issues of the day in exchange for neoliberal economic policy. Three main legislative aims were made clear in the party's manifesto: sex discrimination, gender-based violence and same-sex marriage. Zapatero's premiership (2004–2011) saw Spain enter a further stage of political integration into the EU or, as Kennedy states, the Socialist party were keen to embrace the political "modernization" and "Europeanization" of Spain (Kennedy, 2001). Zapatero was also keen to symbolically heal the wounds of the past too by removing the surviving Franco statues and establishing memorial commission to resolve the horrors of the "white terror" (Franco's mass killings, and the disappearance of thousands of women). The eradication of gender stereotypes in advertising is therefore merely part of the wider picture of legislation that was adopted under a gender equality reforms. Laws on employment rights, political and economic representation, and gender mainstreaming, same-sex marriage law including adoption rights, childcare and paternal leave law, gender identity and transgender rights were all enacted within the first parliamentary term.

11.4 The Gender Violence Act 2004

On 7 October 2004, Zapatero's socialist party had secured a strong majority of 320 votes from members across the political divide in the Spanish Congress to ensure his first piece of legislation as prime minister of Spain would enter the constitution. The full title of the legislation "Integrated Protection Measure Against Gender Violence" gives some indication of what the legislation entails; however, as the list of measures is vast, I will concentrate on providing analysis of significant elements. Firstly, contextualising this legislation is necessary to understand how the act became

Zapatero's first constitutional change but also paint a picture of the magnitude of the task.

There are numerous problems when discussing historical gender-based violence from a Spanish context. Firstly, due to the dictatorship, there is very little data or literature on the subject, and, secondly, due to censorship and cultural control, some of the stories that have been told since are either misunderstood or today deemed as political propaganda (Heras, 2006). What is certain is that women's position under the regime was one of persecution, forced labour, sexual violence and *las mujeres desaparecidas* "the missing women" (Mendiola Gonzalo, 2013). The civil war had brought feminism to Spain but life for women under Franco reverted to pre–civil war conditions: legislation influenced by Napoleons Civil Code positioned women as minors, prohibited contraception and divorce, and gender segregation in school and work was enforced (Davidson, 2011). In Franco's Spain, domestic violence was treated strictly a private sphere or a family matter, and, hence, post-Franco this traditional view remained despite early legislative attempts in the 1980s to combat gender-based violence. Because of this traditional view and the 40 years of a dictatorship that followed, there have been very few government policies, regulations or legislative measures to tackle the problem. According to the United Nations,[2] prior to accession to the EEC in 1986 Spain had adopted was just one preventive measure—the constitutional amendment of 1983 on equal opportunities at work. Various pieces of legislation have been passed in Spain but were nonetheless limited to outside the private sphere—victims of violent crimes Act 1995, EU directives such as the anti-trafficking law. Segregated education under Franco and the state educational programme *Formacion del Espiritu Nacional* (formation of the national spirit) produced essentialist binary ideals: men were trained for either the military, politics or hard labour and women for home life and motherhood. Therefore, the history of state-induced violence against women and the educational impetus to segregate sex in Spain influenced and shaped the political agenda of this period. The Socialist Party's motivation to combat gender-based violence and define the representation of women (i.e. in advertising) as a form of gender-based violence came as part of these rafts of measures. In addition to the stigma from the Franco era, the second influence for legislation was spike in the number of victims of gender-based violence in Spain during the 1990s and early 2000s. One particular case, of Ana Orantes, caused a public outcry when the 60-year-old was thrown off her balcony and set alight by her husband.

The Gender Violence Act was therefore a product of escalating intimate partner violence, increased public discourse and political parties' engagement with women's groups in Spain (Martin-Llaguno, 2016). The act covers numerous provisions that seek to tackle gender-based violence in Spain and establishes a new court *Juzgados de Violencia Sobre la Mujer* (Violence Against Women Court). Despite initially established as a criminal court to hear victims of violence cases, it has slowly mutated and now deals with civil and family cases. The act diverges from Spain's past in positioning gender violence as a public problem that all institutions must address through prevention, protection and sanction (Alberdi & Matas, 2002). As part of the drive to place responsibility on state institutions, the act places obligations upon advertisers and prohibits specific adverts in two broad ways: (a) the use of a woman's body (or part of it) that is detached from the advertised object ("reification") and (b) uses an image that portrays women in stereotyped behaviour(s). Within the act's preamble, this provision falls under the educational sphere; however, the main provision, Article 10, positions the prohibition of sexist advertising as a human dignity facet. The main provision is an amendment of Article 3(a) of the Advertising Act 34/1988, which now prohibits advertisements which "act against the dignity of persons or are contrary to the values and rights enshrined in the Constitution" such adverts shall depict "women in a degrading manner, either by directly using their bodies or parts of the same as a mere object unrelated to the product being promoted" or "associating their image to stereotyped roles antithetical to the principles of our law". The most significant and important element of the act is that it depicts sexist advertising as contributory to the violence referred to in the act.

As the Gender Violence Act is positioned as a fundamental right embedded within the constitution, the Spanish prohibition on certain advertising is divergent to most EU member state's notion of market-driven freedom of expression (i.e. self-regulation agencies, authorities and watchdogs) as it endorses the ban as a constitutional human right to dignity. The act also provides more powers for *Observatorio de la Imagen de las Mujeres*—Women's Image Observatory (OIM). The observatory was established in 1994, six years after the initial Advertising Act (34/1988) was implemented. The new powers provide that the OIM can advocate on behalf of the complainant. The act also included the launch of the National Advertising Plan whereby all public authorities must produce and promote information and awareness campaigns on how to raise a complaint under the legislation. Awareness programmes have been the most effective element in the implementation of the act. Through the work of women's groups and NGOs, protests and sit-ins have become regular occurrences in Spain. This dualistic approach—targeting the general public as well as the regulators—has led to the foregrounding of gender violence in public debate and vilification of sexist advertisements.

Women's groups, along with NGOs, were quick to identify the advert and co-ordinate small protests, but, most importantly, to film the sit-ins and share them on social media platforms. Aside from out-of-court settlements and protests, the act has provided a formal legal remedy. The RyanAir calendar case in 2014 was one of the first to be tested in the courts and has provided legal principles and tests.

11.5 The RyanAir Calendar Case

The origins of the RyanAir calendar case is in the UK. The calendar advertising campaign had previously run in most EU member states since 2008 and had caused controversy, in particular in the UK and Ireland. The calendar depicted female airhostesses in lingerie representing different countries for each calendar month. Some of the adverts that ran simultaneously with the campaign also featured airhostesses or models in lingerie and one advert depicting an adult model in school uniform. The advert prompted three responses in the UK: an online petition initiated by a RyanAir hostess, which received 11,000 signatures; an inquiry from the UK's Advertising Standards Authority (ASA), which received ten complaints; and an investigation by the UK's Office of Fair Trading (OFT). The advert campaign continued to run over the four years until it was investigated by the ASA.

Adverts linked to the calendar were subsequently banned in the UK by ASA in 2012. The case received attention from Spanish NGOs, which subsequently ignited public debate on misogynistic advertising, the links to domestic violence and how offending companies should be sanctioned. At the time of the UK ban, there was a spike in the number of general complaints made about sexist content to the Spanish advertising observatory (OIM). In November 2012, the RyanAir calendar was released and advertised across most EU member states both online and in print. In Spain, a women's group, Tyrius, and consumer group, Adecua, issued a joint formal complaint to OIM and requested a test case at the new Violence Against Women Court using the Gender Violence Act and

Advertising Act. The joint complainant's argument maintained that the advert contravened Article 3 of the act, which prohibits the "reification" of women, arguing that the women are positioned as "mere objects" with "no connection" between the image and product/service (air fare prices). The advert featured the slogan "Tarifas al rojo vivo. ¡Y la tripulación!" ("The tariffs are red hot and so are the crew!"), which the complainant argued as misogynistic and carried clear sexual connotations.

In the judgement, the court agreed that the advert reified women by positioning the stewardesses in "clear sexual invitation". The court also agreed with the juxtaposition argument made by the complainant, that the stewardesses had "absolutely no connection whatsoever" with the product or service. The use of a female body was deemed artificial, and the calendar was used as a tool to website traffic. Most importantly, the court indicated that although it was apparent that the average citizen would not be offended by women in bikinis, they might be dismayed to see the reification, the juxtaposition and the dignity of women under attack. As the women in the RyanAir advert were reduced to objects to attract attention, regardless of the content of the adverts' content, the court condemned the airline and asked for the removal of the advert from the website and online advertising. The significance of the complainant's "reification" argument is important when compared to the earlier decision made by the ASA in the UK and shows how the significance of the term anchored within the Gender Violence Act. In the UK, the SRO (ASA) sanctioned a pause in sales of the calendar and banned the advert merely being "offensive" and the "stance and gaze" of the models sexually suggestive.

11.6 Self-Regulation

Autocontrol, the self-regulatory body of Spain, supplements the Gender Violence Act in tackling sexist content and eradicating gender stereotypes. Autocontrol operates in a similar way to most European SROs—an industry regulating itself. It emerged at a time of satellite TV, cross-border broadcasting and the Court of Justice of the European Union's attempt to regulate the market as well as freedom of expression case law in the European Court of Human Rights. A product of the Advertising Act of (1988), it was established in 1997 as an independent organisation that loosely follows both the International Chamber of Commerce's ethical standards of advertising and European Advertising Standards Alliance[3] but was set up to fill in the gaps left by the Advertising Act. Article 10 of SRO code provides specific remedies for the sexualisation of women and adverts that use outdated gender stereotypes to sell a product. Autocontrol is bolstered by the Gender Violence Act, and consequently has numerous ongoing cases on the reification of women and gender stereotypes in advertising. Autocontrol's jury is quasi-independent of the SRO, and is made up of industry insiders: broadcasters, advertisers and media regulators but not lawyers. The jury reaches a decision based on the SRO's ethical framework, but it may also wish consult further industry-based regulators such as the beer and spirits advertising regulatory bodies. Although there are numerous individual advertising agencies attached to various industries, the current trend indicates that the majority of complainants are passed over to Autocontrol. If an advert is deemed to have breached the either the SRO code or Advertising Act, the advertiser is asked to modify or terminate the advert. The RyanAir case therefore highlights the involvement of NGOs and outsider organisations in this process, in particular OIM, one of the largest organisations and now runs parallel to Autocontrol, and however, watchdogs such as Siamura[4] are also filling the void. The industry-led jury, the NGOs and women's organisations very much reflect the *quis custodiet ipsos costodes* approach to self-regulation.

The most significant facet of Autocontrol is the non-binding pre-screening provision, Copy Advice that assesses an advert's suitability prior to its production and distribution. Unlike other SROs, Copy Advice therefore acts as a quasi-guarantee that the advert will at least not fall foul of the legislation or regulatory code. At the time of the RyanAir case, Copy Advice published its first Women's report with 0.24% of consultations resulting in a breach of the ethical code or what may be deemed as reification of women. Of this, 43% were related to the "dignity" of women and 37% to the juxtaposition of women's body, and 20% involved outdated gender stereotypes. Despite this pre-screening advice centre, the actions are limited to advisory role and numerous companies pursue with their advertising campaign irrespective of the advice. Moreover, the advice can cynically be deployed by advertisers as a defence when an advert receives complaints.[5] The Autocontrol division of the Spanish regulatory system has in the recent years come under fire for failing to raise awareness about its powers as an SRO. Autocontrol also has a public image and legitimacy problem with frequent relaunches; in particular, in 2010 the SRO received heavy criticism from the European Commission as it failed to meet the expected targets from the Roadmap to Equality Programme.

11.7 Austerity, Sexual Violence and Femicide

Since the Gender Violence Act, Spain witnessed radical economic, political and social change which unfortunately placed gender equality concerns firmly on the backburner. The fallout of the Madrid terrorist attacks in 2004 followed by the 2007 economic crisis pushed Zapatero's government's wider raft of social reform to the side and was replaced by tighter security measure, austerity and cuts to public services. In 2008, conservative opposition leader Mariano Rajoy enjoyed the support of Nicolas Sarkozy and Angela Merkel, and by the end of the decade, the PSOE were all but replaced by Spanish conservativism. In 2011, Spain had one of the highest unemployment rates in the EU, and the general election was won by Rajoy's promise to decrease the deficit, increase employment rates and deliver educational reform. Gender equality reform switched to regression, particularly abortion rights and cuts to women's key services. Although there is no clear correlation between austerity and femicide in Spain, there has been a sharp rise in deaths and a general increase in the number of reported domestic violence cases. Arroyo and Coronas (2017) have highlighted that in certain autonomous regions femicide and domestic violence have fallen. However, the recent Pamplona gang rape case in 2019 has reignited the call from campaigners and NGOs to increase budgets and secure changes to the Gender Violence Act.

Amendments to the Gender Violence Act do affect the advertising section, and irrespective of RyanAir Calendar test case there appears to be little progress in tackling sexist advertising in Spain. The core problem lays in the foundations of the act—namely, the legal ambiguity of the terms "reification" and "gender stereotypes" which have hampered attempts to bring an action as well as the application of law (Martin-Llaguno, 2016). Despite numerous training programmes and public awareness campaigns set up by Autocontrol, there has been little guidance on what is meant by the terms covered in the act: "reification", "sexualisation" and "gender stereotypes". Beltrá and Martin-Llaguno (2012) argue that precedent has been set on the definition of objectification and sexualisation in advertising by the work of Autocontrol and its decisions since 2010. However, neither Congress, the Gender Violence Act or Autocontrol have yet to provide separate explicit and unequivocal guidance on how the terms in advertising should be interpreted by the courts (González, 2008). According to Llaguno, the act's application is inadequate: if it is applied broadly, it will inevitably catch all forms of gender stereotypes that may or may not appear sexist—if applied narrowly, then advertisers are at liberty to breach both the act and the SROs code. The same criticisms of the gender violence therefore apply to Autocontrol. The lax and vague definitions of reification, sexualisation and gender stereotypes are problematic, and the case law of Autocontrol rarely develops these terms. The monitoring of the case law of the SRO has shown that the jury often overcomplicate the definitions (e.g. reification), which leads to confusion in the decisions. The most problematic definition with Autocontrol and the RyanAir case seems to be the broader term of gender stereotypes. Tato Plazo (2006, p. 5) argues that the code should strike down gender stereotypes if the gender representation is found to be playing a role traditionally associated with women such as cooking, caring and cleaning. The untangling of the definition of gender stereotype is slowly changing through the case law of Autocontrol and the Cillit Bang case is a good example of the problems with the act and Autocontrol's lack of guidance on sexist content, lack of scope for online content and issues surrounding the pre-screening legal team within Copy Advice.

11.8 Cillit Bang Case

In 2015, Cillit Bang produced an advertising campaign depicting 32 women discussing their cleaning experiences via the use "vlogging". Of all 32 of the vlogs, not one featured a man using the cleaning products. Using the Gender Violence Act in conjunction with the Autocontrol Code, Consumidores en Red challenged the advertiser based on the following: (i) the adverts exclusion of men performing cleaning chores and using the product; and (ii) using outdated stereotypes that portray women as cleaners and carers ("with the new thicker foam, you wipe the washcloth and see how clean and shiny. And it lasts for days and days. With Cillit Bang, I can spend more time with the kids"). In its ruling, Autocontrol agreed with the claimant and stated that the lack of men in the advertisement provided a clear breach of Autocontrol code and that the advert featured outdated "stereotypical behaviours with a clear allocation of role by gender". Autocontrol specifically highlighted two elements that had led to the breach of the code: firstly, the advert campaign (of three separate adverts) each featured exclusively women; secondly, all the advertisements had common characteristics, a collage of photographs of the alleged product users (all of them women) and a voice-over of one of the users explaining how to use the product; finally, during the closure of the advert a woman's voice says, "Try it and tell us yourself!".

The advertisers' defence to the complaint was that despite the advert featuring only women, it did not position women as inferior, and the cleaning products are mainly bought by women. This last factor is quantified by multiple online surveys, questionnaires and focus groups collated by the advertising company. Cillit Bang also gained the clearance of Autocontrol's pre-screening service, Copy Advice. Cillit Bang's argument was rejected, and the advert subsequently banned. The significance of this case is partly in Reckitt's marketing research and its defence that the advertisement is a reflection of Spanish society. Cillit Bang's argument is that it neither reifies/objectifies women, and because it reflects Spanish women's everyday lived experience of cleaning and caring, there is no harm offence caused as the portrayal of women in the advert emulates a housewife's daily routine and is therefore not an outdated stereotype.

11.9 Conclusion

This chapter has set out the ways in which Spain regulates gender stereotypes and misogyny in advertising and does so through the prism of violence against the woman legislation. The Gender Violence Act (2004) identifies the corelation of stereotypes and violence by including a section specifically on prohibiting sexist content in advertising. Unlike most EU member states that rely on predominantly on SROs and regulatory codes, the Gender Violence Act provides a statutory definitions of gender stereotypes by prohibiting adverts that either use a woman's body when it is detached from the advertised product (reification) or when an image of a woman is used in relation to stereotypical behaviour. The statutory inclusion of reification attempts to reduce legal ambiguity and provides Spain's SRO "Autocontrol" with extra scope to extend its reach. The two test cases have provided some much-needed indication as to how the definition might be interpreted by the SRO jury in future cases. The RyanAir case provided substance to the reification test whereby women were portrayed as detached "objects" with "little or no connection" to the product and service offered. Similarly, the Cillit Bang case highlights how women are exclusively represented as in charge of housework chores and cleaning, thus contributing to perpetuating to gender stereotypes and role assignment. To obtain material gender equality, the Gender Violence Act has sought to show the links between media representations of women and gender-based violence. The inclusion of sexist advertising in the act is a symbolic one, and the subsequent precedent set by the two test cases indicates how the Spanish approach substantiates the links between representation and violence against women. The inclusion also has a symbolic role in guiding Autocontrol and the ways in which the SRO tackles gender stereotypes in advertising, moving beyond the language from "soft" regulatory codes towards a more substantive approach.

Notes

1. Section 14 provides for equality between men and women, and Sect. 35 provides for non-discrimination in the workplace and Section.
2. United Nations Global Database on Violence Against Women (Spain) http://evaw-global-database.unwomen.org/en/countries/europe/spain.
3. The ICC along with the EASA provide basic principles and guidance for regulators. Articles 2 and 3 of the ICC code cover social responsibility and decency. https://iccwbo.org/ (accessed 3 May 2021) The EASA code ensures that advertising should be "legal decent, honest and truthful [and] prepared with a due sense of social responsibility". https://www.easa-alliance.org/ (accessed 3 May 2021).
4. Siamura is primarily a Spanish advertising observatory collating evidence and complaints against advertising with sexist content. See http://siamura.eu (accessed 21 April 2021).
5. RyanAir sought advice from Copy Advice prior to their campaign. As the company has a history of complaints, the Spanish SRO asked the company to seek advice prior to the campaign. The advice was later used as a defence in the RyanAir calendar case.

References

Alberdi, I., & Matas, N. (2002). *La violencia doméstica: informe sobre los malos tratos a mujeres en España*. Fundación La Caixa.

Arroyo, A., & Coronas, C. (2017). Intimate Partner Violence in Spain: Medical and Legal Aspects. *GSL Journal of Forensic Research, 1*, 103.

Balfour, S., & Quiroga, A. (2007). *The Reinvention of Spain: Nation and Identity Since Democracy*. Oxford University Press.

Barbé, E. (2000). Spain and CFSP: The Emergence of a 'Major Player'? *Mediterranean Politics, 5*(2), 44–63.

Beltrá, & Martin-Llaguno, M. M. (2012). A Systematic Review of Gender and Advertising Studies. *Catalan Journal of Communication & Cultural Studies, 4*(2), 171–183.

Cubells, J., & Calsamiglia, A. (2018). Do We See Victims' Agency? Criminal Justice and Gender Violence in Spain. *Critical Criminology, 26*(1), 107–127.

Davidson, J. (2011). Women, Fascism and Work in Francoist Spain: The Law for Political, Professional and Labour Rights. *Gender & History, 23*(2), 401–414.

González, R. (2008). Aportaciones de la Ley de medidas contra la violencia de género a la prohibición de publicidad discriminatoria. *Revista de derecho de la competencia y la distribución, 2*, 145–160.

Gonzalo, F. M. (2013). Forced Labor, Public Policies, and Business Strategies During Franco's Dictatorship: An Interim Report. *Enterprise & Society, 14*(1), 182–213.

Heras, M. O. (2006). Mujer y dictadura franquista. *Aposta. Revista de Ciencias Sociales, 28*, 1–26.

Juste and Sío-López. (2016, July 8). *Spain and the European Integration Process.* https://www.cvce.eu/content/publication/2010/5/11/bf91b328-fbed-4a65-9a3b-eadc21a7e831/publishable_en.pdf

Kennedy, P. (2001). Spain's 'Third Way'?: The Spanish Socialist Party's Utilization of European Integration. *Journal of Southern Europe and the Balkans, 3*(1), 49–59.

Lopez-Zafra, E., & Garcia-Retamero, R. (2021). Are Gender Stereotypes Changing Over Time? A Cross-Temporal Analysis of Perceptions About Gender Stereotypes in Spain. *International Journal of Social Psychology, 36*(2), 330–354.

Martin-Llaguno, M. (2016). Regulating Sexist Advertising in Spain. In M. Edström, A. T. Kenyon, & E. Svensson (Eds.), *Blurring the Lines: Market Driven and Democracy Driven Freedom of Expression.* Nordicom.

Roberts, S. G., & Sharman, A. (2013). *Echoes: The Cadiz Constitution in Hispanic History, Culture and Politics* (p. 394). Cambridge Scholars Publishing.

Svensson, E. M., & Edström, M. (2016). Market-Driven Challenges to Freedom of Expression and the Interaction Between the State, the Market, and the Media. *Nordicom Review, 37*(2).

Tato Plazo, A. (2006). Violencia de género y publicidad (Gender Violence and Advertising). *Revista Autocontrol, 107*, 1–6.

Villiers, C. (1999). *The Spanish Legal Tradition: An Introduction to the Spanish Law and Legal System* (pp. 8–9).

Wallace, W. (1976). Wider but Weaker: The Continued Enlargement of the EEC. *The World Today, 32*(3), 104–111.

CHAPTER 12

Conclusion

Gizem Guney, Po-Han Lee, and David Davies

12.1 Introduction

This book started off its analysis with the promise of finding out whether states, which were handled by the contributors, present similarities or differences in the way that they fail in achieving gender equality. As demonstrated in each chapter, the states have taken progressive measures in addressing gender inequality over the last few decades, yet challenges and backlashes remain. Discriminatory legal practices and social norms are still pervasive; women and sexual and gender minorities continue to face unequal treatment, prejudice and violence. On this final note, by drawing upon the case studies presented in each chapter, we aim to bring together the patterns that the states present in how and why they fail in achieving

G. Guney (✉)
University of Portsmouth, Portsmouth, UK
e-mail: Gizem.Guney@port.ac.uk

P.-H. Lee
National Taiwan University, Taipei, Taiwan
e-mail: PoHanLee@ntu.edu.tw

D. Davies
University of Sussex, Brighton, UK
e-mail: D.Davies@sussex.ac.uk

G. Guney et al. (eds.), *Towards Gender Equality in Law*,
https://doi.org/10.1007/978-3-030-98072-6_12

gender equality. We observe that there are four overarching reasons why the states studied in this book fall short in bringing justice to gendered matters: (1) the states' tolerance of friction and ambiguity in laws, (2) the states' inertia in fully pursuing a human rights-based approach, (3) the states' oversight of intersecting marginalisation of women as well as sexual and gender minorities and (4) the states' problematic approaches towards gender-based violence. Each of these themes will be discussed in turn below.

12.2 Understanding State Failures: Friction and Ambiguity in Laws

12.2.1 Friction Within Laws

One of the most prominent findings that this book repeatedly reached is that the friction within the normative systems of the state plays a significant role in states' failure in achieving gender equality. The friction that we call here, and that can also be identified as disharmony, discord or inconsistency within the law, presented itself in mainly two forms throughout the book. The first form of friction is the one where national laws are not synchronised at subnational, regional and local levels. Eskelinen's analysis of Chinese land law and Davies' analysis of gender equality guarantees of Spanish constitutional law clearly illustrated such incompatibility between the national and subnational planes. The second form of friction is the one where laws that promise gender equality are present alongside the laws and policies that pose a threat to gender equality at the same time in the same jurisdiction. Guney's chapter on Turkey's implementation of the Istanbul Convention and Love's analysis of the UK's legal framework on the parenthood of trans men demonstrated reflections of this type of friction, and we will unpack the particularities of these cases below.

With regards to the first form of friction, Eskelinen's chapter has been illustrative of the incompatibilities of law between national and local levels. She demonstrated that there are national laws in China in line with the government's international commitment to women's rights and eliminating socio-economic inequalities suffered by Chinese women, especially those in rural areas. At the local level, however, state agencies have been reluctant and ambivalent in implementing these laws. The main cause of this failure in implementing national laws is that gendered social norms and local customs in rural counties are preserved by governmental agencies and village councils in China. Eskelinen demonstrates that these norms and customs are embodied through local and family practices that deprive rural women of land contractual rights and land operation rights. These women's precarious situation has been aggravated by the *hukou* (household registration) system in China (Liu, 2005), which institutionalises gender stereotypes against women, including those about wives, daughters, divorced women and widows.

In a similar vein, Davies' chapter demonstrates that in the decentralised state of Spain the creation of *Stado de las Autonomías* (state of autonomies) with their own legislative character and competence has led to confusion and uncertainty over legal precedence on matters including gender-related laws. This tension between federal and autonomous states' laws is observed in RyanAir calendar case, which questioned the legality of gender stereotypes in Rynair advertisement campaigns. The case was taken to a Spanish regional court in Malaga to apply the progressive definition of gender stereotypes from the Gender Violence Act (2004). The conflict here was that the Gender Violence Act (2004) was a national law, and yet the applicants took the case to a regional court. This raised the question regarding whether or not the court in Malaga could interpret national legislation, such as the measures within the Gender Violence Act (2004). In the end, the court's jurisdiction over the Gender Violence Act was confirmed, and the act was successfully applied to the case, where the court decided that RyanAir was in violation of the act. Although, the tension was resolved on behalf of women through a progressive reading of gender stereotypes and sexism in advertisement on the grounds of the Gender Violence Act in the end, this case still illustrated how the distinction between national and regional (or local) laws and practices can raise confusion over jurisdiction on gender-related matters.

The second form of friction within the normative systems is when oxymoronic policies and laws that are adopted simultaneously by states. This book provided insight in these instances in both Turkish and the British contexts. With regards to Turkey, Guney's chapter revealed that, in implementing the Istanbul Convention, Turkey has been taking a twofold approach in addressing gender inequality which fundamentally contradicts with one other. She argued that the 6284 Law (2014), which was enacted following the ratification of the Istanbul Convention, brought effective measures in the special context of gender-based violence against women by taking a woman-centred approach, granting legal protection to women on an equal status regardless of their marital status, and ensuring a wide range of civil measures, such as prevention and protection orders. In particular, civil measures were broadened to the extent that the monitoring body of the Istanbul Convention (GREVIO) expressed its appreciation on this matter in its country report to Turkey. Although this law was promising in challenging violence on many fronts, Guney demonstrated that the Turkish government, at the same time, took controversial political and legal initiatives that seriously endanger women's equal status in society. These included the statements of high-level representatives of the Turkish government on limiting women's behaviour in the public sphere, diminishing women's social role to only motherhood as well as legal attempts to re-criminalise adultery and prohibit abortion. This presented a clear portrayal of Turkey's twofold approach where gender equality is simultaneously promoted and yet threatened at the same time.

On the other hand, Love's chapter, analysing *repronormativity* and how it is embedded in English law, presented a picture which can be interpreted as a form of contradiction in a similar vein to the one in Turkey. In Love's chapter, we heard about the story of Freddy McConnell, a trans man who gave birth to his son and wanted to be registered as the child's father. His request was rejected by the General Register Office, and later this decision was upheld by the high court on the ground that the term "mother" is the "status offered to a person who undergoes the physical (…) process of carrying a pregnancy and giving birth" with reference to the Human Fertilisation and Embryology Act (HFEA) (2008).

The McConnell case presents two distinct approaches in the UK that are inherently contradictory in achieving gender equality. On the one hand, it becomes clear in this case that the law legally recognises McConnell as a man, and this is not debatable. Indeed, McConnell's legal gender identity is that of a man, as per the Gender Recognition Act (2004), which allows people to change their legal gender. Although this law has been subject to criticism on numerous grounds, particularly due to the medical evidence that it requires, this legislation is still a significant achievement for transgender rights in the UK. This law is undeniably progressive and is a huge step towards gender equality, considering that there is no such right given to transgender people who experience gender dysphoria in many countries. Yet, on the other hand—via the McConnell case—the UK fails to marry the legal gender and the parenthood status by explicitly rejecting the possibility of registering McConnell as a "parent" in the birth certificate. This presents a bizarre discrepancy in the UK, where, on the one hand, the social gender is recognised and legalised (via the Gender

Recognition Act (2004)) and on the other hand, as noted by Love, it is entirely disregarded in the context of parenthood (via the Human Fertilisation and Embryology Act (HFEA) (2008)) through a biological view that sees parenthood as being exclusively defined as a physical/reproductive experience.

These two chapters are indicative of the fact that complex, and sometimes contradictory, laws and policies exist in a country simultaneously and symbiotically. This also reminds us that law, as a body of norms and authority, is not always a coherent entity in itself, and it could exist and survive with its inconsistencies. In terms of gender equality, certain positive developments in law do not guarantee the departure of negative laws, policies and administrative practices. Guney and Love's chapters therefore remind us of the need to evaluate gender laws and policies not on a strict case-by-case basis, but from a holistic point of view.

12.2.2 *Ambiguity of Law*

In addition to the frictions or inconsistencies within law and policy, this book demonstrated the challenges that the ambiguity of law poses to gender equality. Throughout the book, we observed that although there are laws in place to promote gender equality, the ambiguity of legal terms, namely legal loopholes, creates a space for the enforcers and practitioners to interpret these laws otherwise. It was seen that these legal loopholes were often filled with ideologies and practices that threaten gender equality, disregarding the original intentions of laws.

Two particular chapters were illustrative of these ambiguities. Davies' chapter demonstrated that although the Gender Violence Act (2004) of Spain is a proactive piece of legislation through its strong measures against gender stereotypes in advertisements, the ambiguity of the terms it encompasses constitutes a problem for its effective implementation. In fact, he underlined that reification, sexualisation and gender stereotypes have lax and vague definitions, and Autocontrol, the advertising self-regulatory body, does little to develop clear definitions for these terms. The courts and Autocontrol therefore fall into a conundrum in applying the law: if these terms are applied too broadly, then courts face the risk of catching all forms of gender stereotypes that may or may not be sexist, misogynistic or harmful, and yet, if applied too narrowly, advertisements may not be caught at all.

Another example of this ambiguity can be observed in Grosso's chapter. She showed us that with legal reforms Tunisia has aimed to address the inequality between wives and husbands in the divorce proceedings. Despite all of these positive developments in law, Grosso revealed that when the laws had ambiguity in defining the harm that the individuals experienced, the courts and judges filled in the legislative gaps by facilitating and safeguarding traditional gender norms in practice. As a matter of fact, the judges have implied that these cases represent not merely legal but also moral and social judgements that involve "ethical work"—an invisible function of judicial settlement of family disputes—in order to maintain social and familial stability. In other words, the obscurity of law enabled the judges to hold up "moral work" against the interests of women that are involved in the divorce proceedings. We should be reminded that although legal ambiguity has prevented the law from realising its full promise for gender justice in the case of Tunisia, as Moscati (2020) notes, it can also be used to promote social change, all at the discretion of the interpreters of law. However, the absence of clear definition of concepts and terminologies is also where arbitrariness of legal practices arises. Therefore, the clarity of laws within the law-making process is essential to prevent forms of potential interpretational problems which would negate the positive intentions of law with regards to gender equality.

12.3 Human Rights-Based Approach to Gender Equality: Where Do States Fail?

The advantages of a human rights-based approach to tackling gender inequality have been studied and discussed extensively. Some of the most apparent positive implications of a human rights-based approach include that the state responsibility for addressing gender inequalities would be reinstated, and, in turn, the rights-holders would possess a stronger hand for their claims. Beyond these benefits, a human rights-based approach could be vital to addressing the problems presented in the previous section—namely, to address inconsistencies in laws and legal practices between national and subnational levels, reform problematic laws that are in force, and interpret vague laws to the best interests of women. This is because a human rights-based approach proposes a holistic and unified perspective and guideline on women's equality and rights, and, therefore, the problems mentioned above can be addressed in the light of the international human rights norms, principles and standards regarding gender equality.

Despite these advantages, states rarely effectively fulfil this approach. This book detected three main reasons for states' failure in successfully implementing a human rights approach towards gender equality, and these are the utilisation of religion and culture as a ground of justification for sacrificing gender rights, states' failure in striking a fair balance between competing rights, and the lack of rights consciousness among citizens. To be more precise, the problems include (i) states relying on the so-called culture, tradition and religion to promote gender policies that are fundamentally discriminatory, (ii) states failing to respond to the competition between rights by tolerating violence against the powerless and (iii) states only paying lip service to human rights without promoting the understanding of human rights at a public level. In fact, various states that are scrutinised in this book are found out to experience, sometimes even to facilitate these problems, and we will reiterate the links between these states below.

Starting with culture defence, it is not strange to learn that states often invoke religious and traditional norms to legitimise the making (or unmaking) of law and policy, particularly regarding the status and rights of women and minority groups. As shown in Guney's chapter, for example, the Turkish government and ministers have referred to the nation's traditional cultural values to justify the limitations set to women's enjoyment of equal status and rights, in the context of implementing the Istanbul Convention. In fact, the Committee on the Elimination of Discrimination against Women (CEDAW, 2016) has expressed its concern about this development regarding Turkey's state report, stating that "high-level representatives of government have, on several occasions, made discriminatory and demeaning statements about women who do not adhere to traditional roles" (para. 28). In her analysis, Guney demonstrates the way in which religious or traditional norms are made into legal instruments—beyond merely social and symbolic tools—despite the fact that secularity is one of the constitutional principles in Turkey (Art 2 of Turkish Constitution).

On the other hand, Rashid and Rashid's chapter demonstrated how the religious and cultural position of the governing powers in Pakistan had a significant impact on policies regarding the status and rights of sexual and gender minorities throughout history. They demonstrated that during the Islamic rule *hijras* and *khawaja siras* enjoyed better social status and legal protection. Yet, this declined dramatically under the British colonial rule, which defined transgender persons as "immoral" and "most shameless and abominable", as culminated in the Criminal Tribes Act (1871) and the Dramatic Performance Act (1876). These colonial laws have changed social norms permanently, even after the partition and in the postcolonial era. Sexual and gender minority persons have thus been suffering such a colonial legacy, which justifies their disenfranchisement and the lack of social acceptability as contrary to the Islamic teaching. As a result, we once again see religion and cultural norms acting as state tools and having a direct impact on the laws and policies on the rights of sexual and gender minority communities.

Rashid and Rashid's analysis also makes a strong case for "postcolonial" critique of transgender rights, by reminding us that sodomy laws criminalising homosexuality exist in many former British colonies, and Pakistan is one of them. The criminalisation of homosexuality with the long-standing effect of British colonialism challenges the presumption that Western liberal values are inherently supportive of gender equality. This also brings into doubt of the so-called *universalism* of human rights which were fundamentally established on Western liberal values (Mende, 2021).

Overall, both Guney's and Rashid and Rashid's chapters are a reminder of the infusion of religion into state laws and policies with regards to gender equality in an explicit or implicit manner. It should also be underlined that in cases of both Turkey and Pakistan, the so-called religious and traditional norms are invoked to limit rather than improve the rights of women and sexual and gender minority members. This also affirms the suspicious approach towards culture claims overall. As noted by Choudhury (2008), culture is almost always invoked and defined by the elites of societies and power holders (who are mostly cisgender, heterosexual men), and thus preserves and promotes existing power structures, dynamics and status quo.

In addition to the culture threat to the universal application of the right to gender equality, the second problem presents that the rights can compete and contradict with one another. To be more precise, guaranteeing an individual or a group's right to equality may interfere with the other rights of different groups. Juggling competing rights stifles legal reform and sometimes leads to inaction. Both Neller's and Davies' chapters demonstrate that the UK and Spain have an obligation on the one hand to uphold gender equality as a fundamental right and yet on the other to also safeguard freedom of expression. In Davies' case, he argues that, unlike most EU member states, Spain has underscored the regulation and illegality of gender stereotypes in advertising by limiting the neoliberal and market-oriented version of freedom of expression in favour of gender equality. In Neller's analysis of hate crime legislation in the UK, however, we observed that women's equality—who suffer from intersecting forms of discrimination—is often sacrificed for the sake of freedom of expression.

There are different approaches towards alleviating the tension between right to equality and freedom of expression. Two decades ago, Bunch (1990) reiterated that human rights are not primarily about civil and political rights (such as the freedom of expression). She noted that granting civil and political liberties with superiority over the other rights would not only constitute a narrow understanding of rights but also ultimately impede consideration of women's rights. In emphasising how gender equality is as important as the so-called first-generation civil rights are, she stated:

> Sex discrimination kills women daily. When combined with race, class, and other forms of oppression, [sex discrimination] constitutes a deadly denial of women's right to life and liberty on a large scale throughout the world. (Bunch, 1990, p. 489)

However, this view which does not supersede civil rights (such as freedom of expression) over equality rights is not shared across every state and every jurisdiction. For example, as Boyle (2001, p. 494)) noted in his analysis of hate speech, "Unlike many other states the US courts to give a higher weight to speech than to the counterbalancing interests", including the protection of others, that is, women. Ultimately, questions over which right trumps the other depends on the political philosophy of that which the normative system is withholding. In a Western-oriented liberal approach such as the US, civil rights are often prioritised over the equality rights, whereas in other jurisdictions (such as South Africa) the constitutions may grant a vast scope to equality rights and guarantees. Within the scope of this book, which focuses on gender equality, we find it useful to note that, as reiterated by Edström and Svensson (2014), gender equality is not any less fundamental for a democratic society compared to freedom of expression, and this is confirmed by the Council of Europe, which considers "democracy and gender equality to be interdependent and mutually reinforcing" (2014, p. 483).[1]

The third problem regarding effective implementation of the human rights-based approach is that more often than not states fail to raise awareness about human rights and promote local rights consciousness in civil society. Awareness-raising campaigns are no less significant than legally available rights. The legal rights lose their practicality and therefore their potential for social change, without the knowledge about them. In Frańczak's chapter, when discussing the challenges against realisation of women's rights, she reminds us of the urgent need for raising awareness to tackle gender stereotypes. She argues that the absence of related educational programmes indicates the state's reluctance to fulfil its commitment to creating the context for gender equality. That is, the lack of campaigns and training has become a central concern regarding the states' failures to promote gender equality.

Similarly, Lukera's chapter shed some light on the everyday lived experiences of sex workers and the problems they encounter in Kenya. The magnitude of issues the sex workers face day-to-day manifest from the wilful lack of human rights knowledge amongst law enforcers and community leaders. Similarly, Davies' chapter demonstrated that this need was also imagined in Spain's Gender Violence Act, which requires all public authorities (beyond just advertisements) to provide awareness campaigns on sexist components of advertising, targeting both the regulators and the public. Altogether, these chapters imply that the law's moral legitimacy lies in law enforcers' efforts and consciousness to promote an understanding of the human rights among the rights holders. As Hintjens (2008) remarks, support for awareness-building is important for human rights protection to an extent that the absence or existence of such indicates the genuineness of a state in its commitment to ensuring gender equality.

12.4 Feminist Thought and Lives of "Others": Intersectionality and Gender Binarism

When it came to drawing out the themes and frameworks for this book, it was palpable that we should identify intersectionality and the exclusory rights of LGBTQI people and other sexual and gender minorities as core refrains. By this we mean that we saw a common thread running throughout the chapters—that despite a state's best efforts to bring about positive gender equality legislation, it often overlooked, misunderstood or forgot the intersecting lives of "others" whilst drafting or implementing law and policy. The two prevailing themes of intersectionality and LGBTQI rights that make up for this omission are apparent in segments of the book. In applying an intersectional lens, Neller's, Winstone's and Frańczak's chapters invite us to consider the power dynamics between multiple co-existing identities and the connected systems that oppress (Romero, 2017). In order to understand how law is projected on to transgender identities, Rashid and Rashid along with Love call for the law to continually adapt to the changing social, political, cultural and linguistic attitudes.

Whilst reflecting upon these themes, we can see the application of intersectionality within Winstone's chapter when she considers the lack of retention and progression of women solicitors in England and Wales. When reflecting upon the co-existing identities that occur within the legal sector, Winstone specifically identifies those women who are often absent, namely Black, Asian and minority ethnic (BAME) and working-class practitioners. This problem has been tangible for the last two decades in England and Wales (Sommerlad, 2002), with the lack of progression and retention only being confronted relatively recently (Davies, 2018; Aulack et al., 2017). Winstone's response is to apply a *practical intersectional socio-legal* approach to the problem that endeavours pragmatic solutions within the workplace: flexible working, job shares, career breaks and "returnships". Solutions to the gaps in the legal sector are frequently grounded on intersectionality, which is perhaps where legislation such as the Equality Act (2010) is lacking. An institution, such as the legal profession, that is dominated by white, male, middle-class, cisgender practitioners is a stark reminder of the chasm between substantive equality such as that imagined in the Equality Act and the lived experience of women within that sector.

In Neller's chapter, we can equally disseminate how intersectionality has been overlooked or forgotten in the drafting of hate crime legislation in England and Wales and the gap between "law in books" and the lived experience of women when they are victims of hate crime. In her chapter, Neller identifies how the UK parliamentary debate neglects the intersection of gender with other categories, notably sexual orientation and race, when formulating hate speech legislation. In this sense, legislators ought to recognise the intersections and malleability of gender if they are to produce "good" and meaningful law. An intersectional understanding of hate crime has long been called for (Mason-Bish, 2014) as has been the need to circumvent the often-hierarchical and the "silo" effect of hate crime categorisations (Mason-Bish, 2014; Chakraborti & Garland 2012; Neller, 2018).

Likewise, Frańczak's chapter indicates the omission of women of colour, women living in poverty, migrant women and non-binary persons when drafting international legalisation that aims to eradicate gender stereotypes (CEDAW, Beijing Platform et al.). Overlooking these intersections has led the law astray and exposed it to liberal feminist approaches that inevitably (re)produce and (re)enforce stereotypes (Cook & Cusack, 2010). By challenging the status quo of universality of women's experience, Frańczak argues that without accepting that gender intersects with other forms of discrimination, the construction of anti-stereotyping laws will inevitably replicate stagnant stereotypes by representing the dominant and "valid" experiences of women.

Applying an intersectional lens quickly reveals fissures in the drafting process and implementation of legislation; it can also reveal how interconnected systems and institutions oppress. For example, in both Love's and Frańczak's chapters, heteropatriarchy shapes and codifies laws relating to transgender identity and gender stereotypes rendering the law as reductive and based on gender binarism. In Neller's chapter, we encounter the same institutional limitations and blind spots: "whiteness" as the standard (racial privilege), thus hindering the progress of hate crime legalisation protecting Muslim women. Across the chapters, it is evident that debates surrounding gender equality quickly become fixed in traditional gender binarism with the legislative process overlooking the rights, voice and experience of LGBTQI persons. What is more is the lack of proper recognition, respect and dignity of transgender persons in legislation; with non-binary identities often misunderstood, forgotten or overlooked in the legislative process. This manifests in the lack of the pronoun "they" in Pakistan's laws on transgender people, as seen in Rashid and Rashid's chapter, and the legal right to father a child, as seen in in Love's chapter. This is of course a very concerning prospect as law is habitually a reference point for which marginalised groups look towards when it comes to non-discrimination and equality claims.

In Love's chapter, this neglect of co-existing identities is revealed within the biopolitics of the state as it legislates not just what is considered as acceptable or respectable bodies, but it also limits notions of family, motherhood and identity as biological essentialist concepts. Love's chapter shows us how legal systems from around the world still do not allow—or make it difficult—for transmasculine and non-binary people to be legally recognised as father or mother of the child. Two recent case studies from Israel and the UK are highlighted, whereby both states' legal framework of the dominant *repronomative* order limits parents as binary (cis) male/female couple, thus excluding the right of transparents to be registered as parents. In Israel, there is no hostile law or policy that disallows a trans man to register as a father; rather, there is a clear lack of positive or gender-friendly law allowing him to do so. Such ambivalence in this area is commonplace. In the UK, Love argues that despite opposition from trans-exclusionary radical feminists, there is a need to reform legislation so that it incorporates the rights of transmasculine and non-binary people so that it allows for a definition for individuals that give birth as fathers. As Love's chapter alludes to, legislative reform in this area is never free from spectacle or problems—reforming legal systems that are built on heteropatriarchal assumptions takes time.

Rashid and Rashid's chapter reflects upon seemingly progressive gender-friendly legislation protecting third genders in Pakistan and how the unique transgender identity of *hijras* and *khawaja siras* have been formally recognised through the Supreme Court Orders and the issuance of national ID cards. As we have seen in other chapters, a progressive "one step forward" approach to legal reform that guarantees rights and obligations is frequently followed by "two steps back" discriminatory implementation or a lack of a viable roadmap to equality. In Pakistan, the transgender community are still positioned as auxiliary or second place. This is largely due to traditional norms and values that still blight the pathway for acceptance and equal treatment of the transgender community (Shah et al., 2018); but it is equally due to the continued stereotyping and pathologizing of trans identity as "disorder" or "disability" (Klinefelter syndrome) that restricts access to key services such as health and education (Fazil, 2020). Moreover, with Rashid and Rashid's chapter, we can also see the familiar "law in books" versus the sociolegal "law in action" maxim (Banakar & Travers, 2005), in which the law is construed as symbolic, short-sighted and insufficient, whereas what is required is a more radical, far-reaching human rights approach reflecting dignity and respect as well as more public awareness campaigns to ameliorate the perception of status of transgender people. Altogether, these are mainly due to the heteropatriarchal understanding of gender stereotypes and law: women as mothers, carers and homemakers.[2]

When it came to drawing out the themes and frameworks for this book, it was palpable that we should identify intersectionality and the exclusion of the rights of LGBTQI people and other sexual and gender minorities as core themes. By this we mean that we saw a common thread running throughout the chapters, and that despite a state's best efforts to bring about positive gender equality legislation, it often overlooked, misunderstood or forgot the intersecting lives of "others" whilst drafting or implementing law and policy. The two prevailing themes of intersectionality and LGBTQI rights that make up for this omission are apparent in segments of the book. In applying an intersectional lens, Neller's, Winstone's and Frańczak's chapters invite us to consider the power dynamics between multiple co-existing identities as well as the connected systems that oppress (Romero, 2017). In order to understand how law is projected on to transgender identities, Rashid and Rashid, and Love call for the law to continually adapt to the changing social, political, cultural and linguistic attitudes.

12.5 Gender-Based Violence and the Criminalisation Paradigm

In its broad analysis of gender equality, this book specifically provided interesting insights into different forms of gender-based violence. Some of the chapters illustrated current patterns in relation to the definitions and scale of *violence* as well as variety of dynamics that surround it. For example, Guney's chapter demonstrated that in Turkey domestic violence rates exceed the ones across Europe, and domestic violence is heavily influenced with gendered practices that are caused by Turkey's unique traditional and cultural practices, such as religious marriages (legally non-recognised), polygamy, arranged marriages and so on. Guney's chapter also demonstrated that Turkey has enacted a progressive law (the 6284 Law) to provide more efficient responses to gender-based violence against women which is a positive step towards the elimination of the problem.

On the other hand, Davies' chapter revealed that Spain defines violence against women in a broad symbolic or zemiological sense (Bourdieu, 1979), so as to include harmful gendered stereotypes in advertisements, more specifically, "the use of a woman's body (or part of it) detached from the advertised object (reification) or using an image that portrays women in stereotyped behaviour(s)". This indicates how states can take initiative to adapt a wide definition of violence in their legislation, and violence does not only have to consist of traditional categories, such as sexual and physical violence but can also include harm, objectification or subordination. In a similar vein to Turkey, Davies demonstrated that Spain has also taken a positive step towards addressing gender-based stereotypes in advertising by enacting the Gender Violence Act (2004).

In addition, Lukera's chapter sheds light on a wide range of types of violence that sex workers experience in Kenya. These include the refusal of payment or payment with fake money, conducting sexual behaviours beyond what was consented, physical violence and so on. Together with the stigmatisation and social exclusion pertaining to sex work, it once again becomes clear that violence has its own dynamics depending on cultural and political environment that it is surrounded with, and the laws and policies should be designed by taking into account these particularities.

Besides these findings in relation to gender-based violence, this book has demonstrated that the *criminalisation* approach is utilised to address gender inequalities via two different paradigms. The first paradigm, which is explicitly related to gender-based *violence*, is that, as Guney's chapter demonstrated, the Istanbul Convention obliges the states, besides ensuring civil law measures, to criminalise various forms of violence against women. Looking at the Convention, the forms of violence to be criminalised include psychological violence (Art 33), stalking (Art 34), physical violence (Art 35), sexual violence (including rape) (Art 36), forced marriage (Art 37), female genital mutilation (Art 38) and forced abortion and forced sterilisation (Art 39). In this regard, the first criminalisation paradigm that the book revealed is that the Istanbul Convention, as an international treaty, requires states to bring criminal legal measures to address violence against women, which is an assertive approach, and constitutes a strong interference in the domestic criminal legislation and proceedings. In fact, Chinkin (2012) stated that the Istanbul Convention is of a hybrid nature, as it can be regarded as a criminal law treaty, as well as an anti-violence treaty and an equality treaty.

At this point, it should be reminded that this approach is not immune from criticism. Criminalisation as a legal method to fight against gender-based inequalities, and violence has been extensively discussed within feminist literature and has encountered heavy critiques (Kethineni & Beichner, 2009; Goldfarb, 2007; Coker, 2001). One of the most prominent objections to criminalisation is its inherent individualist view of justice (Meyersfeld, 2010). In other words, criminal law views the violence as an act occurring between particular individuals at a particular time, disregarding the social circumstances and structural dynamics that leads to the act in question. It is merely interested in bringing justice at an individual level for each particular case by losing the sight of the root causes of violence (Gruber, 2009). As a result, patriarchal social structures and social injustices amounting to the disproportionate victimisation of women are ignored, and therefore the law is reduced to a level where it is unable to address gendered structures, which, nonetheless, should be the main purpose of law (Gruber, 2009). Also, this approach would fail to contribute to empowering women in society overall and hence to eliminate the subordination of women, the main cause of violence (Gruber, 2009).

Although it is true that criminal law is inherently individualist, it is doubtful whether it would fail to empower women. On the contrary, criminal law can be utilised to achieve this goal, and thus can be considered as an effective tool. If violence is perceived from a monopolised point of view, which suggests that women do not have power while men do, and violence is simply a reflection of the power inequality between women and men, a firm state interference is necessary in order to correct this situation that negatively affects women as a whole. By criminalising gender-based violence and punishing the perpetrators, the state actually plays the role of neutralising this power inequality on behalf of women (Gee, 1983). In each conviction, the state once again gives the message that violence cannot be tolerated, and that when it happens, the state mechanism is there to punish the perpetrator. This in turn contributes to the destruction of the institutionalised male dominance (Gee, 1983).

The second *criminalisation* paradigm that this book presented was not specifically about gender-based violence, but rather was a reminder of a long-lasting problem and a prevalent practice, namely stripping LGBTQIs persons and sex workers of their rights by criminalising homosexuality and sex work. Rashid and Rashid highlighted that homosexuality is still criminalised in Pakistan, and Lukera showed that sex work is criminalised under the Penal Code in Kenya. It is true that the criminalisation of homosexuality is not a rare phenomenon. According to ILGA's (2020) report on *State Sponsored Homophobia*, although some states, including Sudan, Angola, Gabon and Bhutan, have taken steps to decriminalise or reduce the punishment over the last few years, there are currently "67 UN Member States with provisions criminalising consensual same-sex conduct, with two additional UN Member States having *de facto* criminalisation" (pp. 24–25).

On the other hand, although sex work is contentious within the feminist literature, particularly between liberal and radical feminist schools,[3] it is well demonstrated that criminalising sex work has dramatic negative impacts on women who live off sex work, including repressive policing, deprivation of sexual and reproductive rights, and lack of employment guarantees and so on. Moreover, both Rashid and Rashid and Lukera showed that there is currently no legal or political initiative in Pakistan or Kenya to decriminalise homosexuality and sex work, respectively. This is concerning, and does not give much hope for a positive change in near future. Furthermore, it should be recognised and borne in mind that the criminalisation of homosexuality and sex work are both discriminatory in nature. As reiterated by the UN Office of the High Commissioner (2011) and as argued elsewhere (Human Dignity Trust, 2015), criminalisation of homosexuality is an explicit form of discrimination on the ground of sexual orientation, and similarly, as argued by Amnesty International (2016), criminalisation of sex work constitute a discrimination on the ground of employment and contributes to the discriminatory practices against sex workers in accessing housing, health and social services (SWARM, 2019).

Notes

1. See Recommendation CM/Rec(2013)1 of the Committee of Ministers to member states on gender equality and media (COE, 10 July 2013).
2. See, for example, the Irish Constitution's inclusion of motherhood: Article 140 (1) proclaims that the state will "endeavour to ensure that mothers shall not be obliged by economic necessity to engage in labour to the neglect of their duties in the home".
3. Overall, whereas liberal feminist approach considers sex work as an individual choice and therefore as a form of sexual liberty and women's empowerment, radical feminist camp argues that sex work is ultimately a form of oppression and therefore contributes to women's inequality and sexualisation. For debates around this issue, see Beran (2012); Sloan and Wahab (2000).

References

Amnesty International. (2016). *Amnesty International Publishes Policy and Research on Protection of Sex Workers' Rights.* Retrieved June 30, 2021, from https://www.amnesty.org/en/latest/news/2016/05/amnesty-international-publishes-policy-and-research-on-protection-of-sex-workers-rights/

Aulack, S., Charlwood, A., Muzio, D., Tomlinson, J., & Valizade, D. (2017). *Mapping Advantages and Disadvantages: Diversity in the Legal Profession in England and Wales.* Final Report for the Solicitors Regulation Authority.

Banakar, R., & Travers, M. (Eds.). (2005). *Theory and Method in Socio-Legal Research.* Bloomsbury Publishing.

Beran, K. (2012). Revisiting the Prostitution Debate: Uniting Liberal and Radical Feminism in Pursuit of Policy Reform. *Minnesota Journal of Law and Equality, 30*(1), 19.

Bourdieu, P. (1979). Symbolic Power. *Critique of Anthropology, 4*(13–14), 77–85.

Boyle, K. (2001). Hate Speech—The United States Versus the Rest of the World? *Melbourne Law Review, 53*, 487.

Bunch, C. (1990). Women's Rights as Human Rights: Toward a Re-Vision of Human Rights. *Human Rights Quarterly, 12*, 486–498.

CEDAW. (2016). Concluding observations on the 7th periodic report of Turkey. CEDAW/C/TUR/CO/7. New York: Committee on the Elimination of Discrimination against Women.

Chakraborti, N., & Garland, J. (2012). Reconceptualizing Hate Crime Victimization Through the Lens of Vulnerability and "Difference". *Theoretical Criminology, 16*(4), 499–514.

Chinkin, C. (2012). Introductory Speech to the Istanbul Convention. *Tackling Violence Against Women: International and Regional Approaches Conference*, London.

Choudhury, C. A. (2008). (Mis)Appropriated Liberty: Identity, Gender Justice, and Muslim Personal Law Reform in India. *Columbia Journal of Gender and Law, 17*(1), 45.

Cook, R. J., & Cusack, S. (2010). *Gender Stereotyping: Transnational Legal Perspectives.* Philadelphia: University of Pennsylvania Press.

Coker, D. (2001). Crime Control and Feminist Law Reform in Domestic Violence Law: A Critical Review. *Buffalo Criminal Law Review, 4*(2), 801.

Davies, M. (2018). Educational Background and Access to Legal Academia. *Legal Studies, 38*(1), 120–146.

Edström, M., & Svensson, E.-M. (2014). Freedom of Expression vs. Gender Equality—Conflicting Values When Regulating Gender Stereotypes in Advertising. *Tidsskrift for Rettsvitenskap, 127*(5), 479–511.

Fazil, H. (2020). Equity and Equality of Inclusive Education for Third Gender in Pakistan: A Case study of Klinefelter Syndrome (Gender Disorder). *Journal of Inclusive Education, 4*, 113–133.

Gee, P. W. (1983). Ensuring Police Protection for Battered Women: The Scott v. Hart Suit. *Women and Violence, 8*(3), 554.

Goldfarb, S. F. (2007). Reconceiving Civil Protection Orders for Domestic Violence: Can Law Help End the Abuse Without Ending the Relationship? *Cordozo Law Review, 29*(4), 1487.

Gruber, A. (2009). Rape, Feminism, and the War on Crime. *Washington Law Review, 84*, 581.

Hintjens, H. (2008). UNIFEM, CEDAW and the Human Rights-based Approach. *Development and Change, 39*, 1181–1192.

Human Dignity Trust. (2015). *Criminalising Homosexuality and the Rule of Law.* Retrieved July 10, 2021, from https://www.humandignitytrust.org/wp-content/uploads/resources/3.-Criminalisation-the-Rule-of-Law.pdf

ILGA. (2020). *State-Sponsored Homophobia: Global Legislation Review Update*. Geneva. Retrieved July 12, 2021, from https://ilga.org/downloads/ILGA_World_State_Sponsored_Homophobia_report_global_legislation_overview_update_December_2020.pdf

Kethineni, S., & Beichner, D. (2009). Comparison of Civil and Criminal Orders of Protection as Remedies for Domestic Violence Victims in a Midwestern County. *Journal of Family Violence, 24*(5), 311.

Liu, Z. (2005). Institution and Inequality: The Hukou System in China. *Journal of Comparative Economics, 33*, 133–157.

Mason-Bish, H. (2014). Beyond the Silo: Rethinking Hate Crime and Intersectionality. In *The Routledge International Handbook on Hate Crime* (pp. 24–33). Routledge.

Mende, J. (2021). Are Human Rights Western—And Why Does It Matter? A Perspective from International Political Theory. *Journal of International Political Theory, 17*(1), 38–57.

Meyersfeld, B. (2010). *Domestic Violence and International Law*. Hart Publishing.

Moscati, M. F. (2020). Negotiating within legal ambiguity: Same-sex partners, family disputes and negotiation in Italy. In: Moscati, Maria Federica, Palmer, Michael and Roberts, Marian (eds.), *Comparative dispute resolution. Edward Elgar* (pp. 146–157). ISBN 9781786433022.

Neller, J. (2018). The Need for New Tools to Break the Silos: Identity Categories in Hate Speech Legislation. *International Journal for Crime, Justice and Social Democracy, 7*(2), 75.

Romero, M. (2017). *Introducing Intersectionality*. John Wiley & Sons.

Shah, H. B. U., Rashid, F., Atif, I., Hydrie, M. Z., Fawad, M. W. B., Muzaffar, H. Z., Rehman, A., Anjum, S., Mehroz, M. B., Haider, A., & Hassan, A. (2018). Challenges Faced by Marginalized Communities Such as Transgenders in Pakistan. *The Pan African Medical Journal, 30*, 96.

Sloan, L., & Wahab, S. (2000). Feminist Voices on Sex Work: Implications for Social Work. *Affilia*. Retrieved June 18, 2021, from https://journals.sagepub.com/doi/pdf/10.1177/088610990001500402

Sommerlad, H. (2002). Women Solicitors in a Fractured Profession: Intersections of Gender and Professionalism in England and Wales. *International Journal of the Legal Profession, 9*(3), 213–234.

Swarm. (2019). *Shadow Report for CEDAW: Country: United Kingdom*. Retrieved June 8, 2021, from https://tbinternet.ohchr.org/Treaties/CEDAW/Shared%20Documents/GBR/INT_CEDAW_CSS_GBR_33658_E.docx

UN Office of the High Commissioner. (2011). *Laws Criminalizing Homosexuality Are Incompatible with International Human Rights Standards and Fuel Homophobia*. Retrieved July 10, 2021, from https://www.ohchr.org/EN/NewsEvents/Pages/homophobia.aspx

INDEX[1]

[1] Note: Page numbers followed by 'n' refer to notes.

G. Guney et al. (eds.), *Towards Gender Equality in Law*,
https://doi.org/10.1007/978-3-030-98072-6

Kolibri 360 GmbH
Ferdinand-Jühlke-Straße 7
99095 Erfurt, Deutschland
produktsicherheit@kolibri360.de